'WE ARE BUT WOMEN'

By the same author

Casement: The Flawed Hero (1984)
Slavery in the Twentieth Century (1986)
Children Enslaved (1988)
The Island from Within (ed.) (1990)

'WE ARE BUT WOMEN'

Women in Ireland's history

Roger Sawyer

ROUTLEDGE

London and New York

First published 1993
by Routledge
11 New Fetter Lane, London EC4P 4EE

Simultaneously published in the USA and Canada
by Routledge
29 West 35th Street, New York, NY 10001

© 1993 Roger Sawyer

Typeset in Garamond by
Ponting–Green Publishing Services, Chesham, Bucks
Printed in Great Britain by
T.J. Press (Padstow) Ltd, Padstow, Cornwall.

Printed on acidfree paper

British Library Cataloguing in Publication Data
A catalogue record for this book is available from
the British Library

Library of Congress Cataloging in Publication Data
Sawyer, Roger
We Are But Women: Women in Ireland's
history / Roger Sawyer
p. cm.
Includes bibliographical references and index.
1. Women–Ireland–Political activity–History.
2. Women–Ireland–History 3. Irish question.
4. Ireland–History. I. Title.
DA916.7.S29 1993
941.5'00442–dc20 93–508

ISBN 0-415-05866-X (hbk) ✓

To Mary Aylmer

Hallelujah

CONTENTS

FOREWORD
Lady Fisher

I feel very privileged to have been asked to write the foreword to Dr Sawyer's masterly book about the role of women in Irish affairs. This painstakingly researched and scholarly account covers an immense field, from the early mists of legend to the present day, when there is a woman as head of state in the Republic of Ireland.

As an Ulsterwoman who has lived most of my life in Northern Ireland, I have read with great interest and some pride of the part women have played in politics, the arts and the internal struggles of an always troubled island. Men have tried for centuries to settle the Irish problem. Where they have failed, maybe women will eventually succeed; their role as peacemakers and stabilizers of society could become even more important as we reach the end of the twentieth century.

It has been said that a woman is to be found behind every successful man. Oscar Wilde wrote that 'All women become like their mothers . . . No man does'. This may or may not be true. But there is no doubt that the women of Ireland have achieved an immense amount in their own right, apart from wielding great influence behind the scenes. There have been militant political women like Countess Markievicz and Bernadette Devlin, and there have been women like Mairead Corrigan and Betty Williams who were awarded the Nobel Peace Prize. At the beginning of this century, women as scholars, artists, actresses and playwrights played a dominant part in Ireland's cultural revival. Ascendancy women, among them the great political hostesses, have always been influential in the corridors of power; Edith, Lady Londonderry's close friendship with Ramsay MacDonald certainly influenced his thinking on Irish affairs. When Michael Collins at last put his signature to the Irish Treaty, he telephoned Lady Lavery and told her, 'I have signed your damned Treaty', knowing he had signed his own death warrant.

The chapters in which Roger Sawyer has written on such complicated issues as divorce, abortion, contraception and segregated education, both north and south of the border, are comprehensive and revealing. They throw light on the attitude of successive governments to these sensitive matters which affect women and family life.

To many people Ireland and Irish people, and also women, have always been enigmas. Roger Sawyer may not have solved all the mysteries, but his book makes fascinating reading and I can commend it wholeheartedly to all those who are interested in, or can claim kinship and historical ties with, Ireland. They will learn a great deal.

Patricia Fisher

PREFACE

At first sight it might be tempting to regard Ireland as a microcosm of the peculiar ways in which social, political and religious forces around this planet have created special roles for women; but this would be totally misleading. Many parallels can be drawn with women's experience in other societies, but at times in its history Ireland has moved against the general trend. In this assessment, while generalizations will be made because they are essential to the semantics of any attempt to analyse society and nationality, their inherent danger is recognized; for into this island, which had no aboriginal inhabitants, came a multitude of racial and cultural ingredients that influenced the genesis of women whose diverse status and role have affected and been affected by every twist and turn in Ireland's history. Furthermore, although the countless peasant wives and mothers, the Queen Maeves, the Grania O'Malleys, the Lady Londonderrys, the Lady Gregorys, the Saidie Pattersons and the Bernadette Devlins (McAliskeys) are all individuals, they are also the products and producers of a many-faceted symbolism which continues to affect the condition and the varied attitudes of all sections of the Irish community – worldwide.

Even if the complexities of a rich blend of races are put to one side, Irishness is difficult enough to define without the added complication of the subtleties, and the not-so-subtle distinctions, arising from gulfs and links between the sexes. Women were no less concerned, sometimes more concerned, than men when it came to coping with confused loyalties caused by changing geographical and political boundaries. What follows is an examination of the roles of women in Ireland yesterday and today, assessed mainly in terms of social, religious and political development throughout the island as a whole: women's effect on Ireland and Ireland's effect on women.

Although it is intended that the principal matter of this book shall begin with the Act of Union, some attention must be given to the early influences which created the situations some enjoyed and some suffered in 1800. This is especially important as so many of the ancient traditions about mythological and early historical female figures have not only coloured the Irish man's view of women, but have consciously and unconsciously influenced the way in which Irish women of all classes have perceived their cultural inheritance. The old concepts, admittedly sometimes distorted almost beyond recognition, are still embodied in the national consciousness.

The introductory chapter moves from the original empty island, through the mythological period, to the time when five quarrelsome provinces (fifths), or kingdoms, failed to defer with any semblance of consistency to the High Kings of Tara. It goes on to consider the impact of Christianity which arrived at a time when the Scots, as they were still called, straddled Ireland (to use its later name) and what is now the only part of these islands to be called Scotland. Not surprisingly St Patrick, with much help from St Brigid, changed Ireland's perception of women for ever, though he did not try to extinguish many of the old pagan stereotypes. Ireland's internal boundaries were constantly in a state of flux and it was inter-tribal rivalry which contributed to one of its two most enduring boundary adjustments: that often shifting line between land held by Irish kings and that ruled by the Normans. Had the invaders from France absorbed Ireland as thoroughly as they had conquered England, they would have made a full-blooded and permanent unity of the two islands; as it was they only partially subdued the smaller one, leaving psychological problems and their political consequences as part of a thousand-year legacy.

The rule of one king over the whole of one island and a limited hinterland of another was an added cause of division to hearts and minds already divided by local disputes. The presence of a common foe did not unite them and it often fell to women to tip the political balance this way or that during periods of elbowing for advantage. An irresistible logic, or so it seems with hindsight, had eventually to bring about a merger between the two nations which had been overrun by their powerful European neighbour. Despite repeated violent disputes between those who resisted Norman law and its consequences and those who accepted the status quo, surely it was desirable to translate the dual entity into a United Kingdom, thereby demolishing the official framework of discrimination and eradicating the root causes of hatred. But the forces of disunity did not wither away and during the next 121 years certain Ascendancy women played key roles in the evolution of the divided island of today – which is not to belittle the part played by 'ordinary' women. The first major Irish convulsion of the twentieth century seemed to turn the wheel full circle to two thousand years ago when Ulster (Ulaid) faced the hostility of the rest of the island bent on conquest; twenty-six counties opted for secession as a 'Free State' and the remaining six, with mixed feelings, followed the path of devolution. Inevitably attention has hitherto been focused on the more flamboyant rebel women who made dramatic contributions to the revolutionary cause and, while they must not be ignored, some attempt will be made to restore balance by giving emphasis both to the revolutionary women who did not become famous names and to the women, famous or otherwise, who opposed the separatist movement. The strong case that could be made for sustaining the Union was not necessarily supported merely out of self-interest by politically active Ascendancy women; they acted out of conviction, as did their separatist sisters.

Because of their access to education, the next aspect of a woman's place in Irish history to be considered was also dominated by the women of the Ascendancy. They were crucial to the Celtic Revival; they paved the way to the Irish Literary Renaissance. Although the movement towards awareness of, and promotion of, Irish culture – which meant Gaelic folklore and mythology, 'Anglo-Irish' literature, and also art, craft, music, dance and drama – took on political overtones, many of its most genuine and capable proponents simply loved Ireland and all things Irish. Politically, and irrelevantly they might have said, many were unionist; to the extent that their commitment to Gaelic literature of one form or another (few of them actually learned the language) put them into the company of their political opponents, their devotion was selfless. Their contributions to the literature of Ireland are disparate; it is difficult at first to find common denominators, other than those of class. Key writers from both sides of the divide, among them those who would have reservations about recognizing a 'divide', include Maria Edgeworth, Somerville and Ross, Lady Gregory, Emily Lawless, Alice Milligan, Eva Gore-Booth, Sydney Owenson (Lady Morgan) and Lady Wilde. Then there were promoters of the revival such as Alice Stopford Green. Definitely no sympathizer with the unionist cause, Mrs Green acted as cultural catalyst for the nationalists, for whom Irish culture was also a means to an end.

The first decade of the twentieth century saw what was by no means the first flowering of feminism in Ireland, but in 1908, when the Irish Women's Franchise League was founded by Hanna Sheehy and her husband Francis Skeffington, the demand for women's suffrage caused feminism to move to centre stage, though its importance was soon to be eclipsed by the separatist struggle. Consideration will be given to the several strands of the suffragist movement, represented by those for or against use of violence, and those whose activities were affected by a wish to preserve, modify or sever the connection with the imperial parliament. The First World War enabled British and Irish women, by different routes, to obtain the vote, and Easter Week, 1916, gave those of nationalist persuasion the opportunity both to prove their value to the cause and to discover the difficulties of discarding some of the essentials of their traditional role. In these turbulent times which became the Troubles, important parts, as will be seen, were played by Maud Gonne's Inghinidhe na hEireann and by the larger women's volunteer organization, Cumann na mBan. The attainment of independence for twenty-six counties and a devolved parliament for the other six brought a sense of anticlimax for some, but for others it meant that other rights, specifically for women, should take pride of place. Those who were encouraged by the new political arrangements renewed their commitment to the feminist cause, while women such as Mary MacSwiney, who were enraged by the Treaty, retained other priorities.

Reactions to the establishment of an autonomous Irish political entity will be the next area to be considered. Despite a major schism over the Treaty, there remained much common ground between feminists who belonged to different political camps. Their aspirations could be affected by the Free State's 1922 Constitution. This went a long way towards reassuring minorities, and women – though often a majority – have long been relegated to the 'minority rights' department of human affairs. However, one phrase put perceptive critics on their guard. Article 8 spoke of 'Freedom of conscience and the free profession and practice of religion' being 'subject . . . to morality'. Who was to be the arbiter when it came to moral disputes? As will be seen, the answer to this question was to be found fifteen years later in the 1937 Constitution.

The remainder of what follows is a consideration by way of comparison of the very different paths that were taken in relation to women's issues by the Free State, subsequently the Republic, and by Northern Ireland. The actual rescue of six counties of Ulster from the clutches of Dublin (and Rome), for that is how many saw it, was greatly influenced by pressures exerted by Ascendancy women, notably by Theresa and Edith, marchionesses of Londonderry. But basic motivation was not seen in negative terms: they and, at the other end of the social scale, thousands of workers – especially the Protestant women in the linen industry – did not wish Ireland to be divided. The new political dispensation was, in their opinion, foisted on them. They believed in the positive values of the Union, and the changes which they observed from north of the border confirmed their worst fears. Because of the influence of the Roman Catholic Hierarchy over the ostensibly secular government of the Free State, education, law and the whole climate of opinion with regard to women's rights diverged from what was assumed to be the northern Protestant position on these matters. The permissibility or otherwise of divorce and contraception, and the general approach to the concept of the family, were issues which drove a series of wedges between the independent state and the separated counties of Ulster.

Divorce and abortion law were to become principal sources of friction between the Republic and the European Commission of Human Rights, though the divorce ban did not actually contravene the existing European Convention. The friction, as well as generating heat, served to distract attention from the effects of cohabitation within a small island of opposing views and inconsistent legal practices connected with other family concerns. For some years, though, different iniquities in the North attracted the interest of those concerned with human rights. The civil rights movement arose because of discrimination against Roman Catholics and, although its energies were eventually diverted into less deserving channels, it did achieve its initial aims. With legalized discrimination on religious grounds a thing of the past, demands for an end to sexual discrimination surfaced again – only for nationalists to have it brought home to them that the position was far worse in the South. A whole host of problems, many of which were to be aired at the New Ireland Forum, awaited solution. They concerned issues such as women's property rights, adoption of legitimate children, mixed marriages, equal rights in the workplace, protection of battered wives and provision of sex education.

Absorption by the Welfare State has not been entirely advantageous to Northern Ireland. There has been a debit side to the social development of the province; moreover, the shift of responsibility from the individual to the state has served to widen the gulf between the two Irelands. Antipathetic attitudes developed as a result of the contrast between Northern Ireland's secularism and the clerical culture of the South. While differences regarding, say, chastity and motherhood, arose naturally from the religious divide on the island, the secular ramifications which came in their wake have been legion. For this reason it will, for example, be necessary to look at the extent to which Irish women generally, and Irish women writers in particular, have suffered at the hands of the South's Censorship Board. On the wider scene it will be found that, until the time of the New Ireland Forum, the outlook for enlightened emancipation of women and for the possibility of bridging divides without sacrificing rights of self-determination was indeed bleak. Since then, though, there have been many changes, especially in the laws of the Republic, which have made realistic the idea of genuine reconciliation between the two Irish cultures.

Unfortunately no examination of the role of women in Ireland could be complete without space being devoted to their contribution to the present Troubles. They are even more active on both sides (and in many capacities in the gap between the main contestants) than they were in the violence which led up to, and followed, the Treaty. But emancipation in the wider sense of the term has broadened the range of their opportunity either to terrorize the innocent or to sacrifice themselves for the principles or the people they love. The feminine/female dimension of 'the armed struggle' and of resistance to it is a complex one, further confused by the ambivalent attitudes of male comrades in arms. However, in the light of the remarkable contribution of some women as peacemakers and stabilizers of society, it may not be straining things too far to suggest that the pacification of Ireland may depend on them. Women's organizations are the most potent force for peace in Northern Ireland today. Whether they can point the way to a solution of the present psychological impasse of the two nations of Ireland depends to a great degree on their ability to distinguish the good from the bad in the social and religious traditions which made them and which they helped to make. And the making of value-judgements is difficult enough for individuals, let alone divided communities.

Roger Sawyer
Bembridge, Isle of Wight

ACKNOWLEDGEMENTS

Not for the first time, my greatest debt is to Patrick Montgomery and to his wife Moskie. Though Irish, Pat and Moskie do not pretend to be experts on Irish affairs, and the task of checking my factual accuracy has not fallen on their shoulders. Their contribution has been in the realms of common sense, clarity, friendship and moral support sustained over many years. And my debt to the family did not end with their generation. Pat's daughter Kathie Davey, who lives in County Dublin, has kept me closely informed about the abortion and divorce issues during a time of change and uncertainty in the Irish Republic.

Lady Fisher has done me the honour of writing a foreword to this book. No one could be more appropriate. As will be seen, she is numbered among that special breed who can rise above sectarian considerations to bring compassion and unity to a community divided by the misconceptions of its history. I express thanks to her, and to all whose help is acknowledged here. One hopes that in some way, however small, the consequence of their combined efforts will not only throw some light on women in Ireland's history, but will indicate peaceful ways to overcome avoidable difficulties.

A number of the families whose forebears, or relatives by marriage, played a part in demonstrating the changing role of Irish women over the centuries responded personally to my requests for information. None were more forthcoming than Tony Aylmer and his wife Shaunagh (née Guinness). In fairness one has to fall back on alphabetical order of surnames to avoid disparities of gratitude, when some obviously proved more helpful than others; nevertheless I am relieved that Aylmer begins with 'A'. Sticking to the alphabet I thank Jolyon Buchanan, June Buchanan, Lady Mairi Bury, Richard and Joyce Colclough, Sheila Crichton-Stuart, Eoin Dillon, Charles Du Cane, Lord and Lady Dunsany, Aideen Gore-Booth, Diana Greenly, the Viscount Harberton, Jaquetta James, Andrew and Tina McMorrough-Kavanagh, Anthony and Ann Pilcher, Major the Hon. Robert Pomeroy and the Hon. Mrs R. W. Pomeroy, the Hon. Rosamund Pomeroy, and Diana Tunnicliffe.

When Routledge first commissioned this book Sir John Biggs-Davison had for some years been one of my greatest providers of information and encouragement. The death in 1988 of this magnanimous and far-seeing Irish Catholic was a national loss (to both Ireland and the United Kingdom) as well as a personal one for family and friends. He opened many doors for me and, above all, introduced me to the former Secretary of the Standing Advisory Commission on Human Rights, John Fisher. John Fisher in turn put me in touch with key figures on both sides of the sectarian divide. Later he and his colleague Brian Porter generously agreed to take on the heavy task of vetting my manuscript for factual errors. It must be emphasized that they are not responsible for my interpretation of the facts.

Then there were others who generally smoothed my path either by putting me in touch with valuable sources of information, by enabling me to penetrate areas which were not easily accessible, or by lightening my burdens in various other ways: Basilia Abel Smith, Sister Mary Albert, Nuala Allason, Monica Ayles, Mark Bence-Jones, the Rt Hon. David Bleakley, Sir Adam Butler, Martin Cooke, James Dearden, Anne de Courcey, Constance de Hamel, the Reverend John Dunne, James and Robina Ellis, Lady Esher, Dr Eileen Evason, Pamela Freeman, Lindsey French, Rowel and Yvonne Friers, Jocelyn Galsworthy, Mary Gavaghan, Antonia Gibbs, Isobel Grundy, Sabrina Harcourt-Smith, Dr Mary Henry, Lord Hylton, Bridget Lakin, Miċéal McGovern, John and Clodagh Maher-Loughnan, George Mansur, Ronald and Eustelle Marsden-Harvey, Elizabeth Mavor, Stuart and Caroline Monard, David and Anne Negus, Bill Nigh, Judy Noyes, Edna O'Brien, Dr John Partridge, Patricia Partridge, Siobhán Pinhorn, Jack Poyner, Joe Savage, Adrian Searle, Hannah Scott, Robert and Elizabeth Shanks, Verity Shaw, Etain Ó Síocháin, Dr Séamas Ó Síocháin, His Honour Judge Jonathan van der Werff, Henry Warren, Lieutenant Commander David Webb, Mairead Wilson, and William Wilson.

Three main public repositories must be used by anyone writing about Irish affairs: the Public Record Office of Northern Ireland, the National Library of Ireland, and the Public Record Office at Kew. I gratefully acknowledge the permissions which I received to quote from the archive material which was put at my disposal. In the case of my research in Belfast formal thanks are owed to the Deputy Keeper of the Records of Northern Ireland. Less formally I thank Dr Anthony Malcomson for unravelling some difficult knots for me, and Robert Corbett and Patricia Kernaghan for much valuable help. In Dublin Gerard Lyne of the National Library of Ireland enabled me to locate elusive material; as did Mandy Banton at Kew. When in Belfast I was allowed – by permission of Edith, Lady Londonderry's daughter, Lady Mairi Bury – to examine hitherto embargoed papers. Acknowledgement is also made for permission to quote from Charlotte Despard's diary which was deposited by the late Reverend Gabriel O'Prey, from Francis Sheehy Skeffington's letters deposited by John Magee, and from the Minutes of the Family Planning Association of Northern Ireland. As far as all three repositories are concerned I apologize to any owners and copyright-owners whom I have been unable to trace.

Naturally many political parties, religious bodies, official organizations and voluntary societies were consulted. In Northern Ireland the Reverend Ian Paisley and Rhonda Paisley of the Democratic Unionist Party were accessible and most helpful, and an obvious wish to transmit a positive attitude to women's rights was made by a host of officials and ordinary members of the Alliance Party, and the Social and Democratic Labour Party. Mary Mac Mahon extended the hospitality of the Workers' Party, and Hazel Bradford, former chairman of the Ulster Unionist Party, and former president of the Ulster Women's Unionist Council, spoke for conventional unionism. In the Republic the most eloquent champion of women's rights, if actions may speak as loudly as words, has been a man: Dr Noël Browne, the former Minister of Health. Otherwise, in order to get at the real truth about the funda-mental issues affecting women, one does best to talk both to those who work for or against current trends, and to those within the priesthood who are happy to discuss the position of the Church at a time when moral values are being challenged. Although they have not asked for anonymity, most principal protagonists would not necessarily be particularly happy to be named here. However, an exception may be made in the case of the Bishop of Meath, the Most Reverend Michael Smith, who was kind enough to give me his enlightened views on mixed marriages.

Some, though, insist on anonymity and, as far as acknowledgements go, this hardly matters. It is not possible to express meaningful thanks to members of illegal organizations, or to those who provide them with a legal voice, when one knows that there has never been a legitimate place for violence in the Irish context. Nevertheless I do appreciate the contribution of the Provisional who had the good grace to denounce the Enniskillen bombing. The Road to Damascus may not reach all the way to Londonderry, or even to Derry, but a few humane voices within the ranks of the Provos, and within the Ulster Defence Association, might help to bring peace a fraction nearer.

Others who gave me the benefit of their knowledge of Irish affairs, South and North, were Paula Slattery, Counsellor, and Judy Minihan, Information Officer, both of the Irish Embassy in London, Mary Clark-Glass and Irene Kingston of the Equal Opportunities Commission for Northern Ireland (the former was until recently Chairman and Chief Executive, the latter is Senior Information Officer), and Annette Fitzpatrick, of the Office of Law Reform in Belfast. Among the most useful providers of printed matter on human rights isues were the Community of the Peace People and the Presbyterian Church in Ireland. Sandra Horley, Director of Refuge (formerly Chiswick Family Rescue), supplied information about fugitive battered wives from the Republic. The history of the All Children Together Charitable Trust was provided by Cecil Linehan, one of its founder-members. Joyce Seymour-Chalk, Honorary Secretary of the Gaelic Society of London, successfully helped me in my pursuit of a most elusive Gael. Thanks to her the thoughts of the Hon. Louisa Farquharson finally surfaced.

ACKNOWLEDGEMENTS

When it came to obscure secondary sources my demands on various library services were met with extraordinary efficiency – and never more efficiently than via my own village library at Bembridge. There Michael Cunliffe, Mary Cullimore and Rosemary Bell not only conjured up the impossible, but on their own initiative ordered extra items which they felt I ought to use. Alan Phillips, of the British Humanities Index, went out of his way to help; as did Christina Mackwell at Lambeth Palace Library. At Southampton University Nicholas Graffy never failed; nor did Mary Doran, Brian Kefford, Jacqueline Pitcher and John Westmancoat of the British Library. And, when the need arose, it was always a privilege and pleasure to visit the library of Quarr Abbey, where Father James Mitchell was in charge.

Finally I thank Andrew Wheatcroft of Routledge for his encouragement and advice, and my wife, Diana, for being the source of the love I have of all – well, almost all – things Irish.

1

FROM THE BEGINNING

It was a woman who founded, or found, Ireland, according to the earliest legend contained in the lost manuscript, *The Book of Druim Snechta*.[1] Banba was there while Noah was building his ark, and the Flood did not reach the top of her chosen peak. But another tradition credits Cessair, supposedly a different woman, with peopling the place. She did so because she and her group of fifty women and three men were all turned away by Noah, who regarded them as a motley collection of thieves, not to be trusted on board his vessel. However, few Irish citizens seem aware of these primordial, mainly female settlers. Such has been the unconscious and conscious selection process leading to the curriculum of Irish patriotism that different heroines have been remembered. Ask an Irish boy or girl who has passed through the Republic's educational system to name the first woman who has influenced the story of his or her nation, and Queen Maeve[2] (Medb) will invariably be mentioned.

From palaeolithic times, when the island had been uninhabited, until about the eighth century AD, the principal source of information about prehistory and early history was, as is usual with ancient cultures, oral tradition. In the case of Ireland an especially rich heritage of stories, female-dominated to a large degree, was handed down by word of mouth almost to the present day. A large proportion of the rural inhabitants of modern Ireland, and many who only recently migrated to towns and cities, are only separated by a generation from a peasant oral tradition which goes back more than two thousand years. This means that, to the extent that they have not assimilated the values of late twentieth-century industrialized society, they have been influenced by a broad spectrum of powerful myths and legends in which females often had the upper hand and were invariably centrally or obliquely crucial to the development of the divers tribes which led to the formation of provinces and kingdoms and, eventually, to the present divided island. Illiteracy undoubtedly gave the story-tellers freedom to embellish; but the scribes of the seventh to the twelfth century (and some as late as the fourteenth century) who devoted their attention to recording traditional narratives had few inhibitions when it came to imposing their own interpretation of events. One of the pursuits of modern Gaelic scholars is to disentangle the tale from the teller.

Some methods of detection also have to be employed if one is to penetrate nineteenth- and twentieth-century distortions made by well-meaning Gaelic revivalists on the one hand and would-be educators on the other. In the twentieth century in particular, because of national – and nationalist – education, coupled with misplaced prudery, the race-memory has been subject to censorship, much of it unconsciously imposed. And yet the consequent ignorance was not suffered by the recent illiterate forebears of the mass of the agricultural community. The story-tellers in their midst carried in their minds the mixture of history and fable that for the first millenium of its existence had not been written down and for the next millenium was only available to most people by word of mouth.

Naturally historians have felt themselves to be under an obligation to separate fact from fiction. Cessair and her followers posed obvious problems, and so did Tuatha De Danann: 'the Peoples of the Goddess Danann'; another group listed among the first five of the early influxes of colonizers was a distinctly masculine tribe, the Fir Bolg, whose name has long been taken to mean 'the Men of the Leather Bag', though it is more probable that Bolg was an ancient deity; then there were two other groups named after their leaders, Partholon and Nemed. Danann was herself called 'mother of the gods' and, in this time of female warriors, her peoples, led by a king, had to cope with rivals, the Fomoire, among whom women outnumbered men by three to one. The Fomorians had four ships' crews, each of 50 men and 150 women. The matriarch of this formidable fleet was Lot, who had swollen lips in her breast, four eyes in her back and strength equal to that of her entire tribe. Not unexpectedly, in their quest to interpret events, historians have reacted differently to this sort of material: some have embraced it; others have seemed to be embarrassed by it. One easy way out has been to consign all these pre-Scottish colonizers, bar the Fir Bolg, who seem really to have existed and to have come from Britain, to the realms of fairy tales. The Fir Bolg might have disappeared too, but for the need to have a native population to serve in Maeve's army.

For present purposes, however, the distinction between fact and fiction is of minor importance. What is of value is the perception of Irish womanhood that led to the creation or exaggeration of the legendary figures and, conversely, the perception that real people derived from larger than life heroines whose supposed deeds generated so much inspiration. One precedent that the legends set which influenced practice for many centuries was the paramount importance of the views of wives and mothers in decisions concerning royal succession. This was seen, for example, when Nuada, King of Tuatha De Danann lost an arm and was no longer regarded as fit to rule. The succession was by no means clear-cut and the choice, a controversial one, was taken against the wishes of the men. The women decided to form an alliance between their tribe and the Fomoire by electing to serve under the son of a Fomorian king.

Women, often in bewildering disguise, were sometimes seen as being in some special way in touch with the supernatural and, because of this, were regarded as either embodying sovereignty or being its source. The medieval manuscripts in which the oral traditions were first encapsulated comprise what are normally referred to as four cycles, labelled the Mythological, the Ulster, the Fenian, and the Historical. In the Mythological cycle one is not surprised to find that sovereignty derives from bizarre supernatural forces and, given that feminine attributes are all-pervasive in the Other World, women must be the dispensers of power here on earth. Male influence may be absent altogether according to Irish and Welsh tradition, as it is in the version given in 'The Adventure of Conle' of the Celtic realm of the supernatural: 'There is no race there but women and maidens alone.'[3] This cycle is characterized by man's wish to obtain knowledge, and therefore power, through magical means; in the Ulster cycle, although magic is still present, the priority shifts to will power: the stories tell of an heroic age, of Maeve and her contest with Ulster's hero, CuChulainn. In the Fenian tales the emphasis moves to the romantic, as is most easily seen in 'The Pursuit of Diarmaid and Grainne', an account of seduction by the female, and elopement, which has more than an echo of Arthurian legend about it. Finally, the Historical cycle, as its title suggests, is not predominantly magical, heroic or romantic; nevertheless it embodies these qualities to a degree as it describes dynastic succession and the fortunes of the royal houses of Ireland. Here women are very much the embodiment of sovereignty. Maeve of Connaught had made at least three kings by offering them 'my own friendly thighs';[4] it is a different Maeve, the Queen of Leinster, who looms even larger in this respect in the Historical cycle. She 'would not allow a king in Tara without his having herself as wife'.[5] In all she was wife to nine kings in Ireland.

Despite Maeve of Leinster's statistical superiority, it was Maeve of Connaught who stirred the imagination of those who followed in the wake of the late Victorian and Edwardian cultural revivalists. The uneducated classes had long enjoyed hearing about the exploits of the Irish Amazons; suddenly, buoyed up by the centenary celebrations of the 1798 rebellion and at a time when reform and extension of education had become an issue, men and women of distinctly superior education became aware of a heritage which included her in the front rank of a large caste of fabulous women. The lid of this treasure trove of literary assets – for such it was perceived to be – had been lifted in 1872, when Standish O'Grady, having nothing much to do one wet day, discovered his country's ancient history on the bookshelves of a country house. However, his enthusiasm did not infect like-minded individuals until 1878, when the first volume of his two-volume *History of Ireland* appeared.[6]

As a result of O'Grady's decision to brush the dust off tales which had always been there, but which few had had eyes to read, a considerable number of worthy writers took up the cause of the Irish literary revival, which had previously been left to a few pioneers (see Chapter 3, below). Unionists (among whom O'Grady was numbered) and nationalists who varied from ardent separatists to simple lovers of all things Irish – all laboured to bring the traditional Gaelic myths and legends into the literary mainstream. There was a vast input, and much of it was hardly worth the trouble, partly because at first the leading lights of what had become a movement were unable to understand the original Gaelic texts, and partly because detailed attention to urination, copulation and other taboo subjects offended against the contemporary moral code; it was not in keeping with the puritan conscience of Ireland – Catholic or Protestant. Nevertheless influential literary figures and their disciples made the best of things, according to their lights. As Lady Gregory was to put it to the people of Kiltartan, 'I left out a good deal I thought you would not care about for one reason or another.'[7]

It was the Ulster cycle which best survived the manner of its rebirth, and which, nearly a century after Ireland rediscovered it, still makes a major impact on those who choose to study it or those who have it thrust upon them; not so much because it tells of a beleaguered Ulster taking on 'Ireland' in ways which, fundamentally, are not altogether different from the position today, but because of the extraordinary women who people the narratives. Apart from Maeve, and Deirdre (whose love-life has a self-contained legend of its own), there is a whole host of peculiar female characters with varying degrees of eccentricity or magic attaching to them: Scathach, Aife, Finnabar, Macha, Nes and many others, down to the meanest bondmaids. Unfortunately, though, twentieth-century readers and listeners, from national school children to university graduates, have been exposed to two completely alien versions of all these figures. Earlier generations of students are likely to have been acquainted with the works of Sir Samuel Ferguson, who ruthlessly suppressed all bawdy elements, or of Lady Gregory who, as was only to be expected, sanitized them altogether. Indeed, if the parent of one of today's Gaelic scholars should investigate his offspring's impressions he would wonder if the old Irish heroes and heroines of his day were the same legendary characters as the ones that are currently being studied.

Sir Samuel Ferguson's Maeve (he spelled her name 'Maev') might well be described as Ireland's Boadicea, but only in the sense that both women were embodiments of the concept of the warrior-queen; Boadicea (strictly 'Boudicca') reacted, Maeve chose to act. With her 'King Consort' Ailill, the Queen of Connachta initiated and carried through a number of epic exploits that have been perceived by many to be reminiscent both of the siege of Troy and of the quest for the Golden Fleece. Much of her time was spent attacking Ulster (Ulaid), a larger kingdom than the province of today. At a time when there were five kingdoms, Maeve was the prime mover against Conor Mac Nessa's kingdom, and CuChulainn was her great adversary. She is best known for those of her adventures which are recorded in 'Tain Bo Cuailnge', variously rendered as 'The Cattle-Spoil of Quelgny', 'The Driving Away of the Bull of Cooley' or simply 'Cattle Raid of Cooley'. The first man to write down the key traditional stories was probably Senchan Torpéist, senior poet in Ireland in the seventh century, and what he and those who followed him recorded just does not square with the varnished representations which became popular some thirteen centuries later.

The early records are invaluable for the light which they throw on the activities and attitude of a pagan and barbaric people; they enable researchers to flesh out an otherwise obscure period. Generally, though, they do not relate epic narratives: much of their subject-matter reveals, not very surprisingly, preoccupation verging on obsession with the various ways in which men and women can fight and kill each other. In short, on the evidence of the authors' accounts of Maeve's and CuChulainn's priorities, the early inhabitants of Ireland, like the early inhabitants of most places, were savages. To that comment, however, must be added the paradoxical rider that interspersed in their savagery were flashes of insight into the human condition as it then appeared, and which one hopes were not merely additions of later minds. Even an ardent admirer of 'this epic material', though, found some elements of it (the same elements which have led to the label 'epic' being withheld by scholars) puzzlingly amorphous: 'why is all this medley amalgamated in this saga in the form in which we now have it?'[8]

At one level too much has been read into what Stephen Gwynn[9] believed was the greatest of these early romances, a powerful mixture of history and myth. The parallel is drawn between the quest for Helen of Troy and the capture of the famous brown bull kept on Carlingford peninsula, efforts to purchase it having led to ill-treatment of Maeve's messengers. It is argued that, just as it cannot have been Helen's face alone that launched a thousand ships, there is much more to Maeve's war than a wish to acquire a bull merely because her husband, Ailill, had one. Surely, at the very least, one should see the contest between the male and female champions in terms of a dual personification: of Ulster beset by the rest of Ireland. But too much can be made of the ingredients which lead to this impression, significant though they are – with hindsight. The romance lacks the Homeric qualities which the Fergusons would have liked to find in it, and so they did their best to add them and, while they were at it, they excised the crude elements. Sir Samuel, who, despite a recent claim to the contrary,[10] 'never mastered the language',[11] regretted what he termed 'turgid extravagances and exaggerations, the additions apparently of later copyists'[12] and lamely defended scenes that might not be so easily explained away by saying that 'much of the material of the best classic literature is as crude and revolting as anything in Irish or Welsh story'.[13]

Today there is no need for such apologies. And, as long as he is aware that there are two Queen Maeves of Connaught (and why this is so) whoever seeks to identify primordial Irish womanhood need not be misled. The original was as brutal and aggressive as any legendary man, and offered her favours to anyone who might advance her ambitions. Having read both the earliest and the refined versions, the reader need have little difficulty in appreciating that, compared with the lot of women in many other cultures, Irish women started from a position of strength. For the stories not only reveal that as a personality Maeve was unique; they show that as an example of a woman's ability to command respect and to influence Ireland's history, she was one of many.

After succeeding in her various martial quests, including making off with the brown bull, Maeve lost the battle of Slewin, in West Meath, after which she escaped to her royal residence. Eventually she was killed by a sling-shot while bathing in the Shannon. Conor, the Ulster king, had been killed by the same method by Maeve's nephew, Keth, having been lured within range by Connaught women who shared some of their monarch's propensities.

Inevitably Maeve has become a symbol of female dominance; but according to other traditions of similar antiquity – looking to Ulster and Scotland, rather than to Connaught – women had also achieved the more effective dominance that is associated with their beauty and subtlety rather than their ruthlessness in conflict. There is more than one symbol of this form of dominance, but the one chronologically closest to Maeve in the surviving manuscripts is the beautiful virgin Deirdre (Derdriu), Conor's protégée, who had fallen in love with a courtier, Naisi (Noisiu), and eloped with him to Scotland. The divergence between the earliest accounts and those of the Victorians is no less noticeable in the treatment of Deirdre than it is in the case of Maeve. A powerful bond of physical love is common to both periods, but there the similarity, apart from the names of the dramatis personae and the geographical locations, ends. In the old account Deirdre's evil influence is forecast before her birth, and she seduces her man virtually by force, while the later version of her story has all the overtones and omissions that one comes to expect. As the climax approaches, the lovers are lured back to Ulster and betrayed, and, in the nineteenth-century rendering of the romance – which is clothed anachronistically in the imagery of *amour courtois*, or courtly love, Naisi is told by Deirdre that a life in hiding has no disadvantages as his presence is all that she needs. His reply conveys a message that directly contradicts all the assumptions that have long been associated with the Maeve tradition:

> Not so with me. Love makes the woman's life
> Within-doors and without; but, out of doors,
> Action and glory make the life of man.[14]

Other distinctions are shown in the exchanges between Deirdre and Naisi at their first meeting. In the Gaelic version, having seen a raven drinking blood in the snow, Deirdre said, 'I could desire a man who had the three colours there: hair like the raven, cheeks like blood and his body like snow.' Told that such a one was at hand, she found him with the cattle and 'made as though to pass him and not recognize him':

6

'That is a fine heifer going by', he said.

'As well it might', she said. 'The heifers grow big where there are no bulls.'

'You have the bull of this province all to yourself', he said; 'the king of Ulster.'

'Of the two', she said, 'I'd pick a game young bull like you.'[15]

The Deirdre story not only illustrates the diverse traditions of the twentieth century's heritage, it highlights the superiority of the ancient approach in certain areas, particularly in its choice of imagery, and it shows why later writers have seen in the Gaelic narratives a patchwork containing raw material for an epic that was never written.

Even allowing for the accretions of later cultures, the main stepping stones of the legends, which are arguably exaggerations of real events, led to a dual concept of women which as well as entering into folklore had its longevity guaranteed by being embodied in noble houses. The Maeves, with their leadership and aggression, gave birth to one stereotype; the Deirdres and Grainnes, with initiatives in the field of passion, gave birth to another. Those of the lower orders are more colourfully represented in the old accounts. They may be called upon to taunt the enemy with their bare breasts, while the Victorian 'peerless maid' is less excitingly one of 'the simple country people'.[16] But such is oral tradition that only the remarkable are likely to acquire names, achieve immortality and become cultural stereotypes; and it has to be remembered that in their time Maeve and Deirdre were not remarkable merely because of their sex, any more than Conor or CuChulainn were celebrated because of theirs – they were famed and honoured for what they were and did. Indeed, Conor, as Conor Mac Nessa, owed his accession to the monarchy to the power and influence of his mother, Nessa.

The very use of the term 'stereotype' diminishes some of the most vivid characters of the pagan era. Maeve and Deirdre, one can be sure, had little that was commonplace about them; later ages have over-simplified these and other larger-than-life individuals, just as striking personalities in subsequent periods have been reduced to their more easily remembered features. Their unconscious contribution to later perceptions of the role of women in Ireland has been based on generalizations of traditions connected with their names. But though the traditions which stem from these very different contemporaries are distinct, they do not necessarily conflict. Each in her own way holds men in thrall. As is only too obvious, they have practically nothing in common with two of their New Testament contemporaries, Martha and Mary, except that they too can be taken to represent two different approaches to life: the female and the feminine. The dissimilar characters of Maeve and Deirdre have accumulated over the years two ways of asserting that, despite the intervention of periods in which women have fulfilled apparently passive roles, fundamentally Ireland is not a man's world. Not far below the surface today

7

– North and South – the idealized dual concept of the primordial woman is still a force to be reckoned with; sometimes it seems to be quiescent, sometimes it erupts.

That the old Gaelic concepts of a woman's place were to survive the spread of Christianity throughout the island can be attributed in large measure to the methods adopted by the Englishman who sought to wean the Irish from paganism, and from the errors of the ancient Celtic Church. If the confused traditions about St Patrick have any basis in truth he shared his Master's respect for civil authority. The property and other marital rights, such as divorce, which women had come to enjoy were no more under threat as a result of his mission than was much of the remainder of the complex legal system which was prevalent. At first sight, because the victims of criminal acts, or their families or witnesses to a crime, carried out the sentences passed, Brehon law appears to have been based on the principle of revenge; on closer inspection its many rules were carefully calculated to achieve just compensation for the plaintiff. The Brehons were a hereditary caste of judges or, more accurately, adjudicators and, as their activities were mainly confined to the secular world, there was no reason why Christianity as practised in the fifth century – when notions such as celibacy had not yet gained widespread acceptance – should come into conflict with their rulings. Unlike the fallacious demands of Druidism, Brehon law could for the time being be conveniently left to one side. Moreover, even when it came to separating superstition from religion, Patrick adopted a positive, if not pragmatic, approach. Wiser than the British imperial missionaries who in another age were to convert much of Africa, he did not seek to destroy all existing cultural traditions; instead he used some of them to serve Christian ends. An instance of this, not far removed from the scene of Maeve's adventures, is to be found appended to a story called 'The Fosterage of the Houses of the Two Mothers', where Patrick is said to have endorsed its value at considerable length, concluding with the verse:

> If you tell this story
> To the captives of Ireland
> It will be the same as if were opened
> Their locks and their bonds.[17]

The impact of Christianity on the place of women in Ireland came some four centuries after the heyday of the pagan heroines and can best be understood in terms of the effect of a very different woman, again of noble birth, called Brigid. Patrick's arrival had coincided with the establishment of a sixth-century dynasty which claimed to rule all Ireland through subordinate chiefs (though it never did). But of more fundamental effect on Irish women than the acquisition by Niall of the Nine Hostages of the High Kingship was the birth into Christianity of a woman of Ulster's hereditary ruling class (though, such is the partisanship of so much of Irish history that it is no surprise to find rival traditions, one claiming that St Brigid was the daughter of a Leinster chief, the other that she was of peasant origin). Brigid was 11 years old when Patrick died and, although little is known of her upbringing, it can be reasonably safely assumed that she was spared any appreciable conflict between heathen and Christian traditions; only the invocation of demons and suchlike magical activities were denounced by Patrick. The respect of the learned for the pagan sagas was not regarded as sinful, and much strife was thus avoided. Maeve's and Deirdre's place in the island's culture was preserved.

Brigid founded a convent at Kildare and, after a monastery had been built beside it, the place became a great religious centre. Starting as a small cell, her foundation grew rapidly and the King of Leinster gave Brigid the whole of the district which encompassed what became the town of Kildare and, centuries later, the Curragh military camp. She is said to have effectively renounced ownership in order to allow most of the area to become common land; though it appears that many already had grazing rights there. The growth of the adjacent monastery was to shed further light on the place of women in fifth- and sixth-century Ireland, for at Kildare the bishop was the nominee and the functionary of Brigid, the abbess, and of her successors. This official relationship derived from a combination of ecclesiastical and tribal precedence; Brigid, possessing both the spiritual and temporal rights of a chief who had become a Christian, would recognize the bishop's authority within his area of responsibility; nevertheless, as the early Church followed the existing organization of society, he was subject to her.

Although Brigid paved the way, other women of the ruling class played crucial roles at this stage in diverting the course of Irish history towards and through the cloister. On the Continent nuns seem to have preceded monks, having appeared in the middle of the third century. In Ireland from the outset they combined authority with humility, and their achievement of a special status was helped in no small way by the aristocratic connections, male and female, of Brigid's contemporaries. One of these contemporaries, the elder sister of the King of Oriel, was converted by Patrick and became a nun before persuading her brother Enda (the saint) to train for monastic life. Another of Enda's sisters was wife of the King of Munster, and her husband granted Enda a site in the Aran islands for his own community; here, in the most pagan region of the country, he trained many of those who earned Ireland its 'saints and scholars' reputation. But, despite Brigid's status and the privileges of other women of the old order, the Christian legacy which these religious settlements introduced was to involve with it a removal from women of the direct influence which they had hitherto exerted on secular affairs. Irish civilization gradually shifted from a tribal basis to a system of communities, each with its own tract of land, and with this change came divisions of labour which, except in certain specialized fields and among the upper reaches of social life, relegated women either to the performance of domestic duties or to the supervision of domestics. The changes affected the lives of freemen, serfs and slaves, though naturally in different ways. The serfs were debtors who had no option but to work their way towards freedom by unpaid service on the land; the lives of the slaves changed but slowly until the Church managed to extinguish Ireland's slave trade shortly before the introduction of Norman law (in Brigid's time a *cumal* or female slave was worth three cows). Like historians of other countries, most chroniclers of Irish history have only made token recognition of the existence of the anonymous multitude that lay at the base of so many nations.

Although social changes during the period of dominance of Niall of the Nine Hostages caused a shift of emphasis in the secular life of women, so that they exerted power not so much from the throne as from behind it, Brigid and those who followed her inspired a rival distinctive role for women, in the perception of both sexes, that still colours the outlook of practically all Irish people today. The closely regulated celibate life of the convent, with its emphasis on self-denial, prayer and contemplation, though to some extent it fostered the domestic virtues that may be ignored by those intrigued by the 'Amazon' legends, was a denial in most other respects of pagan habits and assumptions.

For more than three centuries after St Brigid's time, life in Ireland was more peaceful than in most European countries. Monastic life throughout this period increasingly influenced what had previously been purely secular domains and, within the orbit of what were to become collegiate towns, arts and crafts flourished as a number of men and a few women consciously or more probably unconsciously were freed to develop their talents by others providing the basic necessities of life. The increase of the servility of most women came by stealth; as if fulfilling the same natural law that obliged them to bear children, the women of this time, other than those who held ecclesiastical office or were of royal blood, now performed menial agricultural or domestic duties. The occupations were by no means new to women and need not necessarily have been disadvantageous to them; the trouble was that institutions were developing, specifically for females, which entailed exclusion from the decision-making hierarchies of expanding local communities. They were victims of a system which had a compelling logic to it, and against which male initiatives were unlikely to be taken.

As with so much to do with Ireland, ambivalence was the rule. A happy geographical accident, coupled with the spread of Christian aesthetics as well as ethics, meant that much of Ireland, despite some outbreaks of tribal, and even monastic, warfare, could prosper intellectually and function pastorally from the fifth to the eighth century while the rest of Europe lost its way. While the women of convents and royal houses remained highly regarded, it nevertheless became clear to leading Christians that women in general were suitable objects for protection, and this led to 'Adamnan's law' exempting them from military service and pronouncing it a crime to kill them in war. In the sixth century women were going into battle as regularly as the men, and many continued to be warriors during the seventh century, despite a decree promulgated by Columba at Drumceatt in 590. However, Adamnan, a nobleman who became abbot of Iona and author of the famous life of St Columba, was believed to have been persuaded by his mother to use his influence in high places to get these measures enforced. According to legend, when travelling with her son she witnessed a fight in which a woman's breast was impaled on a hooked pike wielded by another woman; she then refused to move until he swore he would prevent such horrors from happening again. Although this story may be apocryphal, Adamnan did convene the assembly which enacted his 'law'.

Because Adamnan acted when he did, the prohibition of killing women in war was not as Utopian as it may sound today. There was already a move away from the secular classification of women as warriors, queens or chattels, while regarding nuns and their abbesses as a class apart. Columba's decree and Adamnan's law were not just plucked out of the air; they expressed a Christian sentiment that had popular appeal, despite ubiquitous domestic slavery and Ireland's peculiar mixture of tribal indiscipline and monastic order. However, though the legal position of Irish women was greatly improved by Adamnan's law, a twentieth-century feminist might argue that, taking a long-term view, recognition of women's special vulnerability did in fact create an invidious form of inequality. It was left to pagan and secular traditions to save Irish women from becoming victims of the sort of paternalism that so annoyed Africans of both sexes at the close of the era of British imperialism. But transient paternalism, at any rate, has something to be said for it: the women of Ireland's monastic period also benefited in practical, more mundane but none the less valuable ways; their rights of property were minutely regulated by laws which were preserved in writing and frequently cited.

When in 795 Scandinavians (usage has imposed the misnomer, the 'Danes') began the raids which culminated in a major attempt at conquest in 830, the drastic setback in Irish development caused by their efforts to re-establish paganism did not unduly affect the political status which privileged women still enjoyed. Indeed, the way in which the invaders chose to assert their own authority over the island and at the same time supplant its religion was to add strength to the idea of a woman's place at the summit: when, for ten years, a Dane set up his own throne in Armagh, his queen, Ota, occupied Clonmacnoise, the famous Christian institution founded by St Kieran, and gave pagan audience from the sacred high altar. Later, when the Danes were losing ground rapidly, and they had depended on an alliance with the Leinstermen, it was the remarriage of a Leinster princess, Gormlaith (whose Danish husband Olaf Cuaran fled) to the High King which ensured that a Gael, her son, became King of Dublin.

11

Gormlaith has other claims to notoriety. Between husbands she managed to bear a child, Donnchad, for Brian Boru and then slid conveniently to the winning side when he broke the six-centuries-old dynasty by toppling her second husband, Malachy. When, in turn, he betrayed her it was she who sought his overthrow by a Danish expeditionary force: the reward for a successful invader was to be Ireland and her hand in marriage. The actual result of this offer was the final defeat of the Danes at the battle of Clontarf. Despite the centuries of Christian influence which lay between them, Maeve and Gormlaith still had something in common.

Until and after the Normans were enticed as mercenaries into the island's military and political affairs, despite the changing structures of society caused by monasticism and the disruption caused by Danish incursions, women were still fulfilling functions that ensured the peaceful conduct of the kingdoms. While the suzerainty of Tara was often little more than a focus of controversy between various claimants, disputes often arose between the male rulers of (or pretenders to) the kingdoms. When this happened it was still customary, as it had been in the legendary periods, for the matter to be decided by mothers or wives. Eighty years before the battle of Clontarf, for instance, when Munster's succession was contested, the queen addressed the assembled nobility and they deferred to her authority by making her son, Cellachan of Cashel, their king.[18] This was not only a question of force of character, though doubtless this aspect of the event played its part; a woman's function as arbiter was to become enshrined in the law: 'In all controversies between O'Neyll and Nelan Connelagh O'Neyll, they shall stand to the arbitration of the Lord Deputy, Rose, daughter of the Lord Deputy, Lord O'Downyll, and Lord McGuyer'.[19] And records show that referring matters to wives was also practised by common consent of the aggrieved parties, as happened when there was a dispute between the Earl of Ormonde and Ulick de Burgh.[20] It happened, too, when argument arose between the earls Desmond and Thomond, about their respective relationships with the Irish tribes: 'we have remitted the hearing of the process to the Ladies of Desmond and Thomond', with some others, 'or to any four of them, so that the said Ladies be two'.[21]

The piecemeal nature of the Norman–Irish entanglement was such that for many years in large parts of the smaller island the way of life of the people was little affected by it. There had always been wars between rivals; the strangers helped to tip the scales one way or another as far as the rule of local hierarchies was concerned. However, for the more mobile classes, that is to say those who could move of their own volition, irrevocable changes would ensue. When chiefs became earls it was much more than the replacement of a label; it reflected a bringing together of the two islands under an aristocratic system that in the long term had a politically unifying effect and this was to continue long after the Flight of the Earls, as Irish nobles became increasingly Anglo-Irish.

Until the Reformation the lives of Irish women tended to fall into the four categories that were the creation of, or were modified by, the Gaelic and the monastic traditions. The celibate life provided such spiritual strength that its adherents would survive the upheavals and the persecution which lay ahead. The married woman, if she were the wife of a freeholder, accepted her responsibilities at the higher level of the domestic scene: she supervised the dairy and the piggery, she saw to it that the wool and the flax which came from her husband's land were spun, woven and then dyed with dyes from the same sources, she might well have been a skilled embroideress (Strafford was to comment that all were 'naturally bred to spinning'[22]) and she made sure that her daughters were taught the use of quern, kneading-trough and sieve. At the lower level of the domestic scene, behind the idyllic picture that is too easily conjured up by descriptions of the principal beneficiaries of division of labour, lay the services of the poor peasants and serfs who made possible the comparatively high standard of living which (at this time) others enjoyed. They made possible, too, the perpetuation throughout the European Dark Ages of the aesthetic skills which were not simply the prerogative of religious orders. Among the fourth category of the women of this period, the noble women, were those who took sensible advantage of their privileged position to pursue Gaelic arts and crafts. An example, and very much a symbol, of the survival of the Gaelic aesthetic tradition was created by the daughter of Rory O'Conor, King of Connaught. When her father died she engraved in his memory a silver chalice and burnished it with gold.

The gulfs between the different levels of society in Ireland grew wider until the devotion to total domesticity expected of the females of the lower orders was in dramatic contrast to the fashion-consciousness of women of the higher strata. There was nothing remarkable about this situation, in that it merely echoed the class divisions of other societies; but it was a change from former times, and it was reinforced by some of the effects of the Reformation. Among these were the material advantages to be gained by the aristocracy of accepting Protestantism, or of avoiding the penalties of not abandoning Rome. A significant number of those now deemed to have been 'Anglo-Irish' perceived Ireland in much the same way, albeit from a different vantage point, as did the common people; they, however, had access to the new religious teachings, as had the people of all classes in England, Scotland and Wales. Not so the Irish peasants who, but for one act and one omission, might have remained indifferent to doctrinal change. The act was the prohibition in the name of the boy king, Edward VI, of the saying of mass; the omission was availability of Protestant doctrine in the Irish language. Irish-speaking clerics could well have paved the way for a peaceful substitution of Anglican for Roman communion. Those priests in sympathy with the reforms knew no Irish.

The faith, when challenged, was seen to affect woman's place in the whole scheme of things infinitely more than it had done when Christendom had seemed to speak with one voice. Now there was not only a Roman Catholic view of women and an Anglican opposing view, the upper reaches of society tended to be separated doubly from the lower orders and the Anglo-Irish were themselves of divided adherence. As the apparent heresy had entered the island from England, whence even the edicts of the Catholic Queen Mary did little to ease things for Irish Catholics, and as the majority of the ruling class were to embrace Protestantism, all the seeds were sown for martyrdom, rebellion, war and civil war. Consolidation of commitment to the Christian ideal of celibacy was an inevitable outcome of resistance to the libertarianism of those prepared to recognize the right of priests to marry. 'Brides of Christ', as they came to be known, were not uniquely Roman Catholic but, especially when viewed against the background of misuse of brides by the recent king of England, they acquired a special sort of sanctity which was to colour Irish attitudes for at least four hundred years. Virtually no effort was made to justify doctrinal changes or legal and ecclesiastical prohibitions and the people, knowing no reason to doubt their traditional faith, clung to it in understandable desperation. Their disillusion was completed when Queen Mary not only failed to do anything for the Irish who lived 'beyond the Pale', or outside the small hinterland of Dublin Bay, but also gave nothing back to the monasteries and set precedents, especially in land confiscation, for the worst aspects of Queen Elizabeth's Irish policy.

By this time the way had long been prepared, partly by an eighth-century Irish litany, partly by the teaching of a saint now no longer venerated in Ireland, for naïve Protestant perception of a specific heresy. Both the heresy, what there was of it, and the perception of it by opponents, were to have profound effects on attitudes to women throughout the island and beyond its shores. As the years passed the major sin of Roman Catholics in the eyes of Protestants of various degrees of reasonableness or unreasonableness was that at best they used Christ's mother as a mediator, at worst they worshipped a usurper of the Godhead who, as it happened, was a woman. An extreme form of this opinion was to lead a Roman Catholic headmaster of a later century to complain, 'They say we worship women.' Put bluntly like that, the very idea is absurd. And yet, strictly speaking, there were among the simple faithful some men and women who were innocently guilty, in the sense that intellectually and culturally they had few options, of the Marian heresies of which they were accused; they allowed Mary to eclipse Jesus. Given the circumstances, one might ask, would Jesus have been particularly upset?

When most of the population were illiterate it was hardly remarkable that some were inclined towards 'extravagances', as the *Catholic Encyclopedia* is pleased to term them ('Mariolatry', as in 'idolatry', is the preferred Protestant term). Had St Thomas Aquinas and St Oengus the Culdee changed places in time and space there might have been no problem. Aquinas in the thirteenth century defined the special honour owed to Christ's mother as 'hyperdulia': 'a veneration which exceeds that paid to other saints, but is at the same time infinitely below the adoration ('latria') due to God alone, which it would be blasphemous to attribute to any creature.'[23] Oengus (formerly Aengus), however, heard no such warnings that his prayers might be in any way excessive, and he became something of an embarrassment to the Irish hierarchy because of the ardour of his language whenever the Virgin Mary's name was introduced. Moreover, he continually referred to Christ as Jesus Mac Mary: an offence against theology rather than propriety in the sense that Mac God would have been theologically acceptable, although somewhat familiar. But then Oengus was steeped in the imagery of the striking eighth-century litany, in which the Blessed Virgin Mary was: 'Mistress of the Heavens, Mother of the Heavenly and Earthly Church, Recreation of Life, Mistress of the Tribes, Mother of the Orphans, Breast of the Infants, Queen of Life, Ladder of Heaven'.[24] Perhaps such verbal excesses are only to be expected from those whose daily discipline required them to fast, to genuflect frequently, and to recite one third of the psalter while immersed in cold water.

If anyone, on the basis of selected 'extravagances' were to argue that Ireland owes its – at times fraudulent – reputation as a matriarchy to association of the female in general with the Virgin Mary, he would be ignoring much evidence of geography and custom. It is true that by the sixteenth century there had developed among some of the people a habit of placing before themselves an idealized female. But this simplification leaves on one side the diversification of clans and provinces which characterized Ireland until 1603, and takes no account of the very different secular worlds in which the island's inhabitants lived. There was no uniform culture. Outside the area of parliamentary rule, which was no more than six hundred square miles, was what might today be termed a buffer state, the Middle Nation, consisting of low born and high born who had to some extent gone native and identified themselves with things Irish; their absorption had been hastened by families following the ancient custom of fostering out boys with leading families, a practice which served to create strong bonds. Then there was Gaelic Ireland, little influenced by strangers and enjoying its own diversities of social tradition and local politics. All three areas contained strong-minded rulers and there arose many conflicts between Brehon and Norman law, and also eccentric compromises between the two caused by the fluctuating degree of autonomy enjoyed by the earls.

A product of Gaelic Ireland in this period was Grania (Grace) O'Malley, a woman bearing little resemblance to any Christian ideal version of woman-hood. She achieved her fame as a pirate chieftainess with three galleys and two hundred fighting men at her command. A latter-day old-fashioned ruler in part of Connaught, she at first appears to be a reincarnation of one the early legendary figures, a warrior chief and the dominant partner in her marriages. But, as an illustration of the multiple traditions of Ireland with regard to women's rights, her attitude to divorce is as interesting as her attitude to marriage. By an idiosyncrasy of history, a reversal of the late-twentieth-century position prevailed, whereby the secular arm of a small state, the enclave of another, imposed a Christian ethic limiting the availability of divorce. At the same time in a comparatively large area beyond the bounds of the Pale, divorce on demand for both sexes was permitted by Brehon law – the irony of the situation being that it was the Protestant power which at that time curbed citizens' rights, especially of women.

Under Brehon law marriage and divorce were simple procedures, comparable in some respects to the practices of twentieth-century tinkers. Grania's first marriage ended in the death of her husband, Donal O'Flaherty, after she had borne his two sons and a daughter. The union had brought about an alliance between two clans, and similar considerations would have influenced her choice of a second husband, Richard Burke. According to tradition the two entered into an arrangement whereby the marriage could be dissolved after a year if either party so wished. Trial marriage seems to have had its temptations for a strong-minded woman; again according to tradition, when Richard Burke returned from some warlike expedition at the end of the initial year he was greeted with Grania's shout from the battlements of Rockfleet Castle: 'I dismiss you!',[25] and refused admission to a property that was no longer his. Whether or not the story can be believed (they did marry, live in Rockfleet and produce a son, and on Richard's death Grania claimed her husband's lands), it conveniently serves to demonstrate the looseness of marital bonds before the old laws and practices were superseded:

> In no field of life was Ireland's apartness from the mainstream of European society so marked as in that of marriage . . . Down to the end of the old order in 1603, what could be called Celtic secular marriage remained the norm in Ireland . . . Christian matrimony was no more than a rare exception, grafted on to this system.[26]

But it should be remembered that, as far as the protection of women went, Gaelic law had something to commend it; it took into account the material consequences of divorce. The prospective husband could be called upon to provide securities for the return of his wife's dowry, should he divorce her and remarry.

Exceptional though she was, Grania O'Malley did not shock her compatriots to anything like the degree that she shocked observers from other cultures. The behaviour of her female contemporaries was a continual source of amazement to those reared elsewhere. Elizabethan and post-Elizabethan settlers, from Edmund Spenser to Luke Gernon, were surprised and often disturbed by all sorts of practices: women were seen presiding over feasts, drinking alcohol and apparently flaunting their sexuality by not wearing corsets. They greeted strangers with a social kiss, and wives are believed to have been promiscuous – though there is some disagreement about this characteristic. Most visitors were impressed by the amount of authority Irish women exercised within the family and often within the community at large. Female confidence during this period was boosted by a woman's right to keep her own name after marriage. She could also still make use of the traditional right of claiming paternity for her child simply by 'naming' a father, who might well be someone of power and influence. This right could be exercised at any time during the child's minority, and could effectively bind him or her to a father previously unknown to either child or mother. In such ways families were strengthened and links were made with the wider world of clans, a tendency not seriously diminished by a counter-tradition in remote parts of Ireland whereby a married woman might continue to live in the house of her birth.

In most of the clans Gaelic tradition favoured choosing the next chief during the current ruler's lifetime on the basis of fitness to rule, and this process had enabled some strong-willed women to exercise power. But as time went by it became more and more necessary for a good deal of oratory, doubtless aided by residual superstition about women and sorcery, to be employed if female ambitions were to be achieved. Unlike women's property ownership rights which had long been recognized as at least establishing a basis for treatment as equals before Irish law, there had been no actual right of female succession until Norman custom had been introduced within the Pale and for a while beyond it. Where this applied a daughter could inherit land and lordship when there was no son. However, a retrograde step was soon taken, one which helped to hold back this aspect of women's property rights in Ireland for centuries: the Irish lords, fearing female succession lest the right of the Crown be exercised to choose the husband and their power be diminished, abandoned the custom. So in Connaught, for instance, the Burkes made it a family rule that only a male heir could succeed.

When, in 1603, James VI of Scotland succeeded to the kingdoms of England and Ireland, everything began to change; his accession to the throne occurred as the last independent Gaelic kingship was destroyed, and not long afterwards the earls took flight. The descendants of the Normans who had come to Ireland at the invitation of the king of Leinster, and had been misnamed 'English', were soon to be 'Old English'. They, like the earlier inhabitants, against whom and for whom they had fought, and among whom they had settled, had retained the old faith. Soon they were to find that 'New English', many of whom were Scots returning to the land whence they had come as colonizers in the fifth century, were to be 'planted' on much of the best land in the north. The 'New English' had embraced a narrow Protestantism, while the general disposition of the 'Old English' was more attuned to that of the old-established Gaelic or Scottish inhabitants. When the term 'Anglo-Irish' was coined, many of the substantial 'Old English' families, Catholic and Protestant alike, did not take kindly to it. They reckoned that they were as Irish as any so-called native. This was not always the case in the regions of the 'plantations'. In these parts it was soon found that there was much profit to be gained from redistributing land on an inequitable basis, leaving only one third of it on which the existing population might be employed. The first consequence of this was an extension of the plantation principle to other parts of Ireland; the second was rebellion.

The Great Rebellion broke out in many parts of Ireland during the reign of Charles I, and inevitably, when the turmoils of the Civil War began, it became difficult to draw a clear line between loyalty and disloyalty among both Catholics and Protestants in the Irish context. By the end of both great events, though, the dispute in Ireland had become much more narrowly a matter of religion than of race; a woman's status would be determined more by her faith and her social class than her supposed ethnic origin, significant though this might be. There are countless examples of this; among them Ellen FitzGerald who traced her ancestry to Gerald of Windsor, Strongbow's most famous companion, and had married into the ancient royal house of Munster. On the face of it her offspring would be unashamedly recusant, but her son Murrough O'Brien, Lord Inchiquin, was Protestant with a degree of zeal which recalled the personality of his most celebrated ancestor, Brian Boru. Being one of the 'native' Irish, if there had ever been such creatures, would not necessarily have been a disadvantage, provided that other criteria were satisfied.

Women whose sense of responsibility was put to the test at this difficult time might react very differently, as two examples may show. Lady Ellen Aylmer, by birth a member of the recusant Butler family and sister of the future (Protestant) first Duke of Ormonde, is said to have taught succeeding generations of Aylmer males 'to eschew marriage with too strong-minded ladies'.[27] Her Roman Catholic husband Andrew, second baronet of Donadea, having been accused of treason was 'under torture' in Dublin Castle in 1641 when she was besieged in Donadea Castle. When offered her husband's life and freedom if she would surrender Donadea, she replied that if her husband were to be hanged in front of the gate it would make no difference to her. Sir Andrew begged her to negotiate with his captors, sending his ring as evidence that the message was genuine, but still she would not yield. Nevertheless he was eventually released and in 1662, under the Act of Settlement, his legal ownership of lands and properties, including manors, castles, villages and towns in County Kildare, was confirmed: an unusual outcome at a time when Roman Catholics were being deprived of their estates, and one that, notwithstanding a degree of apparent heartlessness on Lady Aylmer's part, owed much to the force of individual character.

County Wexford was one of the principal areas of unrest in the mid-seventeenth century, and it was there, at Tintern Abbey, that the plight and behaviour of a dissimilar though no less striking personality, Lady Colclough (Alice, daughter of Sir Robert Riche), illustrated the peculiar admixture of loyalties which affected the overlapping politics of the two islands.[28] Alice had been a widow for four years and was alone at Tintern at the outbreak of the rebellion. Immediately she set about putting the abbey into a state of defence and preparing it as a place of refuge for the two or three hundred Protestants who lived in the neighbourhood. She arranged for it to be garrisoned by a detachment of troops from Duncannon Fort under the command of a Major Aston, and together they withstood siege for some five months. In June 1642 she gathered together those of the Protestant gentry who had English properties to which they could go, and left for England. Years later, when the rebellion had been suppressed, many Wexford Protestants were indicted on the specific charge of not having left the country with Lady Colclough.

While Tintern Abbey was being besieged the Civil War began in England and the Protestant holders of office in County Wexford, all Royalist, immediately offered Alice's three brothers-in-law and two of their friends the sum of £400 if they would take the abbey from the English troops. Three Colcloughs then undertook to attack the very place that their sister-in-law had so recently defended; and, with a force of some three hundred rebels, the Colcloughs proved that the family was as good at attack as it was at defence. After several months of sieges and assaults, Major Aston surrendered on condition that his men might go freely into Munster, and this was allowed. Colclough motives during this episode had been mixed; a prime consideration seems to have been prevention of the house and contents being sacked and looted by their new allies, the rebels. When the day of reckoning came only the Catholic brother-in-law suffered exile and forfeiture of possessions; there is no evidence that the two Protestants were punished. Nothing more is known of Alice's experiences, except that after spending the rest of her life in England she was buried at Tintern. In her rescue of the Protestants of Wexford she was, of course, behaving as an individual of courage and compassion; she was also fulfilling the role that might be expected at this time of the daughter of a knight and (until 1637) the wife of a baronet.

According to Burke[29] Lady Colclough had two sons: the elder, Caesar, who, if the account were to be believed, was born five years after his father's death, and Anthony. The younger son, again if Burke were to be believed, was drawn full-bloodedly into things Irish and Catholic. Not only did he take the oath of the 'Confederate Catholics of Ireland', he became a member of its supreme council. But Burke is wrong.[30] It was another Anthony Colclough, whose mother Honora was the daughter of the Lord of the Walshe Mountains, who although a Protestant took the oath of the Catholic Confederation and was a member of the Supreme Council of Kilkenny. The membership of this body, which included those Roman Catholics who might be termed 'Old English' and others who might regard themselves as native Irish, sought peace with a view to establishing a Roman Catholic nation, and acted as loyal subjects of King Charles. Unfortunately, while Cromwell's victory on both sides of the Irish Sea reduced all Confederates to the level of disloyal papists, the restoration of the monarchy did not restore to them the lands and the influence which Cromwell had taken away. Moreover, introduction of the penal laws confirmed that henceforward, despite all the other factors of origin and commitment, most Irish men and women were to be categorized as either disloyal papists or loyal Protestants.

Implementation of the Penal Code imposed by the Irish Parliament brought most Catholic families down to the lowest level of subsistence and the women, as child-bearers, suffered more than the men. The situation of the Catholic poor was made even more intolerable by a succession of potato famines that have been largely obliterated from memory by the Great Famine of 1845–9. Although during the next century those penal laws which did not pose a direct threat to Protestant monopoly of power were repealed, the peasant workforce of Ireland suffered alternative legislative penalties which destroyed the woollen trade. Important consequences of this were a widening of the gap between north and south and, as time went by, the creation of an industry based in Ulster that was manned almost entirely by women.

William III rewarded the people of Ulster for their part in placing him on the throne by promising to encourage the linen trade. This developed throughout the eighteenth century as a cottage industry which augmented the pathetic income which farmers could derive from their small plots. A full night's work is foreseen in the couplet:

> My wife the house trims up full-tidy
> And in her wheel sits down beside me . . . [31]

Such domestic scenes could only too easily conjure up a phoney idyllic conception of the peasant husband and wife at their loom. Throughout much of Ulster the facts were not too harsh; elsewhere it was a different story:

> Half a dozen children, almost naked, were sleeping on a little straw with a pig, a dog, a cat, two chickens and a duck. The poor woman spread a mat on a chest, the only piece of furniture in the house, and invited me to lie there. The animals saluted the first ray of the sun by their cries and began to look for something to eat . . . I got up very soon for fear of being devoured.[32]

The arrival of the mechanized cotton industry heralded the end of Irish linen-making as a cottage industry and for a while it seemed as though linen manufacture itself was doomed. But Irish linen was saved by Lancashire cotton; the English industrial giant destroyed its Irish rival, leaving a legacy not of unemployment but of a technology that was ideal for making profitable the manufacture of linen. The linen-mill was born, and with it a new type of Irish: working-class females.

By the end of the eighteenth century the role of women in Ireland no longer appears to lend itself easily to generalizations; women were fulfilling a variety of roles depending on where they lived, their religion, occupation and class, and on the overlapping of these categories. Despite later impressions to the contrary there was still a Catholic landed gentry, and the ladies of this class, as the next century was to show, were as skilled at manipulating their husbands as were their Protestant counterparts. There was more intermarriage between the Catholic and Protestant great houses than has been recognized and, while nearly all were to subscribe to the Union which was about to come into being, an increasing number of the ruling class felt – rather than thought – that one's primary loyalties were to Ireland and the Crown; a secondary loyalty, albeit an important one, would be to the United Kingdom. The 'native' side of this equation was subtly developing the characteristics first noticed by Sir Henry Sidney when he described Grania O'Malley as 'a most famous feminine sea captain'[33] and observed that his son, the poet Sir Philip Sidney, had been captivated by her charm.

When one looks below the level of the well-documented classes, whose letters and diaries help to explain motives and actions, one can be better served by the novel than by the Blue Book. The ebb and flow of trade in the eighteenth century had seen the development of a middle class which was outwardly male-dominated, but the significance of the female dimension of this was not to become clear until pockets of Ireland emulated England as a nation of shopkeepers, and daughters became poorly paid, or unpaid, assistants. It was the rural Irish woman, the wife of a poor tenant farmer, who was first sympathetically and effectively (though sometimes sentimentally) portrayed in the novels of Maria Edgeworth, Sir Walter Scott's chosen literary model.

The peasant farmer's wife, as exemplified in the Edgeworth novels, is an object of respect shown at the humblest level of society. She is in the direct line of the bondmaid of the old legends, but it is clear that a long infusion of Christianity of a type that gives women a special place, if not a certain sanctity, has brought her a means of control or influence. It is as if, emboldened by their mythical heritage and the Marian emphasis of Roman Catholicism, women, though no longer the repositories of supernatural power or of sovereignty, enjoy a special status within the family as the source of wisdom that is not always limited to domestic matters. The word 'matriarchy' is sometimes bandied about, though not by Maria Edgeworth. The appropriateness of this label, however, may be found in the past and again in the future, not on the eve of the Union.

2

IN THE ASCENDANT

After the 1798 rebellion, for a mixture of motives, it suited more than just the aristocracy and the Protestant landed gentry who ran the Irish Parliament that a complete unification of Great Britain and Ireland should occur. The rebellion, like so much violence in later times, was counter-productive to the attainment of rebel aims; the majority of the people, sick of troubles, made no significant protest. The Catholic bishops, many of whom had been trained in France and had witnessed the horrors of the French Revolution, shared the general mood and saw the Union as an opportunity to gain emancipation for members of their faith. It was left to William Pitt the Younger, who saw the practical realities of the independence which the Irish people nominally enjoyed, to decide that with a liberal distribution of cash and peerages he could peacefully redress injustices by uniting the two parliaments. Like the Norman Conquest before it, had the Act of Union gone the whole way it might have reduced the Irish Question to an acceptable level of bickering about the respective rights and duties of local councils and central government. As it was, it brought to an end the Protestant Ascendancy as a legal governmental entity. Henceforward Ascendancy was to be a social and economic phenomenon, its power and influence much diminished though never extinguished.

It has been pointed out that 'The meaning of Ascendancy implies the inevitability of a fall'[1] but the fortunes of the Ascendancy throughout the 121 years of the existence of the United Kingdom of Great Britain and Ireland did not follow the regular pattern integral to a geometrical way of looking at history. During the nineteenth century the Ascendancy families were put through a series of arduous tests, none more severe than those arising from famine and from reform of tenants' land rights. As the years went by benevolent aspects of the bonds between landlord and tenant were sorely strained, and some snapped. As is well known, often the villain of the piece was the agent of the absentee landlord, for whose sins the absentees must accept their share of responsibility. But, as is far from well known, a serious misreading of history has led to what amount to racist theories of responsibility, and therefore blameworthiness, becoming the accepted wisdom. False interpretations of events have been so widely purveyed that even the old unionist families, loyal to their principles through thick and thin, eventually came to accept them.

The tragedies endured by the peasantry, mainly during Queen Victoria's reign, were not the result of the English being beastly to the Irish, aided and abetted by rich, fellow-travelling Irish, some of whom spoke with English accents. They were caused partly by the absence in the mid-nineteenth century of an infrastructure which would have enabled swift amelioration of large-scale human disasters. Then the consequences of this disadvantage for which none were to blame were compounded by the incompetence of over-centralized government: its inability to cope, even when ignorance or wrongheadedness were not integral to decision-making, with problems of any magnitude when these arose outside the boundaries of the Home Counties. The government consisted of a healthy mix of races, drawn from all parts of the British Isles. Few would deny that on many occasions the powerful exploited the weak and, as the centre of government was on English soil, the language of nationalism was soon the lingua franca of friend and foe alike. The seemingly inevitable outcome of this was that a social revolution was mistaken for a national revolution; and in its course the chance was lost of making a sensible and humane political entity out of a coherent geographical unit: the British (and Irish) Isles.

Both sides, unionists and separatists, having mistaken a struggle for fundamental human rights for a conflict between races, the myth to all intents and purposes took over from reality – just as, even today some, among them ill-informed Englishmen, see Northern Ireland as England's last colony. Against this background the vices of the Ascendancy families have been exaggerated, and their actions frequently misinterpreted. Nevertheless there are some features of Ascendancy life which have not been exaggerated, of which extravagance is one; and women can take their share of responsibility for this. Moreover, in the long term, and sometimes in the short term, the outcome could be disastrous for estates when there was a clash between certain standards in England and those which could be maintained on a heavily mortgaged Irish estate receiving artificially low rents from the tenants. When, for instance, Henry Herbert of Cahirnane had found himself a wife in Hampshire, Katherine (daughter of a clergyman who had married into a wealthier branch of the Herbert family, the Herberts of Muckross) was appalled to discover the absence of basic indoor sanitation at Cahirnane and made it quite clear that she disliked everything about the place. In the end her husband felt that he had no alternative but to build her a new house, later described as 'a monster of grey cement',[2] at a time when his rents were decreasing; while such was the strength of tradition that a vast entourage of servants, together with horses and carriages, continued to be maintained as the overdraft at the bank steadily increased.

The extravagance of the 'Anglo-Irish' had decided benefits for Ireland's architectural heritage. But during times of hardship or famine the incongruity of the magnificent edifices in which some lived could prove to be a source of resentment. The dilemma facing those who seek to interpret the values of those who built beautifully and grandly in the eighteenth and nineteenth centuries in Ireland is similar to that facing priests and imams today as they look at grandiose cathedrals and mosques attended by the starving faithful of South America or West Africa. It has been noticed that anyone so misguided as to seek to remove 'Englishness' from Ireland (happily this phase seems to have passed in the Republic) would have to start by razing to the ground the best of Dublin. Outside the city boundaries the 'Big Houses', from those ancient castles which had been well maintained to Palladian mansions of considerable splendour, fortunately had chatelaines whose responsibility was by no means confined to keeping an eye on the servants; it extended to initiating the beautification of landscapes on a scale that compares favourably with England's Blenheim, especially where Irish acreages were more generous.

Naturally recognition of family responsibilities and duties went far beyond caring for the physical properties of estates, and not everything else fell into the categories of local or national politics; inevitably some were to find the cultural and social heritage into which they had been born something of a straitjacket. Transition from government by the nominally independent Parliament of Ireland to that of the United Kingdom would eventually lead to awakening of separatist ideas and sentiments in the minds and hearts of well-known women rebels of the Ascendancy, such as Countess Markievicz. But 'Big House' independence of spirit, outside the constraints of political ideology, had been seen in Georgian times, and this was exemplified in the feminist life-style – though they would have been horrified to hear it so termed – of the Ladies of Llangollen, whose lives spanned much political change which they chose to ignore.

In two of the relevant genealogies, Kavanagh (better known as Mac-Morrough Kavanagh or 'The MacMorrough', a title given to the kings of Leinster) and Ponsonby, Burke[3] describes the running away together of Lady Eleanor Butler and Sarah Ponsonby as an 'elopement', and such it was in accordance with both principal meanings of the word. However, the Ormondes, Eleanor's family, in their entry in the *Peerage*,[4] have used the old genealogical trick for concealing embarrassments by hiding their offspring in the phrase 'had issue, with three daus'. Traitors, of one sort or another, can easily be disposed of by such expressions;[5] and in the Irish context one man's traitor tends to be another man's patriot. But when Eleanor and Sarah fell in love with each other they were only discreet when discretion was forced upon them; as soon as circumstances allowed they behaved boldly until they had achieved their aim. Eleanor, the masculine one, came from the highest level of ancient Catholic aristocracy; the family seat was Kilkenny Castle, and she had been educated at a French convent. Sarah came from a younger, but equally powerful, Protestant line, the Bessboroughs: her grandfather was the second son of the first Viscount Duncannon, whose brother, as well as succeeding to the viscountcy, became the first Earl of Bessborough.

Today some of Eleanor's relatives attribute her unconventional behaviour to an understandable wish on her part to escape from the only two options allegedly open to a woman of her class, creed and age: a suitable marriage or life in a convent. But this theory just does not square with the evidence; the love that dared not speak its name was, and is, writ too large in diaries and journals, and in the living of two lives that sought to conceal only the most intimate details. Moreover, in France at that time, as Eleanor must have known only too well, convents provided plenty of scope for a woman to express her love for a woman;[6] prejudice against such deviant behaviour was nothing like as marked as it was against homosexual men. Sarah had her own reasons for taking flight. She had been orphaned at the age of 7. Superficially privileged, as orphans go, she had excellent connections and after the death of her stepmother, Lady Staples, when Sarah was 13, her late father's cousin, Lady Betty Fownes, assumed responsibility for her.

All was well while Sarah attended a congenial boarding school in Kilkenny, where she was befriended by Eleanor Butler, who had been asked by Lady Betty to keep an eye on her. Things changed, however, when at the age of 18 she left school and moved into Woodstock, the Fownes's country seat. There she was to suffer from the attentions of her ageing foster-father, Sir William Fownes, who wanted a son and imagined that his wife would soon die. He 'cast his eye on Miss Ponsonby after she had lived in his house for a year or two'.[7] Thus began the 'hot pursuit'[8] which drove her to Eleanor. For better or worse the two women fell in love, and that was not especially remarkable. They proved to be unwitting and remarkable pioneers in the way in which they chose not to hide the fact of their mutual affection, and in their ability to make such a success of their 'retirement', as they called it. One might wish that their twentieth-century successors, of both sexes, would emulate the good manners which they displayed in what amounted to an unorthodox form of marriage.

Neither at Borris House in County Carlow, where Eleanor was briefly imprisoned in the care of her elder sister Susanna, wife of the Catholic 'Monarch' Kavanagh, nor at Llangollen in North Wales, where the pair lived and held court, are they forgotten. The view from the study window at Borris still evokes some of the domestic drama: 'It was across those fields that Eleanor ran away to join Sarah Ponsonby at Woodstock',[9] the attempt to force her to give up her romantic relationship with a woman sixteen years her junior having only strengthened her determination to elope. At Borris, the relationship between the two having already gone far beyond the point of no return, the convent solution proved to be a counter-productive threat made by understandably desperate families who had begun to sense, though hardly to comprehend, the true nature of the bond which they were trying to break.

The most remarkable achievement of these two products of the Ascendancy in Georgian Ireland was the extraordinary degree of respectability which they achieved at Plas Newydd, their Welsh retreat. Because of its scandalous origins, their life together has given birth to an industry of stories that often bear little resemblance to reality; and yet there is no excuse for inaccuracy as a wealth of evidence exists in Eleanor's journals, Sarah's recipe and account books, letters, and much other documentation which reveals most of the details that posterity needs to know. The couple's papers are silent on one issue only: did they, or did they not? Certainly they occupied the same bed; but this is hardly shocking. As the dominant partner, Eleanor wore masculine clothing from an early point in the relationship, Sarah only doing so when a disguise was needed:

> Miss Butler is tall and masculine. She wears always a riding-habit. Hangs up her hat with the air of a sportsman in the hall, and appears in all respects as a young man, if we except the petticoat, which she still retains.
> Miss Ponsonby, on the contrary, is *polite* and effeminate, fair and beautiful.[10]

This description, which appeared in an article of malicious intent in a July 1790 issue of the *General Evening Post*, when Eleanor was 'shortish, inclined to be fat and all of fifty-one',[11] nevertheless had some truth in it. As time went on and the age gap between the 'Ladies of Llangollen' became less apparent, written descriptions, of which there are many, testified that Sarah was dressing in clothes identical to Eleanor's. Prince Puckler Muskaus, writing in 1828, stressed their similarity to one another:

> Both wore ... a gentleman's round hat, a gentleman's cravat and waiscoat, instead of the 'inexpressibles' however, a short *Jupon* and gentlemen's boots. The whole was covered by an overdress of blue cloth of a quite peculiar cut, keeping the middle between a gentleman's overcoat and a lady's riding habit.[12]

Other descriptions spoke of 'not one point to distinguish them from men ... black beaver men's hats'[13] and 'crop heads'.[14]

These Establishment figures, as they would be termed today, disgraced the Irish Establishment only to be adulated by Establishment figures of several nationalities for the rest of their days. Quite why two women who had scandalized their families, and – for those who were aware of their behaviour – their nation, should be so rewarded in their lifetime is not easily discovered by looking at the written record, which reveals neither genius nor consistency. When a note came from William Wilberforce,[15] Eleanor decided to preserve it, being 'proud of this distinction from a character we so highly respect'. She respected him, to her credit, despite her conviction that the slave trade should not be abolished. She believed that humane methods of transportation should be adopted, and that after some years of 'general attention to their morals, manners and health'[16] and sound instruction in religion, the slaves should be released. She was at least consistent in her views about despatching people to the colonies, for elsewhere she related how she had received a letter from a

Welshman convicted of sheep stealing, asking for intercession to 'get him off from Transportation'. He had not reckoned with the Ladies' unsympathetic attitude to quite a few of his class: 'Threw his letter into the fire as we cannot consider a noted Sheep Stealer entitled to much lenity even had we interest to get him off.'[17]

Nor was there much sympathy at Plas Newydd for servants who fell short of demanding standards; though the loyal Mary Carryll, who had aided the elopement and lived and died with her two mistresses, was accorded the privileged status of an altogether different species, and there were others who qualified for special appreciation. Not so Peggy, the undermaid, who lived in for three years until 'Her Pregnancy she could no longer conceal, nor could she plead in her excuse that she had been seduced by promises of marriage.'[18] Summary dismissal followed. 'What is to become of her?' What, indeed? A week later there was comment about 'the rapine and plunder of Servants'[19] in another household. And gipsies fared no better: 'Gypsy came to the door, wanted to tell fortunes. Dismissed her. Hate such people.'[20] But a different sort of caller, Lady Lonsdale, found Eleanor 'the greatest flatterer I ever met with'.[21] Although the obvious interpretation of the contrary reaction is tied up with social acceptability, there is a little more to it than that. The Ladies had in a narrowly material sense come a long way down in the world from Kilkenny Castle and Woodstock; at times they instinctively felt the need to identify with, and to please, those they felt to be of similar stock. Conversely, they might be hasty or dismissive when distancing themselves from the lower orders. Sarah's account book is instructive in this domain:

Expenses
July 2, 1800 . . . to the Mother of the Boys whom we caught in our part of the Cufflymin, for Whipping them 1s.

July 3   6d. to the one 6d. to the other, and 1s. to Mrs Davies Son John in compensation of our unjustly suspecting them of taking our Strawberries 2s.[22]

Sarah's expenses entry of 3 July is reassuring and, in its way, helps to explain the Ladies' local popularity. It is more difficult to explain the extraordinary national – and even international – following which they attracted. Curiosity will have drawn people in the first place; but that would not have sustained the constant stream of men and women of distinction who sought to meet, to befriend and to correspond with the Ladies. These included Edmund Burke, Queen Charlotte, Lord Castlereagh, Charles Darwin, Sir Humphry Davy, Lady Caroline Lamb, Southey, Wordsworth and the Duke of Wellington; friendship with the last-named extended to finding badly needed financial help for Sarah after Eleanor's death: 'the King was yesterday graciously pleased to grant you a Pension on the Civil List of 200 a year net'.[23]

The intimacy of the Ladies' relationship is brought home to one most vividly by the entries in Eleanor's journal. The daily record is peppered with references to 'the darling of my heart', 'my beloved' and 'my Sally', while for her part Sarah's letters echo her devotion with her simpler 'my B'. The transparency of their outrageous and yet at the same time rather beautiful relationship, which they managed to make public without giving offence to any but a few of the older members of their own families, was clearly an important element of their fascination for people; another was the remarkable house and garden which they created around themselves; and another was Eleanor's powerful presence, fortified by Sarah's acquiescence and admiration. Their peculiar contribution to this world was best summed up by Susan Butler, a member of Eleanor's family, 140 years after Sarah's death: 'They threw over their sheltered existence and became, not too self-consciously, the archetypes of female independence.'[24] She went on to argue that the fact that they were sustained by 'an invisible but none the less influential "good family" network should not diminish their credit in modern democratic eyes'. She praised them for their 'aristocratic carelessness of public opinion', and might have added that they were well-read, as well as well-bred. For these and doubtless for other less definable reasons Plas Newydd, the refuge of 'the two most celebrated virgins in Europe',[25] as Prince Puckler Muskaus described them, became 'a place of pilgrimage for admirers from all walks of life and both sexes'.[26]

Unknown to the Ladies, who imagined that in Wales they might shut out, or rise above, the politics of the world – they were, after all, fugitives – the testing time for all who might exercise power in Ireland was beginning; though none took action to avert disaster until it was too late. It is easy to be wise after the event, but part of the rationale of a union of the two islands had been the mutual advantage of coping with disparate needs by the uninhibited flow of resources. In the first half of the nineteenth century the United Kingdom contained within its borders a mixed agricultural economy with sufficient resources to overcome the failure of the potato crop, that is, if unnatural hindrances had ceased to exist. Too much, though, would depend on finding able administrators with common-sense priorities.

Throughout the 1840s, the decade which followed the elimination of the last major obstacles to Catholic emancipation, any Ascendancy women resident in Ireland who might secretly have envied the independence enjoyed by the Ladies of Llangollen would have had to reckon with some unexpectedly pressing moral obligations before leaving the island. At a time when separate strains of the community might have begun to grow together in harmony, they were prized apart by a series of potato famines which culminated in the Great Famine of 1845–9. During this dark period, but for which – and the execution of the Easter martyrs – the United Kingdom might have stayed united, the compassionate action undertaken by some Ascendancy women provided most of the few rays of light. In rent-collecting their record is of tempering their husbands' conception of justice with some mercy; in famine relief the same motives led them, additionally, to intervene in a practical way. Unfortunately, though, when it came to the sort of eviction that amounted to pronouncing sentence of death, a woman could be more heartless than the despised Earl of Leitrim, whose habit of shooting tenants' stray goats led in part to his assassination on the way to an eviction. When looking at this period of Irish history hackneyed sayings may pull one in opposite directions. Were ruthless evictions carried out on the instructions of a woman 'exceptions which proved the rule' or evidence that 'the female is deadlier than the male'? Or is the sex of the perpetrator irrelevant? Proverbial wisdom can be rejected at once, if only because it can be used to justify anything.

The credit side of the landlords' activities has tended to be lost in the overall calamity and equally the part played by women has tended to be subsumed within their husbands' performance. Whereas in ancient Ireland women were to the fore, by the middle of the nineteenth century, although a woman's power might be no less, within the constraints of her class it was more often than not exerted off-stage. Nevertheless the merciful acts of some women were visible. At Ross House, County Galway, the Martins, the family of Violet, the 'Ross' of the Somerville and Ross literary partnership, worked ceaselessly to feed all who depended on them, and all who turned to them for help. Violet's aunt Marian, who was in charge of the household throughout the famine years, caught typhus from pupils at the school which the family ran on the estate. In desperation her husband Robert bled her, and it was little short of a miracle that she survived. Meanwhile, outside the gates, Violet's mother and father, Anna and James, set up a soup-kitchen which saved lives as it drained away some of their extremely limited income.

And elsewhere, whenever mercy was most plainly to the fore, a feminine factor was usually found to be at work. At Castle Leslie in County Monaghan Christiana and Charles Leslie 'fed their own tenants and distributed stirabout and turnips from a huge cauldron in the courtyard to all who chose to come';[27] while at Harristown in County Kildare, John and Maria La Touche's deer-park 'ceased at this time to have any deer in it; all were made into food for the starving people'.[28] In County Sligo when Sir Robert Gore-Booth went down with cholera his wife Caroline, who was already touring the neighbourhood by pony, distributing food from paniers, 'took over the relief work and on returning home was so exhausted she had to be lifted off her horse'.[29] Her early death has been attributed to overwork during the famines. In more recent times it has been far too easy for such efforts to be sneered at for their piecemeal nature, and as the self-congratulatory antics of Lady Bountifuls. Piecemeal they were, seen in national terms, but there is no evidence to suggest that any ulterior motives were at work, and certainly the tenants did not see things in that light. Drumcliffe's parish priest took it upon himself to express to Lady Gore-Booth the gratitude of the Catholic tenantry: 'It will be consoling to her Ladyship to learn that the humble prayers of God's humble creatures were offered every night in every home for the spiritual and temporal welfare of every member of her Ladyship's family'.[30]

But, as J. S. Mill pointed out, motive has nothing to do with the morality of an action, even though it tells us much about the worth of the agent. It was the system which failed all levels of the community and hurt some more than it hurt others. So what was the condition of those, particularly the women, who were hurt most? If they did not die or emigrate, mothers, wives and daughters had to find some way of surviving and coping with family responsibilities. Famine problems did not deplete the growing Catholic middle class, nor their Protestant counterparts with whom increasingly they made common cause. The vicissitudes of the landlords were to do with land and money, rather than life and death; some 'had devoted themselves and their whole resources to the work of relief. All had suffered economic loss; and some had been brought to bankruptcy.'[31] In the eyes of the world at large, though, all stood condemned; regardless of their financial standing, and this varied widely, they were identified with those partly responsible for the deaths of nearly a million people because some of them had taken advantage of the disaster; they had thinned down overcrowded estates by evicting the poorer tenants.

The example of the notorious Mrs Gerrard is instructive, not only because it shows a member of the supposedly weaker sex persecuting the weakest members of a poverty-stricken community, but also because it led to a special enquiry by Lord Londonderry, who exposed with some force the consequences of pursuing a policy of 'evictment' for the purpose of profiteering. In 1846 Mrs Gerrard wanted to change the holdings of seventy-six families into grazing land, and arrangements were made for a detachment of troops, accompanied by the sheriff and his staff and many police, to evict 300 individuals from Ballinglass, a village in County Galway. Had the tenants been in arrears with their rents her decision would still have been a savage one, for 'scalps' or burrows, hastily dug in the earth, were the only alternative accommodation and the effects of the famine were getting worse. But, far from being in arrears, the peasants had increased the value of the land in those parts by reclaiming about 400 acres of bog.

The full force of the law was employed. After the people had been told to leave their houses, the roofs were removed and the walls demolished. The women either ran about hysterically, clutching pieces of their property, or hung on to doorposts until they were violently removed while their children screamed with fright. For one night the families were allowed to camp down in the ruins but such generosity was short-lived; the following day they were forced to leave and attempts were made to prevent their return by the removal of the houses' foundations. Because those who lived nearby were forbidden to take them in, shelter was improvised in 'scalps' or 'scalpeens'. The scalp was a simple hole dug to a depth of about three feet, covered by branches and pieces of turf; illogically, as 'een' is a diminutive suffix, the scalpeen was a larger burrow made where the foundations of a razed house had been. As discovery of either kind of refuge meant that the former tenants were evicted again, it is difficult to escape the conclusion that death by exposure was the object of the enterprise, regardless of whether or not the people were starving in the first place.

In his speech in the House of Lords,[32] Lord Londonderry emphasized that Mrs Gerrard's tenants had had no intention of withholding rents, and commented that, after such behaviour by the authorities, no surprise should be expressed if outrages were to occur. Shortly after this event, when news of the evictions was followed by news of starvation and the connection between the two became manifest, it was women who were prominent in the law-breaking that ensued. A large crowd of them, accompanied by their children – about a hundred in all – intercepted carts carrying government supplies of maize to a store in County Cork, ripped open the bags, and stole about two tons of meal. The presence of children in food riots served to underline one of the causes of the famine: over-population.

Among the problems facing those detailed to carry out the census of 1841 was the need to track down 'the community of evicted and unemployed who existed in caves, sod huts and under tree-roots',[33] and, of course, many were missed. As a result, the overall population figure of 8,175,124 for that year was regarded as an underestimate, and an independent check, using County Clare as a sample, suggested that, by 1845, when famine had begun to take its toll, the true figure was probably more than 9,000,000. Comparisons with Third World countries today are a help towards understanding why the Irish peasants, despite their poverty, were such prolific breeders. One reason, common to the Irish Catholic and the Hindu, is that until the rudiments of a social security system exist children are their parents' only insurance against the hazards of old age or infirmity: Irish Poor Law provision did not begin to take effect until 1838 and even then was scanty. While it may be true that tradition and family influence played their part in encouraging large families while the mortality rate was high, other aspects of peasant culture have to be taken into consideration.

It should be remembered that before the combined effects of eviction and famine led to disease and death on a monstrous scale, where and when these factors were not operative the lot of the Irish peasant could in some respects, not least diet, be compared favourably with that of contemporary English, Scottish and Welsh peasants. Travellers of repute[34] bore witness to the sound physique of a race reared on ample supplies of potatoes and buttermilk. They saw too how the simplicity and monotony of rural life in a dubious climate made the consolations of married life attractive, especially to young couples. It was not a question of easy virtue. Traditions introduced and fostered by the Church were strongest in rural Ireland, and Irish girls were 'very correct in their conduct'[35] and there was, or so it was said, no need for the Poor Law 'to make provision for bastards';[36] that was one fiscal advantage of precipitate marriage. However, it has to be said that there are grounds for believing that illegitimate births,[37] and infanticide committed to avoid disgrace, may have been commoner than contemporary observers appreciated. Even so, given the low material expectations of many couples, there were few bars to an instant union, blessed by the Church. The rural tradition (still extant) of the *meitheal* – a number of strong men who gave their combined efforts and simple skills to a member of their group – meant that a cabin could be built within a few days; then a pot, a stool, and perhaps a bed, would be added, and the new household would be complete. 'They cannot be worse off than they are and . . . they may help each other',[38] commented the Catholic Bishop of Raphoe; and other oral evidence received by the Irish Poor Law Enquiry of 1835 (admittedly not supported by census findings six years later) was to the effect that the peasants were more enthusiastic about marriage than the bishop's words may suggest. The girls, it was said, married at 16, the boys when a year or two older, and babies followed in quick succession for the next twenty years. Certainly this was the pattern for many.

It seems to be some sort of heresy to say so, but the conditions of the pre-Famine Irish tenant farmer, provided that he was not evicted, stood comparison with the plight of peasants worldwide. Adverse criticism of his standard of living is better justified on social rather than on national grounds, and such criticism was made increasingly loudly whenever subdivision of land, often caused by excessive breeding, made subsistence more difficult on the diminished potato patch. His wife commonly brought forth a dozen children in under twenty years, into a cabin kept warm by the perpetually burning peat fire. At this time in Irish history there was little opportunity for the wife of a cottier to do other than work on the rented plot, do some textile outwork and fulfil the stereotype of a victim of 'total domesticity' within her own dwelling. This was likely to be her life unless the extended family and outside circumstances allowed her to enter service, possibly in the Big House. Whenever she could, until machine production made her redundant, she added to the family's means by weaving. She dressed simply, but warmly, in clothes that she had probably made for herself. Her husband and her children seldom lacked warmth either. Many of her class slept on the mud floor, which they sometimes shared with pigs and other animals. The family ate a lot and their diet was a reasonably healthy one, until the blight struck.

The primitive warmth and comfort which was the basic consoling feature of life in the cabin disappeared altogether from the lives of most peasant families in the winter of 1846–7, when Ireland's normally wet but fairly mild climate was interrupted by a Siberian blizzard. In England the freezing conditions were to be remembered for the amount of ice in the Thames. In Ireland, although the peat fire might continue to burn night and day, the intense cold proved fatal for some who customarily stayed indoors and relied on the previous season's potato harvest; adequate clothing became inadequate as starving people left their warm cabins to labour for their new employer, the Board of Works. The Board's original decision to pay a fit man a fair wage for a fair day's work, in order that he might pay his rent and buy food, proved wholly unrealistic, and other criteria for selection had to be considered; destitution became one of the keys to employment. Among the Irish peasants of the 1840s it might be difficult to decide who was more destitute than another, but women, especially widows with families, were an identifiable group; to them was awarded the privilege of 'breaking stones at 4d a day'[39] (2d would buy a pound of maize). Contemporary reports complained that 'old, feeble and very young persons were engaged';[40] a Board of Works official spoke of 'women and children on the roads, with spades and shovels, completely unfit for work'.

Suffering was not evenly distributed throughout the island. Some areas, thanks to enlightened landlords who waived rents or concocted employment, escaped virtually unscathed. In County Kildare, for instance, the tenants of the Aylmers of Donadea Castle were lucky that Maria, née Hodgson, the eighth baronet's wife, was altogether unlike the second baronet's choice of spouse – whose strong-mindedness about her husband's fate so impressed succeeding generations of Aylmers. While the Board of Works' employment projects are mainly remembered for roads which led to nowhere, Maria's influence led to useful 'good works'; she encouraged her husband to employ tenants in the construction of stone cottages for their own families to occupy, and in the development of drainage systems which were among the first successful attempts to reclaim tracts of the Bog of Allen.[41] Another woman who came to the rescue of those hit badly by the Famine was Frances Anne, second wife of the third Marquess of Londonderry. Under her guidance several projects created employment on the Antrim coast: a harbour at the village of Carnlough, a castle on Garron Point, and an inn, the Londonderry Arms. Below the castle an inscription was carved into the limestone stating that she had had it built because of her links of birth and marriage with Ulster and because she wanted to 'hand down to posterity an imperishable memorial of Ireland's affliction and England's generosity in the year 1846–7, unparalleled in the annals of human suffering'. Local nationalists have since obliterated the words 'and England's generosity'. To most of their persuasion the English race had to be blamed for the failures of central government, and their hatred was fuelled by false rumours of Queen Victoria's mean attitude to the victims of famine.[42]

The effect of Ireland's affliction on town-dwellers was mixed. Parts of the industrial north-east fared comparatively well, but in 1852, four years after the 'Great Famine', blight was destroying potatoes around Belfast; elsewhere crowding together in search of food or work meant that typhus was easily transmitted by the ubiquitous lice which infected those whose dwellings made few concessions to bodily cleanliness or to sanitation in general. And yet, while the country's population was being dramatically reduced by starvation, disease and emigration (about as many left as died), a great industry was becoming greater and a new class was developing in the eastern half of Ulster. It was a working class with a difference: in the linen-mill women outnumbered men. Here was poverty of a different sort, suffered by women with religious and cultural differences from the inhabitants of cabins or burrows. They, too, experienced the consequences of overcrowding and unreliable wages, but they were predominantly Protestant and their loyalty to the Union steadily grew as the years went by, despite the dangerous conditions in which many of them worked:

> On Saturday . . . a worker in the mill . . . at York Street sustained a very severe accident . . . She was engaged at the carding part of the machinery and her head became entangled in the machinery, in which the greater part of her scalp was removed from the head and the skull severely injured. Little hope was entertained for her recovery.[43]

This accident was one of many. Poverty was widespread in the red-brick streets that mushroomed in the shadow of the mill stacks and the workers, many of them first generation town-dwellers, were easy victims of exploitation. To make ends meet the children had to work as well, and apprentice girls were the most vulnerable members of a workforce exposed to lung and skin diseases caused by the flax dust in the air. The majority of workers died before reaching the age of 45 years.

The sufferings of the working women in Ulster, though great, were not such that blame would instinctively and necessarily be attached to 'England'. Even taking into account appalling accidents and limited life expectation, the Belfast working class had an easier time than the peasants further south, and in any case it was only natural and logical to blame local bosses for every misfortune connected with the mills. So, given their religious adherence and wide acceptance of belief in their distinctive mythological and historical antecedents, perhaps it is understandable that within living memory of Ireland's darkest hours the linen industry's workforce was to the fore in the opposition to Home Rule. As soon as the threat was perceived, under the presidency of the Duchess of Abercorn the 'Ulster Women's Unionist Council' was formed; within a year some 40,000–50,000 women joined, and in West Belfast 80 per cent of the 4,000 who joined the local branch in its first month were mill-workers and shop-girls.

At the other end of the social scale loyalty to the Union and, more specifically, to the Crown, meant adherence to a traditional way of life which was not to be allowed to be jeopardized by natural or unnatural disasters, even of national proportions. Those, however, who maintained extravagant standards when the Famine was nearing its terrible climax have been censured by those best qualified to do so: 'The Dublin season, noted for its gaiety, was as lively as ever in the grim spring of 1847.'[44] In happier times the social round of the nobility, Catholic and Protestant, enabled Irish women to display a talent for style and extravagance that must be the envy of all who have ever aspired to gain acceptance within the ranks of the fashionable and the well-bred. Big House extravagant expenditure in the bad times is more easily understood when construction of follies and other buildings, and design and decoration of elaborate gardens with lakes, bridges and islands, created employment, especially when a consequence was that a large number of domestic servants could look forward to a reasonably secure future. But only a minute proportion of the population of pre-Famine Ireland could be saved by such means. The future, moreover, would be by no means secure when the apparent wealth of Ascendancy families was found to hide an ever-increasing burden of inherited debt.

The Ascendancy is seen by most in terms of decayed grandeur or of the profuse and exciting social round which was partly the cause of the decay. Throughout much of the nineteenth century the reality of the life that was led by the wealthiest 'Anglo-Irish' came nearest to what is still associated with them in the popular imagination; a sizeable proportion of income, or of capital, was devoted to providing everything necessary for attending viceregal balls at Dublin Castle and, given the energy, in fulfilling the rituals of the Dublin season in February and March. Then, if the means was found, there was the London season in May, June and July, and Cowes Week in August. The practical implications of playing one's part might have proved daunting, had not most of the families involved been accustomed for centuries to the pace and expense of living life to the full. Whilst the burdens of running the estates were delegated to trusted servants, the first social priority of the families was to ensure that all the girls, even if they were already married, and regardless of whether or not they had already been presented at court in London, were presented at the viceregal court. To make this and attendance at other social events possible, the better-off Ascendancy families owned Dublin houses; others rented properties for the season or stayed in hotels, such as the Shelbourne on St Stephen's Green. The luckier ones were invited to stay at the Castle itself.

For those whose social calendar included England, travel arrangements were elaborate. For example, great pains were taken to see that Lady Ardilaun's journey from Ashford Castle in County Galway or from the family's Italianate palace, St Anne's, beside the northern shore of Dublin Bay, to Carlton House Terrace in London was as comfortable as possible. The head coachman, with a groom and a carriage and pair, would make the crossing a few days before her departure; then the second coachman would drive her to Kingstown (now Dun Laoghaire) and she would be met at the boat by her husband's agent who would escort her to the cabins reserved for her and her maid. She would find her accommodation filled with flowers from her own garden. On these journeys a footman invariably travelled on the box of her carriage and kept his distance on the boat. On arrival at Holyhead he took her and her maid to a reserved compartment on the train; at the main stops on the journey he had to appear at the window to see whether or not his services were needed. When the train arrived at Euston the party was met by the head coachman and the journey was completed in the same manner as it had begun. Arrangements were even more congenial for the return journey. After the boat had docked at Kingstown, Ascendancy passengers would rise when it suited them and then breakfast at the Royal St George Yacht Club.[45]

High standards of travel were complemented by high standards of dress; while the men often exhibited sartorial extravagance at the Dublin Horse Show or at Punchestown Races, their wives took the opportunity to parade in fashionable clothes, as they did with great style in anything connected with the season, whether in Ireland or in England, at hunt balls or at private parties. Entertaining was lavish, and at Christmas in a good year the workers on some estates could expect considerable largesse, as when Lady Coote at Ballyfin in Queen's County (now Laois) 'distributed many useful and suitable gifts of clothing, etc.'[46] to the wives and families of about a hundred workmen on the Ballyfin estate. But it is for its performance in the realms of eccentricity that the Ascendancy is most remarked upon today and this is another area which, despite a cultural tradition of hyperbole, has been less exaggerated than some might suppose. One has only to visit late twentieth-century survivors of the Ascendancy – and there are far more of them than is generally realized – to be convinced that even the least credible tales may be believed.

Women's role in the field of Ascendancy eccentricity was not so much bound up with being eccentric as with coping with the strange behaviour of men, either of their husbands or of their servants. Generally speaking those women whom most people would once have regarded as eccentric had characteristics which nowadays would have a different explanation: such as those of the elder of the Vere Foster sisters, who wore men's clothes and was known as John. But, on the whole, it was a woman's handling of male absurdity which could impress and gain her the upper hand in the social sphere. One such occasion was when the Countess of Caledon's butler over-indulged himself in the wine-tasting and proposed marriage to her while serving at one of her dinner parties. As she remarked later, she accepted his proposal as a matter of course and asked him to continue serving the meal. The following day it was as if nothing had happened. Another drunken butler, who was serving tea at Blarney Castle after the funeral of Sir George Colthurst's widow, came into the drawing room nude, carrying the tea tray. The late Lady Colthurst's former companion swiftly suggested that a little more sugar was needed, and he left the room at once. It is, of course, just this sort of minor incident, the lighter side of Ascendancy life and excellent material for novels, which can be scathingly used by modern commentators wishing to denigrate the families which dominated Irish life for so many centuries. It is too easy to suggest that they added colour and little else to a long and sometimes tragic tale.

Because of the ostentation of some members of the upper layer of the

Ascendancy, the wealth of the entire social edifice from the lowest level of the gentry to its upper reaches has been overestimated. Looking at Ascendancy antecedents one can see both the position of great strength which had been built up and how the behaviour of ancestors led to financial decline. Instead of ploughing back income into estates, forebears of the Victorians adopted or vied with the life-style of their English relations who, in general, had greater resources. Moreover, they were slow to modify agricultural methods and some spent too much on charitable enterprises. Their most harmful legacy was the combined effect of the habit of overspending with the heavy burden of a large mortgage that hung around the necks of so many landlords. Impecunious gentry often succeeded in keeping up appearances, as when the daughters of James Cooper of Cooper Hill took it in turns to go to balls because there were not enough dresses for them to go together. But the sons of the same family had to go barefoot until they were 12. Anna, the Countess of Kingston, somewhat higher up the social scale, found Mitchelstown Castle expensive to run. She had to cope with mortgage interest of some £10,000 a year, to be subtracted from an annual income of about £18,000. So, when her tenants demanded rent reductions and withheld rents when she did not comply, there were evictions which called the tenants' bluff. Virtually all paid up immediately and went straight back into their cottages. Mitchelstown was thus spared the horrors which the evictions brought elsewhere.

From time to time compassion on the part of Ascendancy women affected Big House budgets in ways that did not meet with the approval of husbands or fathers. Elizabeth Cole Bowen, of Bowen's Court, used secretly to slip the rent to tenants who, she believed, were unable to pay, and her daughter, Sarah, to whom the task of rent collecting was sometimes delegated, proved to be as hopeless at the task as her mother would have been. But obviously compassionate intervention on the part of Ascendancy women diminished in proportion to the amount of time which the families spent away from their estates; and although four-fifths of the principal landlords were resident in Ireland for most of the year during the late 1880s, by that time the tenants' period of greatest suffering was over. The landlords were now definitely on the losing side of the land war. Soon the tenants would own the land, and paying, or failing to pay, the rent would cease to be the national preoccupation.

At this point it is essential to move away from a consideration of the two extremes of nineteenth-century Irish womanhood, as exemplified by Ascendancy women of the minority landlord class on the one hand, and the peasant wives and daughters of the majority tenant class on the other. Fine gradations of social strata were moving into the middle ground. The problems of this region were called to mind provocatively in a recent study: 'Can "going mad" and "joining the nuns" be seen as two very different responses . . . to the intense psychological pressures which their social and economic position imposed upon women in prosperous, modernising nineteenth-century Ireland?'[47] – a question partly prompted by the coincidence in time and place of an increase among females of mental illness and a proliferation of convents. Such an impression might easily have been explained away or summarily dismissed had it not been for other indications that there was something in it in terms of negative and positive response to an intolerable environment.

The Great Famine has understandably loomed so large in the minds of people in general, and of historians in particular, that one may be forgiven a moment of disbelief before coming to terms with the idea of 'prosperous, modernising, nineteenth-century Ireland'. It rather depends on which part of the century (and, of course, which part of the country) one has in mind if 'prosperous' and 'modernising' are to achieve credibility. In the 1841 census 62 per cent of working adult women described themselves as textile and garment workers, the percentage including numbers of cabin-dwellers whose contribution to overall production of this cottage industry was minimal. After the Famine the figure had fallen to 22 per cent. Industrialization in the north-east was one factor which had previously helped to cut back earnings from this occupation elsewhere, from 5d. a day in 1817 to 1d. a day, at best, in 1836, for the same personal output. During the first twenty years of the century, until the industrialized centres commandeered the market, women in most parts of the country – aided by children and husbands – could be counted upon to dress flax, to spin, to card, to weave and to bleach in accordance with a fairly steady demand. Some areas had their own textile or garment specialities: the women of the West were famous for knitting, Athlone had a thriving felt-hat industry. But when one of the consequences of competition turned out to be unemployment there was a marked increase in the number of women turning to begging and prostitution. This happened despite what the Bishop of Raphoe had to say about contemporary morality – but then he had the bottom layer of the rural community in mind, not those who had some distance to fall. Doubtless many of the fallen women would have turned to another chief source of female employment, day-labouring in agriculture, had opportunities not been so narrowly restricted by the seasons.

The economics of pre-Famine nineteenth-century Ireland were such that if a labourer and his wife had three children it was up to the wife and the children to bring in half the family's income in order to subsist. As circumstances changed, the wives tried alternative means of ensuring family survival. The amount of professional or semi-professional work available to those who had managed to acquire some sort of education was negligible. As a general rule the options open to women, other than caring for their own families, were domestic service, in which 22 per cent were working during 1841, and labouring and herding, which accounted for another 10 per cent.

Except for the commanding heights of the Ascendancy, and the poorest of the poor, the social order which appeared after the Famine bore little apparent relation to anything that had gone before it. The eighteenth century had seen the development of a middle class; the nineteenth century saw that class adopt bourgeois values and habits in direct proportion to its acquisition of wealth. Soon women at the lower end of this new scheme of things were more likely to be domestic servants than to spin and weave; by the end of the century only 3.2 per cent of them were agricultural labourers. Many members of the affluent middle class, Catholic and Protestant, now began to treat their servants as *nouveaux riches* the world over are wont to do; they used them, or abused them, in order to distance themselves from their own origins, of which they had become ashamed. Visitors commented on the way in which Irish servants were dependent on the 'whims and notions'[48] of Irish middle class mistresses: 'the mistress of nearly every little house in Ireland who owned a maid-of-all-work or a kitchen slavey had her cup of tea in bed in the morning like the grandest in the land'.[49] It is the use of the word 'owned', not the example of service given, which emphasizes the nature of an employer–employee relationship which might be little better than domestic slavery. As always, those least accustomed to power and responsibility were most likely to abuse their new-found authority.

But there were other places than private houses which depended on a supply of women for domestic duties and, after spending some time in them, a woman might be able to choose a more responsible and worthwhile occupation. Prosperity (which, it must be borne in mind, persisted even while famine recurred from time to time) meant that there was a need for more hotels, and, as Irish society diversified, a woman's talents – as conventionally understood – were required in hospitals. Unfortunately, though, as gradual development of educational provision helped women to qualify as nurses and schoolmistresses, to become nuns, or to assume secretarial, clerical and various other white-collar responsibilities, numerically women's employment opportunities actually diminished. While white-collar jobs for women quadrupled between 1880 and 1910, humbler occupations, such as those of washerwoman or small-time dressmaker, were undermined by modernization. Figures for shop assistants are not available for the same period, but in 1841, 0.25 per cent of working females were employed in this capacity. It may be confidently assumed, though, that expansion in retail trade in the late Victorian period increased numbers greatly and helped this form of female employment to break away from the nepotism which inevitably characterized it at village level.

Whether or not education was to provide the key to occupational emancipation of women was to depend not only on access to schools, but on the curriculum which society as a whole thought fitting to perpetuate its traditional notion of a woman's role in the family and in the community at large. Before the Great Famine, although basic education was made available to the humblest Catholic girls, even when its provision was technically illegal, domestic circumstances were such that a negligible proportion of girls took advantage of it; and the few who did, like their sisters of the Protestant lower orders, could hope for little more than needlework and religious instruction. Moreover, when the National Board of Education was established in 1831, and most existing schools became associated with it, what was taught changed little. After the Famine Ireland was no longer the same place, but although the educational needs of the entire populace were taken seriously it was not until the Irish Education Act of 1892 that, at the most basic level of schooling, girls achieved equality of opportunity with regard to access to school premises.

Throughout and after the century the convent schools largely catered for the growing number of middle-class girls, and, as demographic changes occurred, played their part in educating the poor. In short, they reflected the existing social structure while, because convent policy, doubtless for sound motives, was to try to accept as nuns only middle-class pupils with vocations (and dowries), one of its incidental consequences was that the middle-class ethos was consolidated. Meanwhile in the secular world several foundations, culminating in that of Alexandra College, Dublin, sought to open up the entire field of education, including higher education, to females. Denominational schools settled on the whole for religion, reading, writing and arithmetic (the four Rs); fee-paying schools for older girls, despite the example of the pioneers in their midst, instead of providing for university admission were content to try to produce 'ladies'. Ascendancy girls, who were ladies anyway, had governesses. In 1891, 37 per cent of those receiving secondary education were female, but by the end of the century this figure was on its way down to 34 per cent. It took no account of the untold numbers to whom secondary education was not even a dream.

Contradictions implicit in educational provision, and the lack of it, arose from a dual concept of a woman's place in society, shared by most classes; and it was all a far cry from the old idea of the overtly dominant Amazon, or the more subtle embodiment of sovereignty. Generally speaking, in the higher echelons of society anything which smacked of the vocational was *infra dig*. For the wealthy there was no harm in taking that attitude; in the end it is the accomplishments which create a distinction between humans and the other primates. Women of the upper classes who needed money badly could go to England, where they would have a better chance of earning it unobserved, either by their peers in Irish society or by their social inferiors. But in Ireland in the latter half of the century, among those without English connections, was a growing army of spinsters for whom finding the means to earn a living was of prime importance. They had several obstacles to overcome, among which were the pronouncements of the Roman Catholic Church and the way in which ordinary mortals modified papal advice to suit their own prejudices. Pope Leo XIII spoke of a woman's relationship to her husband, 'the chief of her family', in terms which ran counter to the impression previously encouraged by the Marian model of an 'all-powerful, compassionate courageous mother':[50] she 'must be subject to him and obey him'.[51] And, although he emphasized that she was a companion, rather than a servant, there was no escaping her subservient place in the scheme of things.

To peasant ears there may have been an element of mercy in what the Pope had to say, for in parts of Ireland men were accustomed to leaving much of the heaviest physical work to the women; much folklore had prevented the concept of the weaker sex from becoming universally accepted. But by the 1870s some women were agitating for democratic freedoms which would not only deliver them from physical exploitation but would eventually have more positive consequences. In 1876 the Irishwomen's Suffrage and Local Government Association was founded, and the next few years saw the rise and fall of the militant Ladies' Land League, followed by the birth of the only women's trade union founded in Ireland during the nineteenth century, the Textile Operatives' Society. Some initiatives came from the shop floor and from its agricultural equivalent but, partly because the extent of Ireland's shop-floor was limited and partly because of the effect on the conduct of the faithful majority of papal pronouncements about a woman's status, when it came to full-blooded political issues it was the Ascendancy women who came to the fore. Home Rule proved to be the ultimate political issue, and Ascendancy women were prominent on the battlefield, whether they were promoting separatism or defending the Union. However, naturally it has been the rebels of their number who have attracted more attention than those who appeared to be doing no more than defending the status quo.

In one way the families of the Victorian Ascendancy were exactly the same as their surviving descendants in Ireland and the United Kingdom today. They constituted the members – often talented members – of an extensive club. Entry to the club was achieved by birth into families which had been in membership for a few generations or, less frequently for those who might not satisfy pedigree requirements, by marriage. Because the club, or the class, was (despite its extent) exclusive, its members tended to live their lives within certain parameters which encouraged most of them to know each other. They were in any case relations; in times of stress, blood brothers. But while, in this respect they differed not at all from the humblest in the land, their great strength lay in knowing who was related to whom; this knowledge brought them solidarity. The club was a species of extended family, held together quite strongly by known genealogical bonds. Of course, this did not prevent feuds and major or petty differences occurring, as they did at all levels of society. However, cement provided by kinship, by education, by a common conception of what was meant by good manners, by the rituals of the social round, by many moral imperatives (even when religion might have been expected to divide), and by much of that vast area of behaviour that is simply taken for granted, held together a large and influential group with a common sense of purpose.

For some free spirits, like Constance Gore-Booth, however, viceregal balls were a bore, and Ascendancy life as a whole proved to be claustrophobic. The

41

crystallization of such thoughts and inclinations did not come to her until after her marriage to the Polish Count Markievicz. Her family had emerged from the famine years with a good reputation. The people appreciated landlords who did not hide in London throughout this difficult time; many of them had benefited in an immediate and personal way from Caroline Gore-Booth's missions of mercy, and that they had survived at all could well be attributed to the £40,000 which the Gore-Booths spent on famine relief. So, some might think that Constance was simply carrying family tradition a stage further. They would be wrong. In the last year of her life, 1926, when asked if she was going to the funeral of her sister, Eva, whom she loved more dearly than any other being, she replied, 'I simply cannot face the family'.[52] Like a number of other Big Houses, Lissadell had found it difficult to come to terms with having a rebel in their midst, though they did not allow the world to see their difficulty. As Constance said, 'I suppose it's very embarrassing to have a relation that gets into jail and fights in revolutions that you are not in sympathy with'.[53] She did not always see the position quite so clearly.

The landmarks of Countess Markievicz's life are an impeccable catalogue of rebel achievement. As soon as her political awareness dawned – the last ray appeared as she read an account of Robert Emmet's death – she joined Sinn Féin and, after some friendly political indoctrination by Bulmer Hobson, joined the Drumcondra and Glasnevin branch. She was chosen to be the branch's delegate to the annual Sinn Féin convention and, in 1909, was elected to its Resident Executive Council. In the same year she launched Ireland's nationalist alternative to Baden-Powell's Boy Scouts, Fianna Eireann, an organization which would have had more than a little in common with the Hitler Youth, had it achieved anything like the same degree of efficiency; as it was, it trained boys in the use of arms in anticipation of the volunteer activity which was to come. She joined Maud Gonne's Inghinidhe na hEireann (Daughters of Erin), and became an officer in James Connolly's Irish Citizen Army. She was sentenced to death for her part in the Easter Rising but, because of her sex, instead served a term of penal servitude. In 1917 she became president of the women's republican organization Cumann na mBan (Irishwomen's Council) which, largely because of her powers of oratory, immediately absorbed Inghinidhe na hEireann. Elected Sinn Féin MP for St Patrick's, Dublin, she became the United Kingdom's first woman Member of Parliament, though she did not take her seat. While in prison she became Minister for Labour in Dáil Eireann's cabinet; she denounced the Treaty and worked actively for the republican side in the civil war. For the rest of her life she was a Sinn Féin abstentionist member of the Dáil; and when she died her funeral had all the attributes of a state occasion, which in many ways it was, despite the presence of armed Free State soldiers to see that a republican volley was not fired over her grave.

Behind a political career which, judged by republican criteria, was exemplary, lay much failure in departments of life in which women have inescapable responsibilities. Marriage was an early casualty; in a story allegedly told by one of Count Markievicz's neighbours, the rebel's husband complained that the last straw was finding guns under the marital bed. Apocryphal though this may be, it encapsulates what it must have been like to have been married to a woman who embodied all the zeal of a convert to the achievement of political aims by violent means. But the failed marriage was not entirely her fault; her husband, who was a widower six years younger than she, had the reputation of a womanizer, and reacted predictably when, after the birth of their only child, his wife lost her capacity for physical love.[54]

The birth of the daughter led to revelation of other signs and symbols of what the future held. Throughout Constance Gore-Booth's youth she had been almost daily reminded, because nearly all the windows of Lissadell gave a view of Knocknarea mountain, that she was growing up in the shadow of the burial place of Ireland's most celebrated warrior queen. Now, in memory of the ancient Gaelic heroine for whom a cairn stands on Knocknarea's summit, the daughter whose birth nearly caused her mother's death was christened Maeve. As so often happens, though, the mother's perception of the daughter – for the choice of name had all the significance that one could possibly attach to it – was simply an extension of her own aspirations; the child Maeve echoed her mother's rebelliousness only in the sense that, deprived of maternal affection, she became disillusioned and sometimes made things difficult for the women placed in charge of her. Her governess, Miss Clayton, was to recall how at the age of 7, she and 'the fiery little girl',[55] were taken by Constance for a picnic on Knocknarea, in order to place stones on Queen Maeve's cairn. On that occasion Maeve, who was to develop a talent for amateur dramatics, recited 'The Triumph of Maeve', a poem by her aunt, Eva. Its opening verse gives an insight into mother's and daughter's fiery spirit:

> I have seen Maeve of the Battles wandering over the hills,
> And I know that the deed that is in my heart is her deed,
> And my soul is blown about by the wild wind of her will,
> For always the living must follow whither the dead would lead –
> I have seen Maeve of the Battles wandering over the hill.[56]

Unlike her daughter, the mother who sensed that the deed in her heart was Maeve's deed, was not successful when called upon by her husband to be an actress. The count who, as well as being a painter, wrote a number of plays and was himself an enthusiastic actor, encouraged her to act while their marriage lasted. She was keen to perform, but could not make her own personality subservient to the part she had to play.

On Constance's marriage her widowed mother moved out of Lissadell and soon took up permanent residence at Ardeveen. It was in this house, while her father and mother spent more and more time in Dublin, that Maeve was to be reared by Lady Gore-Booth and educated by Miss Clayton. Her mother found other things more important than the responsibilities of motherhood, which in some ways is understandable. But Constance seemed unaware of a dilemma, and unaffected by the stress that absence from one's child would bring to anyone who experienced love in the natural way. She did visit Ardeveen sometimes, when she behaved as though she were an elder sister, rather than a mother. These visits, however, served only to widen the gap; after she had left, Maeve pronounced her verdict: 'Well, that's over. She won't think of me for another year.'[57]

What little maternal feeling Constance had only surfaced under extreme circumstances, such as when she was in prison; otherwise her daughter's welfare was too often taken for granted. When, in 1922, Maeve called on her mother in a London hotel, she failed to recognize her, despite having been given a description and told in which room to find her. All Maeve's thoughts and opinions had been affected by her having been brought up by a grandmother for whom the Union was right and normal; but the gulf between mother and daughter really owed nothing to ideological differences. Rather it was the logical result of the abandoning of maternal obligations for an ideology; the choice, which had instinctive and rational aspects to it, was both selfish and selfless, and represents the eternal problem – less and less recognized today – confronting women who attempt to combine motherhood with any demanding activity which takes them away from their children.

Some other Ascendancy Sinn Féin activists were spared such choices. The Hon. Albinia Brodrick, an IRA nurse who was the daughter of Viscount Midleton, and the Hon. Mary Spring-Rice, gun-running daughter of Lord Monteagle, both died unmarried; and poor Ada McNeill, cousin of Lord Cushendun, had the misfortune to fall in love with Roger Casement. One who was associated with the Ascendancy though not, strictly, of it, had her own reasons formed when her illegitimate children were born in secret, for defending abdication of maternal responsibility. Maud Gonne, Constance Markievicz's English alter ego, believed that Constance 'was so unselfish she sacrificed everything for Ireland, and . . . did what she thought best for the child'.[58] In general, women of the Ascendancy who were politically active in defence of the Union were not faced with this problem. They were not breaking with the established order of things, they operated within the law, and, until their world began to crumble, they continued to use their traditional ways of sustaining family relationships. These included the use of nannies, governesses and tutors, as supports, not substitutes, for maternal love. Moreover, by the turn of the century, turbulence connected with the prospect of Home Rule had forced virtually all to realize that Ireland was their first love, and this realization in no way diminished their loyalty to, and affection for, the monarchy.

From the Catholics of the Ascendancy deep devotion to Ireland seemed only to be expected but, as the old order began to change, the bonds of class usually proved stronger than those of religion and politics. It was Daisy, the Countess of Fingall, absurdly nicknamed 'the Sinn Féin Countess', whose signature appeared at the head of some 165,000 others in the six volumes of welcome addressed to Queen Mary in 1911. Of the Protestants, Theresa, Marchioness of Londonderry, is generally held to have been the most skilful intriguer for the unionist cause. Skilful she was; intriguer she was not, for her tireless efforts to protect a legally constituted political entity were legal and free from deception. A woman of influence, she used all her considerable powers of persuasion, sometimes flamboyantly, to strengthen the position of the loyalists and limit the effects of separatism. Her husband had been viceroy from 1886 to 1889, and she had seen to it that his, and her, viceroyalty had been a brilliant one. Working through the marquess or on her own account, at the County Down country seat, Mount Stewart, or in Dublin, or at Londonderry House in Park Lane, she cultivated all those most likely to save as much as possible of the society in which she believed; the Carsons and F. E. Smiths were all grateful for the 'enduring friendship and support of this remarkable woman, almost the last of the great feminine influences in politics',[59] as F. E. Smith's son, the second Lord Birkenhead, was to recall. There were, however, subtler strains of influence emanating from viceregal circles. The Hon. Catherine Rowan Hamilton, sister-in-law of another viceroy, the Marquess of Dufferin and Ava, preferred to spread the unionist message more discreetly. She was to marry Sir Arthur Nicolson (Lord Carnock) and her third son, Harold, was to write that his mother, 'although descended from one of the most excessive of Irish rebels, was herself a gentle little loyalist'.[60] The rebel in question was Archibald, one of Wolfe Tone's associates, known as 'Mr Rowan'.

As the Victorian era came to an end, the only common denominator of the Irish woman's condition – common, that is, to all levels of society and among those to whom the possibility of change provided cause for hope or despair – was frustration. Even those at the summit, the powerful women of the existing regime, and those on the other side of the political divide, who sought a lot more than Home Rule seemed to offer, were frustrated by the way in which events were forcing them to compromise on matters of deeply held conviction. For many their worst fears were to be realized two decades later when unionists lost twenty-six counties, and the separatists lost six – the reaction of women when this happened was, as will be seen, much more virulent than that of their brothers-in-arms. But lack of educational opportunities for women meant that political awareness was in short supply, whereas perception of social constraints was brought home to every woman who accidentally or intentionally stepped out of line. Over the centuries women of every background had been aware that there was something special in Irish culture about the wife and the mother; oral tradition and much of the teaching of the Roman Catholic Church had seen to this when formal education was lacking, while members of the educated classes had been able to discover it for themselves.

Polarization of ideas caused by the conflict between culturally aroused aspirations and social and religious repression meant that the organizations which articulate women founded in the last twenty years of Queen Victoria's reign – which laid blame for Ireland's ills at England's door – had an important feminist motivation, although this might not form part of their *raison d'être*. Anna Parnell's Ladies' Land League (the committee established in 1881, when male Land Leaguers became liable to imprisonment under the Protection of Personal Property (Ireland) Act) is a case in point. Through it, women who were still without votes embarrassed their male allies, especially their founder's brother, Charles Stewart Parnell, by excelling males in fields which in recent history had been reserved for those with so-called masculine virtues. Their aggressive, well-organized resistance to the authorities on behalf of labourers and small-holders, showed effectively how women could excel men in taking collective decisions and acting on them. But they, too, were frustrated: Parnell had the Ladies' League suppressed in 1882, but not before it had 'provided a political baptism for a generation of radical Irishwomen who spoke on platforms, organized tactics, were denounced by the clergy and got arrested'.[61] After their disbandment, many former members of the Ladies' Land League were to find a vocation in the quest for emancipation as soon as opportunities arose for them to become involved in suffragism and Sinn Féin.

In some ways the frustration felt by some Irish women of all walks of life was shared by women elsewhere in the United Kingdom; but the cultural inheritance and the uncertain political future of Ireland meant that there were differences of kind as well as degree. The largely unconscious initiative of the Ladies of Llangollen made it necessary for them to leave the island; both rebel and unionist women of the Ascendancy had strong psychological pressures placed upon them by the limited room in which the traditions of their class and the prospect of fundamental change allowed them space to manœuvre. At the other extreme the post-Famine female was doomed to spinsterhood or to late marriage by new peasant attitudes to the sub-division of land that a son's marriage might cause. And between the high and the low was a growing body of literate women who hoped for wider horizons. As emigration, famine and changed marriage habits took their toll, between 1841 and 1901 the number of Catholics in Ireland almost halved; and yet, during the same period, the number of nuns increased eight-fold. One's interpretation of these two statistics is bound to be coloured by personal religious conviction. There is no doubt, though, that a life of self-denial had a remarkable appeal to many girls – or to their parents – during this period of equivocation about the place of women in society. But, while some women sought fulfilment by renouncing personal secular responsibilities and consolations, others realized that the answer to feminist and wider political yearnings might be found in or through the Irish cultural revival which was beginning to blossom on all sides.

3

IRISH CULTURAL REVIVAL

Ireland's cultural revival has been variously described and defined; the accounts of its origins and the emphases of its labels, embracing as they have done a wide range of concepts, from 'literary Fenianism'[1] and Celtic or Gaelic Revival to Irish Renaissance, have varied so much that it is often difficult to decide when it began and what limits to place on its subject-matter. Although most would agree that literary activity which generated sufficient interest to be termed a revival occurred in the early 1880s, such dating ignores the work of those whose earlier research or original authorship sparked a later conflagration, as well as making valuable contributions to scholarship and literature in general. It has been argued[2] that to single out women authors is to 'marginalize' them unfairly, and frequently there is much truth in this argument – which need not be limited to the literary field; but the dominance of Irish women as practitioners, exemplars and catalysts of what became a movement with a cultural impact felt far beyond the shores of the British Isles was so marked that it commands attention.

Although Maria Edgeworth's novel, *Castle Rackrent*, appeared in 1800 it had been written some years before the Act of Union. As a product of the distaff side of the Ascendancy, it is more interesting for present purposes than any of her other writings partly because she wrote it in secret, therefore independently of her father's often excessive influence, and without any intention of having it published. As has already been observed, the end of the eighteenth century was not a time when Ireland was conspicuously a matriarchal society; consequently the way in which Maria Edgeworth approached her task and the perspective of her account of the conduct of the Rackrent family tells the reader something about the constraints felt by female authors, and the attitudes of educated women of her class. Had she been a man she would, no doubt, have taken for granted her right and duty to comment upon the great issues of the day; instead her experience of life had taught her that public pronouncements on matters of social and political consequence were customarily left to men. If women wrote, their natural or assumed literary material was limited to family concerns, preferably as seen in the context of the drawing-room.

Castle Rackrent, as its shortened title suggests, is about the Big House; albeit a comparatively modest example of one is used. The full title was *Castle Rackrent, an Hibernian Tale: taken from the Facts, and from the Manners of the Irish Squires, before the year 1782*, and already the author had made a political comment – a rackrent being an extortionate rent. The title page gives no hint of the author's identity; in search of clarification the reader may turn to the Preface, where he will only discover that one Thady,

> the author of the following memoirs . . . was an illiterate old steward . . .
> a few notes have been subjoined by the editor, and he had it in
> contemplation to translate the language of Thady into plain English; but
> . . . the authenticity of his story would have been exposed to doubt if it
> were not told in his own characteristic manner.[3]

Thus the author has doubly distanced herself from her sex. Not only is the tale told by a man, but the fictitious editor she chooses to employ is also masculine. Gender reversal may be an acceptable or commendable literary device (as was use of an 'editor', during this period), but in this author's case it provided the route to what, in her day, was a rare opportunity to give a transparent and vivid account of an important area of social history.

This story, set in the last years of 'the independency', has received much praise for its literary merit. It pioneered the portrayal of regional characters using regional English, and brought to life the rural Irish from the Squire downwards; without it the world might have been deprived of the Waverley novels and all that derived from them. Moreover, as the 'editor' stressed, it is essential to look behind the façade that prominent men present: 'it is from their careless conversations, their half-finished sentences, that we may hope with the greatest probability of success to discover their real characters'.[4] The narrator, the only character in the book admitted by the author to be drawn directly from life (he was based on John Langan, the Edgeworths' steward when Maria first came to Edgeworthstown, the family estate in County Longford), relates the sad history of the Rackrents 'in his vernacular idiom',[5] wholly aware of all the faults of the family, yet remaining loyal to the end. But Maria Edgeworth was aware that other characters in her story were more real than she herself chose to reveal; there was a family history, known as *The Black Book*,[6] on which she drew heavily, and in a postscript the 'editor' indiscreetly announced that every characteristic described had been 'taken from life'.[7] Thady, in the freedom of his anonymous soliloquy, describes the decline and fall of a family previously known as the O'Shaughlins and related to the kings of Ireland.

Thady's casual reference to his master's origins makes it clear to readers that the Rackrents, though as Irish as anyone on that island had – in part – concealed their Irishness in order to make life more comfortable for themselves. There is more than a suspicion that they abandoned the old religion when it was politic so to do, and it is in passing asides like this that the author makes her oblique political and social commentary. The fall of the house of Rackrent is mercilessly described by a fictional narrator whose affection for the family is never in question. When Sir Condy Rackrent drinks himself to ruination and the end comes, it is Thady's son, Jason, who buys out the estate, much to his father's consternation.

The Ascendancy author did not flinch from revealing frankly and in great detail the short-sighted self-indulgence and absurdity of some members of her class, but recently too much has been read into her supposed sympathy with those who were to displace most of the Rackrents. It is going too far to say that 'her book illustrates a private and subtle protest against all forms of "absurd authority", of which the British Empire may be considered the most obvious and public manifestation'.[8] This comment was made in connection with what were assumed to be Maria's views on the great issue of the day, the imminent Act of Union. However, the Edgeworth family, including Maria, were in two minds about the merging of the two parliaments. Maria's father, a member of the Irish Parliament, spoke for the Union, and voted against it. He usually tried to impose his views on Maria, and, despite *Castle Rackrent*'s having been written without his knowledge, the last two paragraphs of the postscript betray her doubts also. She wonders whether the Union 'will hasten or retard the amelioration of this country'. Then she shrewdly asks whether certain English who came over to Ireland taught the Irish to drink beer, 'or did they learn from the Irish how to drink whiskey?'[9]

Maria Edgeworth had a keen sense of the absurd, but she did not categorize the empire as an absurdity. Much of her literary output, in partnership (as junior partner for much, though not all, of the time) with her father, Richard, was educational material, the full value of which was not to achieve recognition until well into the twentieth century. Her message for Ireland was closely related to her educational philosophy and was to do with 'amelioration' of the status quo. She was not happy about the dismantling of existing structures, hence her uncertainties about the Union: was it building or destroying? Her attitude to landlordism was quite clear: although few were more aware than she of its shortcomings as practised in eighteenth- and nineteenth-century Ireland, she believed that there was nothing wrong with it as an institution. The widespread abuses needed to be rooted out, and one of her contributions to society was to expose them. This was done with touches of humour in *Castle Rackrent*, and more seriously in *The Absentee*. The device of the anonymous male editor gave her the opportunity to fire away in footnotes at iniquities that Thady was simultaneously complaining about in the main text. Within the parameters of his role as faithful retainer he was not blind to terrible things that went on in the district, but his criticisms were necessarily limited to what could reasonably be known by an old steward.

In anticipation of a full-blooded treatment of the hazards of landlordism in *The Absentee*, the 'editor' of *Castle Rackrent* makes an attack on 'middlemen' that is part didactic, part tragic and part humorous. The didacticism lies in a succinct description of the hierarchy of rural Ireland; the tragedy lies in the way tenants might be exploited to the extent of paying their rent twice; the humour in the tongue-in-cheek flattering modes of address used by potential victims when speaking to the middlemen: 'your honour's honour' and the like, at the beginning and the end of every sentence. These expressions were never used when speaking to 'the good old families'. And the editor adds, 'A witty carpenter once termed these middlemen *journeymen gentlemen*'.[10] Writing well before the Famine and the horrors of the nineteenth-century evictions, the 'editor', in reality the daughter of a model landlord, can be forgiven for taking an indulgent view of a system which could so easily be abused. Furthermore, as landlordism evolved into the benign system which survives in much of the United Kingdom today, her opinions were, in the long term, vindicated.

Because of the manner of *Castle Rackrent*'s birth, very different works from the same author's pen found their way into print first. In *Literary Letters to Ladies* (1795) Maria Edgeworth advocated the provision of education for girls; in the *Parent's Assistant* (1796) she used the observations of her first stepmother, Honora Sneyd, on education as an experimental science (based on the progress of Maria's siblings) as the basis of a series of instructive tales; and, in partnership with her father, she produced *Practical Education* (1798). Richard Edgeworth, who had by his four successive wives nineteen children, not counting those which did not survive infancy, encouraged his eldest daughter's literary aspirations. However, it is he who must take much of the blame for the deterioration in her style which has led to the majority of her novels lacking popular appeal because of their obtrusive didacticism. Influenced by *Émile*, he was encouraged by Honora, and by the convenience of having a large family, to try to employ Rousseau's educational principles. Remarkably, his relationship with Maria did not suffer from the notoriously risky practice of trying to experiment with one's own offspring.

Didacticism is very much a feature of *The Absentee* (1812), which, as its title suggests, describes the consequences, and indicates the predictable cures, of absentee landlordism. Like many of Maria's other novels, it is a love story intended to provide an accurate portrayal of the fashionable life of her day; enlightenment of the reader is sought by demonstrating the contrast between false values encountered in the salons of London and what can be found in the healthier environment of Ireland. The hero, an extraordinarily naïve landlord, comes to his senses after he has been exposed to the beauty of Ireland and the good nature of the Irish peasantry, and discovers the shocking things that have happened in his name because of his absence and, of course, finds his true love. Some awkward construction and cardboard characterization mean that here, as elsewhere in her writings, Maria falls short of the standards set by her contemporary, Jane Austen. But, then, her aims were different, and she succeeded where even Jane Austen might have failed; the Edgeworth achievement lay in giving literary acceptability to the minds and lives and speech of the lowly Irish. At the same time she gave a perceptive exposé of contemporary attitudes to the relationship between the two halves of the kingdom, giving the advantage to Ireland. Both *Castle Rackrent* and *The Absentee* escape the charge of pessimism, but by different means: the former shows a sorry state of affairs which is said to have disappeared for ever; the latter ends with a letter from a sympathetic character, whose last remark is 'and you see it's the fashion not to be an Absentee'.[11]

Maria Edgeworth was not a lone female figure writing to the advantage of Ireland. While she was getting across a social message, sometimes with subtle obliqueness, sometimes with clumsy directness, as the Union came and its effects were felt, there were others whose purposes were more overtly political. Lady Morgan was one of these. The daughter of an Irish actor and an English woman from Shrewsbury, she was a writer with a very different approach. Remembered now principally for one novel, *The Wild Irish Girl* (1806), originally published under her maiden name, Sydney Owenson, she gained much notoriety at a time when Irish fiction writers were enjoying a boom. Before the 'cult of Tone' began, she alone mentioned the rebel hero in her work. A prolific author, she tackled political issues head-on, both in her fiction and in her attempts at straightforward analysis. Thirteen years after her marriage to Sir (Thomas) Charles Morgan and after the Edgeworthstown landlord's daughter had published her romance, *The Absentee*, the Irish actor's daughter produced *Absenteeism*, a matter-of-fact examination of the problem. Then, two years later, came another of the easy-to-read romances which accounted for her excellent sales: *The O'Briens and the O'Flahertys*. She lost few opportunities to praise Ireland for its beauty and its history, and she bluntly ascribed all its ills to misgovernment, injecting into her novels frank portrayals of Irish causes, as she saw them. Her grammar was eccentric, as her critics were quick to point out; but it was her satirical character sketches, and the favour which she found with the Whig aristocracy, which brought her both friends and enemies. The source of much nineteenth-century literary entertainment – who, for some of her descriptions, was praised by Lord Byron – she at least helped to consolidate women as an accepted feature of the literary scene. She had definite feminist opinions: one of her unfinished works was entitled *Woman and her Master: a History of the Female Sex from the Earliest Period*.

Lady Morgan had more impact on the general readership of her day than she had on her fellow authors. In several important ways Maria Edgeworth's influence had a direct effect on the literary values of others, especially on two who devoted much of their energy to writing from an assumed masculine standpoint. Major Yeates, RM, whose reminiscences have been under-valued on both sides of the Irish Sea, was the creation of two women who chose to relate his experiences in the first person singular. Violet Martin, whose family had acquitted themselves so well at Ross House during the Famine, was a great-grandchild of a close friend of Maria's, Nancy Crampton; using the name

Martin Ross, she combined her talents with those of Edith Somerville, another great-grandchild of Mrs Crampton. While in the Ascendancy generally speaking everybody knew everybody, and one's friends were often one's cousins, the ties of class and blood which drew Somerville and Ross together proved to be unusually fruitful. Violet inherited the Edgeworth–Crampton correspondence, and both authors idolized Maria. They were proud of their family's link with the famous writer, and proved their admiration of her methods and achievements by following her example in much of their work. After Violet's death, Edith wrote,

> Miss Edgeworth had been the last to write of Irish country life with sincerity and originality, dealing with both the upper and lower classes, and dealing with both unconventionally ... [she] ... had the privilege, which was also ours, of living in Ireland, in the country, and among the people of whom she wrote.[12]

It was in their ability faithfully to render the natural speech and attitudes of mind of country people, the high and the low, that Somerville and Ross showed that their talents were equal, or sometimes superior, to those of their idol. They shared her social background, and yet like her they found it easy to cross bridges that others did not even know were there. Maria deserves credit for finding, and sometimes building, bridges, and her disciples were always aware of this debt. Nevertheless, it remains something of a puzzle that they have received nothing like the same degree of acceptance from critics of serious literature. One can put forward several suggestions to account for this. A likely explanation is that the experiences of the Irish Resident Magistrate, which are amusing stories whether or not one is interested in the social significance of the content, have stolen the limelight, while serious works, like *The Real Charlotte*, have been left in the shade: it may be difficult to slough off the stigma of frivolity. Another possibility is that, to those who did not, or do not, know Ireland at first hand the whole scenario of the reminiscences may appear to be ludicrously far-fetched. The magistrate's adventures have stubbornly remained centre stage, and moreover, it is probable that the characters he remembers will be disowned by some who have their reasons for denying that Ireland or the Irish were ever like that. The personal foibles of a Victorian peasant may seem quaint, to say the least, and many Irish are understandably touchy when stage Irishness is suspected. A simpler explanation is that between *Castle Rackrent* and the writings of Somerville and Ross occurred the Famine and the worst of the evictions; after these events it was difficult for anyone to accept that the products of the upper strata of society had genuine rapport with 'ordinary' people.

When what may be termed the mainstream of the Irish literary revival was in spate, Somerville and Ross were not part of it. They belonged neither to the political tradition of it (Violet's unionism went some way to cancelling out Edith's nationalist inclinations), nor had they sympathy with the creation, that often masqueraded as a rediscovery, of a supposedly glorious Gaelic past, nor with drama which purported to give dignity to humble folk, but which sometimes drew its inspiration from too little acquaintance with its subject-matter. This is not to demolish at a stroke a movement which in many ways rejuvenated Ireland and, looked at as a whole, inspired much of the best that has been written in English during the last century – to say nothing of parallel stimulation of art, crafts and music. It is, however, to underline the fact that hitherto the canon of the revival has too often been limited to the output of the circle, some would say clique, associated with the names of Lady Gregory and W. B. Yeats. Among their number were a few whose contributions were misbegotten and, naturally enough, even the greatest authors and artists of what was by no means a coherent movement lost their way from time to time.

Another significant source of the affinity which existed between the joint authors and Maria Edgeworth lay in the part which formal education played in their lives. In Maria's case, she easily assumed the exceptional attitudes of her unusual father and her first stepmother, and, between them, the family's efforts in this field still find their way into works of comparative education today. But she was denied the fulfilment which some members of the next generation of women were to enjoy. It was not until three years before her death that an educational qualification for women became available, when, in 1846, the Diploma for Governesses was established by the Governesses' Benevolent Institution.

Apart from the convent, the governess remained the standard educator of well-placed women until 1866, when the school which both Edith and Violet were to attend, Alexandra College, was founded. Education there, subsequently thought of as respectable and conventional, breached a succession of dams that had previously held women's potential in check. Coincidentally with the founding of similar colleges in England, it awakened minds to possibilities that had long been hidden, and it provided the means to change futile, confused yearnings into realistic aspirations. But it was not a mere shadow of English institutions and it knew that it was different. An Irish Society immediately blossomed, more Irish than 'Anglo-Irish' and producing a regular magazine with sections written in Irish. The day was to come when Patrick Pearse would be teaching Irish there.

Comparisons between Somerville and Ross, who cohabited mainly at Edith's family's house, Drishane, Castletownshend, in County Cork, and the Ladies who lived out their lives in Llangollen, are inescapable. Here again were two spinsters who had chosen to live their lives together under the same roof, and to turn their backs on the traditional ways of women of their class. They, too, shared beds, and their insight into the minds of men was astonishing. Inevitably, it seems, a case has been made to prove that their relationship was a lesbian one;[13] but the evidence put forward has been thoroughly sifted, and the argument soundly refuted.[14] The paths of the two female couples did, in fact, cross, and the reactions of the younger pair to the

Ladies was hostile, as they revealed in print and in private correspondence: there was no sympathy for the way in which Eleanor and Sarah had decided to leave their families, their life-style was described as a 'grotesque romance'[15] and, as Violet said in a letter to Edith, she 'could never tell the wearisome grind of those blessed hags of Llangollen'.[16]

Bed-sharing was fairly commonplace among the women who lived in the large, often inadequately heated, scantily carpeted houses beyond the Pale – when dilapidation had begun to set in among the lesser gentry – and there was no reason to read anything odd into it; though whether one could stretch this point to include the sleeping arrangements in the cosier bedroom of Plas Newydd is another matter. One would do so, if this were the only possible clue one was considering. But refutation of a charge of lesbianism (as it happens, neither then nor now an offence under British law) has been achieved both negatively and positively, by shredding the arguments put forward by its principal advocate,[17] and by producing written evidence of Edith's reaction when approached by an aggressive lesbian. Ethel Smyth, under the mis-apprehension that the relationship between Somerville and Ross had a physical dimension, propositioned Edith in no uncertain terms, protesting, when rebuffed, that she could achieve experiences of that nature 'far more cleverly and energetically than any man would be capable of doing'.[18] Nevertheless, Edith's and Violet's feeling for each other – a sublime unity of mind and spirit – undeniably had something in common with the chemistry that made Eleanor and Sarah special people. There was a shared commitment to the principle of a woman's right to follow her own chosen path, and in both cases an emotional predisposition to join forces preceded practical con-siderations (with the Somerville and Ross combination it was Violet who took the initiative). In Llangollen, companionship was enough; luckily for posterity the couple who chose to stay with their roots channelled their passions to yield literary rather than human fruit. They never felt the urge to divorce themselves from the issues of their day and 'retire' into a retreat. Far from it: they pooled their resources to further the cause of women's suffrage, and their successful career as authors added strength to the feminist cause.

Excluding those who were engaged solely in Gaelic research, Somerville and Ross were, after Maria Edgeworth, true precursors of the revival, though they sought to distance themselves from it; their work was much appreciated by Lady Gregory and Yeats. Despite her claim that 'I was the first to write in the Irish dialect – that is, the English of Gaelic-thinking people',[19] an aberration which must be attributed to vanity, Lady Gregory not only read the Resident Magistrate's reminiscences to Yeats, much to his delight, but held the authors in such high regard that she sent books of her own, and of others engaged in the revival, to Violet for criticism. That she did so is much to her credit, for she was practitioner, inspiration, and, especially, influential promoter of the Irish drama that eventually dominated the revival. It says something about the close-knit nature of Big House society at that time that, as the correspondence went to and fro between Coole Park and Castle-townshend, not far away the former Miss Charlotte Payne-Townshend, one of Edith's many cousins, was revisiting her childhood haunts. She had married George Bernard Shaw and was not only midwife for his prolific outpourings but, many years later, performed a similar service for Lawrence's *Seven Pillars of Wisdom*, which, despite the author's Anglo-Irish paternity, is not a work that one would expect to have had links with the Irish literary revival.

The men of the revival seem to have owed most of their achievement to women, and this is true of none more than W. B. Yeats. Lady Gregory's part in his development was part inspirational, part educational and part practical. She it was who made him listen to the country people who lived near her at Coole, she was his confidante, and she lifted the revival to the level of a Renaissance by agreeing to be a founder of the Irish Literary Theatre, which, with the financial help of another woman, Annie Horniman, became the Abbey Theatre. But she was really the woman behind the entire movement. For better or worse, she invented 'Kiltartanese', rural dialect based on the speech of the inhabitants of the village near Coole (jotting down some 200,000 words in the painful process), she wrote more than forty plays, including *Spreading the News* and *The Rising of the Moon*, and generally kept everyone up to the mark. In Yeats's life though, she was an alternative – one of several women to whom he turned when Maud Gonne had spurned him yet again. Lady Gregory was more than a dozen years older than he, and their bonds were to do with common interests and attitudes. By contrast, the inspiration of his life had a strong sensual hold over him, held views that were not always consistent with his, and periodically drove him to distraction.

Born in Aldershot, Maud Gonne was the daughter of a man who rose to the rank of colonel in the British army, and when her sister, Kathleen, married Captain Thomas David Pilcher, who was to become Major-General, she became connected with a family that was as respected in England in her time as it is today. This 'English' respectability, for she was ever the racist, as her anti-Semitic remarks were to underline, riled her, and she did her best to disguise it in that collection of half-truths and instinctive misrepresentation, her autobiography.[20] But she found it difficult to escape. When, for instance, she was particularly waspish in her comments about Queen Victoria, she read in the *Irish Figaro* that her conduct was 'all the more to be regretted when it is remembered that she is related by marriage with that most gallant officer, Colonel Pilcher'.[21]

Maud Gonne's background was completely different from that of Countess Markievicz, with whom she is frequently compared, but the two rebels had experiences in common, and shared attitudes to life, that are sufficient for parallels to be convincingly sustained. Seemingly small details, like Maud Gonne assuming the name 'Maeve', supposedly for security reasons, at the meetings of the women's organization which she founded, Inghinidhe na hEireann, become more significant when seen in terms of the importance attached by the more articulate rebels to the power of symbolism in their struggle. The sanctifying of names for the sake of the cause was to achieve a climax for Maud when her would-be lover, Yeats, was to 'write it out in a verse' that included the name of her recently-executed estranged husband, John MacBride:

> MacDonagh and MacBride
> And Connolly and Pearse
> Now and in time to be,
> Wherever green is worn,
> Are changed, changed utterly:
> A terrible beauty is born.[22]

That both women should choose the name Maeve, one for her daughter and one for herself, may not be especially remarkable. Nevertheless, it can be seen as a symbol of a wish to pursue a role other than that ordained by custom, and hence of the dilemma facing women who choose to take an active part in public affairs. For Constance and Maud there was a constant conflict of interest between political commitment and personal, especially maternal, obligations. When Maud defended Constance's record as a mother, to what extent was a guilty conscience guiding her pen? A letter to the countess's stepson was written when she knew that the marriage of the surviving offspring of her relationship with a married man, her illegitimate daughter Iseult, was a failure. Buried in her mind somewhere there was also the knowledge that her first-born son, Georges, had died of meningitis when she had not been with him:

> Constance loved children and it was a great sacrifice when she sent Maeve to be brought up by her mother because life's evolution had made things too strenuous for the child at home. I have heard people . . . speak of her as a neglectful mother. Nothing could be falser than that . . .[23]

These words could as easily have been written to defend one who, as she waited outside Mountjoy prison to provide aid to newly-released civil war prisoners, was to hear a taxi driver shout at her, 'Go home and take care of your bastards!'[24]

Maud Gonne's influence on the cultural revival was strong and beneficial in some of its achievements, harmful in others; it owed as much to her vices as to her virtues. As with her attitude to the conventional view of a woman's place in society, she had few qualms about using any means at her disposal to achieve her chosen ends. The dubious morality which marred Yeats' play, *The Countess Cathleen*, in which Ireland's mother figure sells her soul to the devil to save starving peasants, was probably a reflection of her own influence on the poet while he was writing it. Taking a cosmic overview, Yeats distorted J. S. Mill somewhat by making an angel say, after Cathleen's death, that,

The Light of Lights
Looks always on the motive, not the deed,
The Shadow of Shadows on the deed alone.[25]

A strong advocate of using violence for the causes which she believed to be just, Maud who, like the real-life Countess from Lissadell, was to be called Ireland's Joan of Arc, seldom shrank from manipulating means to serve her ends, and from time to time, in her disorganized life, attempted to manipulate Yeats. But the most powerful influence she had on his life and his writing she did not seek. Her beauty in his eyes, and in the eyes of others of their time, was breathtaking. It was his lifelong obsession, it inspired some of the best of his writing, and it encouraged him in some of his sillier activities, from dabbling on the lunatic fringes of spiritualism to admiring the false face of Fascism.

Like Countess Markievicz, Maud Gonne was a woman of action, never happy except when in the thick of things, opposing evictions, organizing rival attractions to diminish the impact of a royal visit, addressing public meetings, establishing committees and societies, and writing angry letters to newspapers. Apart from her limited talents as an actress, and her ability to rouse the emotions of a crowd by her own style of oratory, Maud added nothing of her own to the output of the cultural revival. But, although she was no Lady Gregory, she shared the older woman's knack of getting other people to give of their best to a movement which to her was essentially the means to hastening the advent of the revolution. To her, the fulfilment of nationalist – and feminist – aims would be substantially assisted by a cultural movement which, to use the title of a famous lecture given by Douglas Hyde in November 1892, recognized 'The necessity of de-Anglicizing the Irish people'. However, such an analysis runs the risk of showing her in much too harsh a light. No more than Douglas Hyde, was she a Philistine; she had aesthetic values of a high order, but they were closely bound up with her glorification of a naïve view of freedom.

As the end of the nineteenth century approached, Dublin Castle became aware, and wary, of three organizations that were cultural in the widest sense of the term. Certainly between them they nurtured and stimulated a high degree of the national self-consciousness that often gave birth to rebelliousness, though it would be a serious mistake to equate them with the cultural revival. The Gaelic Athletic Association had been founded in 1884; the Gaelic League and the Celtic Literary Society did not appear until 1893, by which time Maud Gonne and Yeats had decided that if a cultural movement was to be of real service to Ireland, such organizations must proliferate. One outcome of their conclusion was that Maud, who had adequate private means, should popularize the idea of a Celtic Revival, not only in Ireland, but in England and on the Continent; her beauty, eloquence and style made her the ideal cultural ambassador. She impressed the *Association Irlandais*, which she had founded in France as a branch of the Young Ireland Society; and she was one of the speakers at the inauguration of the National Literary Society of Ireland which she and Yeats co-founded in 1892.

Yeats was slow to discover that the object of his love had an illicit relationship with the French journalist and right-wing rebel supporter of General Boulanger, Lucien Millevoye; otherwise he would not have been so happy about the ease with which, in 1892, the beautiful orator went to and from the Continent. There were many speaking engagements in France, mostly sponsored by student clubs, and after returning to Great Britain for similar meetings in the north of England and in Scotland, Maud was visiting France again, and giving lectures in Belgium and Holland. In terms of oratory, her performances were resoundingly successful, and worthy forerunners of an even more dramatic, and certainly more controversial, tour which she was to undertake in the United States five years later. However, the outcome of the lectures showed that promotion of Irish culture, as such, was wholly submerged in nationalist rhetoric: after one of her meetings, for example, her listeners were so excited that they demonstrated outside the British consulate at La Rochelle until the police dispersed them.

For Maud Gonne, promoting the nationalist cause meant seeing the political position solely in terms of the blackness of England and the pure white of Ireland; for Yeats, the grey shades were realities to be faced, and in any case art transcended politics. While she laboured to raise funds for providing village libraries, he refused to remain silent about flaws which he saw in Thomas Davis's poetry, and he expressed his unhappiness about Charles Gavan Duffy's selection of books to be published by literary societies in Dublin and London, thus incurring her wrath for his supposed treacheries. And yet, despite her double standards, she continued to bewitch him and in a seemingly arbitrary manner succeeded in organizing other people's lives, even when her own affairs were chaotic. Hers was an inherently restless disposition. In her haphazard way, motivated partly by a desperate patriotism, partly by her craving to be always in the public eye, and partly by her need to keep her mind off the tragic confusion and deception of her private life, her constant implementing of new ideas brought together other minds. The contribution these minds made to feminist, nationalist and cultural development left permanent marks on Irish history.

The bond between Maud Gonne and Yeats, formed at a respectable level of society, may be contrasted with another union, in most respects anything but respectable: between James Joyce and Nora Barnacle. The two couples could hardly have been more different; and yet the power exerted by the runaway chambermaid who cared nothing for the printed word was no less than that of the British Army officer's daughter with artistic notions. Each achieved the upper hand, each begat bastards; but, whereas Yeats's great love was never reciprocated in any satisfactory sense, Joyce and Nora Barnacle loved each other passionately, and the illegitimacy of their children was no accident. The

'Joyces', for though they lived in sin for twenty-seven years (contrary to James's entry in *Who's Who*) they eventually married, are examples of a parallel literary movement which consisted of Irish *émigrés*. Nora had been reared in Galway, surrounded by all that the literati romanced about, but to natives with a modicum of ambition emigration was an attractive means of bettering oneself, and to some it provided the means for family survival. Alice Milligan was one who urged that landless labourers and domestic servants should be content with their lot; Pearse called emigrants traitors and fools.[26] Nora, daughter of a baker and a seamstress, had no pressing financial reasons for leaving Galway; her decision was to do with being a free spirit.

Joyce, a lower-middle-class Catholic by birth, had strong intellectual reasons for leaving Ireland, as well as subjective ones which he shared with Nora. Above all, from the age of 16 he rejected, and increasingly despised, the Roman Catholic Church, and this meant that he appeared to reject Ireland:

> This lovely land that always sent
> Her writers and artists to banishment
> And in a spirit of Irish fun
> Betrayed her own leaders one by one.[27]

But as an exile Joyce cheated: Nora was his Ireland; more than a lifeline, her whole life, her Catholic faith which she put into suspension for his sake, her personality and vocabulary, gave him the substance of his greatest works, after *Dubliners*. Molly Bloom's monologue at the end of *Ulysses*, maddening though it is to those who cherish punctuation (Nora had next to none), is a seminal, if controversial, feminist outburst with deeper roots in Ireland's troubled psyche than some might care to admit. Except in his relationship with Nora, Joyce was outwardly a misogynist. But contrast between surface behaviour and inner conviction is nothing unusual. Molly is composed of many of Nora's elements and, among other things, Nora was to Joyce the epitome of Irish womanhood. As a literary source she was used by him throughout most of his work to refute phoney Irish claims about national purity 'which linked a wholly false notion of the Gael to the equally false notion of the sexually and racially pure Irish person – to be more specific, the pure Irish woman'.[28] To Joyce, Lady Gregory and her set were hypocritical; her friends of the Irish literati were oblivious of the real Ireland; the Irish Literary Revival was contemptible:

> That they may dream their dreamy dreams
> I carry off their filthy streams.[29]

For all that, Joyce unwittingly made Nora into yet another 'dreamy dream': 'Nora Barnacle is as much a part of Irish mythology as Queen Maeve.'[30]

Joyce being an enemy of the Irish literary revival did not prevent the Joyces and the Yeatses from becoming good friends, and dining together in Paris. The Joyces were financially able to socialize at this level because of two of James's other female supporters: throughout his literary career a rich English spinster, Harriet Weaver, was his generous patron, and for much of the time Sylvia Beach was his indulgent publisher. Yeats, who had eventually settled for marriage with Georgie Hyde Lees, having failed to marry either Maud Gonne or her daughter Iseult, regarded Joyce as a genius. He made the recommendation that led to Ezra Pound publishing *A Portrait of the Artist as a Young Man* in serial form in the *Egoist*, and helped to get him a grant from the Royal Literary Society. But Yeats had never been allowed to put art before politics in all things; nor did he experience fulfilment in love. His relationship with Maud Gonne was at its best when their aesthetic motives carried them in the same direction; it was shaken when nationalism slipped into second place, as, for example, when Yeats adversely criticized well-meaning, but pathetic, patriotic literary efforts. The Parisian dinners were encouraging links on a personal and intellectual basis between the rebellious pioneer of Ireland's wider literary empire and the man who had become one of the acknowledged leaders of the mainstream of Irish literature. But Yeats, despite his instinctive refusal to take a narrow nationalist view of writing was often tugged that way by his emotional servitude to Millevoye's mistress.

Yeats disagreed with Joyce's obsession with the urban scene, believing that great art could only come about when nature held sway. Joyce dismissed the older man's views on this issue as useless generalizations of a man of letters, and put them down to his age. Considering the frankness of Joyce's writing, and his distaste for the literary revival, it does at first seem remarkable that Yeats – and Lady Gregory – recognized his talent from the beginning. The attitudes of the two men to women were not as different as their reputations might lead one to believe. The frankness of some of Yeats's last poetry has more than a Joycean touch to it, and neither man chose to obliterate contradictions in outspoken declarations about a woman's place in the scheme of things. In his final phase, collaborating with his friend Dorothy Wellesley, Yeats developed a traditional tale in such a way as to confuse or enrage feminists, socialists and conventional thinkers alike. The basic idea, which evolves from the ballad 'The Three Bushes', is that a lady in love sends her chambermaid to sleep with her lover because she wants to preserve her chastity; there are three songs of the lady, one of the lover, and two of the chambermaid. The lady's second song, with its Christian refrain 'The Lord have mercy upon us', ends with a question which would not have worried Joyce, whose chambermaid gave him everything:

> If soul may look and body touch,
> Which is the more blest?[31]

Yeats, though, whose love proved to be unattainable, made his lady a victim of the Irish approach to celibacy:

He shall love my soul as though
Body were not all.
He shall love your body
Untroubled by the soul . . .

Speaking to her maid, she wonders what sort of man will be coming to lie between her feet.[32] But she does not wait for an answer: 'What matter, we are but women.'

It was typical of Maud Gonne's priorities that it was at one of the meetings of the Celtic Literary Society that she initiated her most significant contribution to female political activity in Ireland. She asked those present to persuade sisters and women friends to visit the society's office in order to discuss the possibility of establishing a women's separatist organization. On the face of it, there may have been much that was 'Celtic' about this move, but the 'literary' aspect seemed to have disappeared altogether. However, although Maud's initiative was feminist and nationalist in its intent, the meeting of minds which began in October 1900, when fifteen young women appeared at the Abbey Street office, led to some genuine encouragement of Irish cultural activity. An agenda had been drawn up by the convenor, assisted by Yeats, and it is possible to discern which of its authors had been responsible for the contrasting subjects of the curriculum. With Maud Gonne in the chair, the decision was taken to provide free lessons for children in Irish history, Gaelic, Irish music and Irish dancing. Inghinidhe na hEireann would also campaign against recruitment of Irishmen into the British army by distributing leaflets to young men, and by dissuading girls from fraternizing with soldiers; a 'Buy Irish' policy was to be promoted; the reading of 'low English literature' was to be discouraged, as was singing English songs and attending English entertainments. Maud was elected the organization's first president, and her racist inclinations were reflected in the condition of membership that all must be Irish, or of Irish descent.

A number of women who became famous on the nationalist side of the struggle, which waxed and waned among those who cared, were 'Daughters of Erin', and there were some who rose above the narrowness that Maud's recipe was calculated to impose. Two poets of some stature, not only marked by the subsequent inclusion of their work in *The Dublin Book of Irish Verse*, were among the vice-presidents: Anna Johnson, alias Ethna Carberry, and Alice Furlong. Another poet, Ella Young, who was also a Celtic scholar, was responsible for teaching children tales of the ancient Irish heroes. As happened at Alexandra College, an altogether different environment, Patrick Pearse was recruited to help ensure that Irish was properly taught; and others who had played, or would play, key roles in Ireland's main period of transition since Norman times were drawn in to help Erin's Daughters. One of those persuaded to address them was Anna Parnell. The educative task that

Inghinidhe na hEireann had set itself was a daunting one, if for no other reason than that initially most of the raw material at the primary level was a largely illiterate body of children from the Dublin slums. Dedicated women did what they could, but this was not what most people meant by a cultural revival. If one looks at the mixture of targets which the organization had erected, it had a measure of success, with a few bull's-eyes; if popularity is among the acceptable criteria by which it should be judged, it can be said to have flourished; branches sprang up in Limerick, Cork and Ballina.

Although members of Inghinidhe na hEireann had something in common with the other two organizations that worried Dublin Castle, the Gaelic Athletic Association and the Gaelic League – like the former they wanted to have a 'Gaelic' influence on young people nationwide, like the latter they wanted to 'de-Anglicize' Ireland – they and their aims owed much more to external factors, such as the Boer War and the aftermath of the 1798 centenary celebrations: the membership was solidly devoted to complete independence from the rest of the United Kingdom. When they held a *ceilidh* or celebrated the sacred day of a Celtic goddess, the set pieces which they performed were statements of separate identity. With Douglas Hyde as its president, the Gaelic League did not suffer from narrow political preoccupations until, well into the first decade of the twentieth century, infiltration by the Irish Republican Brotherhood (IRB) was complete. True, it suffered from other narrowing influences, and they eventually led to disputes and a split in the revivalist movement, but the arguments themselves stimulated literary development of a high order. Moreover, evidence that the league was more Gaelic than Irish can be found in its links with the Scottish Gaelic Societies, especially the Gaelic Society of London. The Hon. Louisa Farquharson, who was to become its Chief in 1908, spent some time in Ireland in the early 1900s and it was she who gave the final tilt to the scales of Roger Casement's allegiance so that he realized for the first time that he was a committed separatist.[33]

It would be an over-simplification to say that disputes within the initially small, predominantly bourgeois, membership of the Gaelic League led to a divergence between language and literature, but there is no denying that separate traditions developed in which beliefs about what constituted Irish writing were far apart. The league's original purpose had been quite specific: to revive the use of the Irish language and to see that it was part of Ireland's educational curriculum at all levels. As the revival gathered momentum, however, and embraced authors who might never dream of joining literary or political organizations, the Irish language could be seen on the one hand as the only doorway through which one passed to a truly Irish literary tradition; on the other as, at best, a source of colourful legends, at worst, an irrelevance or a stumbling-block. It could be argued that the only true Irish literature must be expressed in Gaelic, but was there not already an Irish national literature in which 'The spirit was Celtic, if the form was English'?[34] The traditions should have been complementary to one another; the language movement could be seen to be a necessary precursor to the literary revival, if only to enable new writers to draw upon the events of the ancient heroic period. But was the language really such a barrier? Lady Wilde, a daughter of Ireland, but no Daughter of Erin, had put matters into perspective in 1888, when she wrote of gaining access to 'the shrouded part of humanity' via language, mythology and the written word: 'The written word, or literature, comes last, the fullest and highest expression of the intellect and culture, and scientific progress of a nation.'[35] Her collection of ancient Irish legends was based on oral tradition expressed, as she put it, 'either in Irish or in the Irish-English which preserves so much of the expressive idiom of the antique tongue'.[36]

Like so much that had gone before, the split in the literary movement had sectarian and class elements that came increasingly to the fore. There was no denying the flowering of what was soon termed the 'Anglo-Irish' literary tradition, and, of course, it was predominantly Protestant and Ascendancy, and not antipathetic to unionists. The best that could be said for the other side was that they were often scholarly. Maud Gonne's part in this was paradoxical, to the extent that the consequences of her inconsistent behaviour towards Yeats benefited his literary performance, and, through him, influenced his friends. She was emotionally unstable, though her heart was in the right place when it came to assuming the role of a real-life Cathleen ni Houlihan, combating evictions or defending prisoners' rights, or to playing that part in the play which Yeats wrote with her in mind. For this reason the Daughters did achieve success in their training of girls for the stage by manifesting the mystique of Erin. Her intellectual powers were another matter; she was incapable of objective judgement.

Eventually – in 1914 – the Daughters were persuaded by Countess Markievicz to submerge their organization in Cumann na mBan, the women's Irish Volunteers. Long before this, however, Maud Gonne's attempts to propagate a mishmash of anti-British Irishness had been superseded by the more broadly cultural approach of Alice Stopford Green and her friends. Maud Gonne's campaign had been presented from behind a screen of cultural activity, admittedly helped by women capable of achieving the positive aims of what masqueraded as a cultural society. Born in 1849, Alice Stopford was the daughter of the Church of Ireland Archdeacon of Meath, and her upbringing had been puritan in a peculiarly Irish Protestant sense. She sought consolation for the bleakness of her environment in intellectual pursuits and, after her father died in 1874 and her family moved to London, she married the historian, John Richard Green. A victim of tuberculosis, he was to die six years later, and as his death approached, the couple worked closely together on his history of England, which it was left to the widow to complete. Then, over the next few years, Mrs Green became a historian in her own right and her London house became a meeting place for many of the more radical spirits of the day.

Although from about 1883, the year of her husband's death, Mrs Green's aims were much the same as those of Maud Gonne and Constance Markievicz, her methods could hardly have been more different. She saw rebellion mainly in terms of the genesis of ideas and, apart from helping with the production of an anti-enlistment leaflet,[37] her main printed contribution to the nationalist cause was her history, *The Making of Ireland and its Undoing*. But she believed in seeing that the ground was well prepared, so that the seeds of Irish culture, which should be sown over a wide area, would be sure to germinate. As a historian, she knew that 1798 had seen another Celtic development, besides all that flowed from Wolfe Tone's rebellion: the Welsh *eisteddfod* had been revived. A hundred years later she lent her support to a group of unionists, separatists and those who simply loved all things Irish and had decided to revive the Irish equivalent of *eisteddfodau* by organizing a series of *feiseanna*. Just as the *eisteddfod* was supposed to be derived from ancient Druid ceremonies, the *feis* had its roots in the distant past, the earliest having occurred at Tara in the sixth century AD. Today the Irish word is often loosely translated as 'festival', but to students of Gaelic, or Gaelic ways, the word 'assembly' would have been a more suitable translation: 'It was a tradition among the greater chiefs, or those who sought a commanding leadership, to gather together the learned men of the whole country in national festivals of all Ireland.'[38] In the rather limited form, the *feis* had never died out (the Gaelic League made much use of them for recitation competitions); but it was felt that much would be gained culturally by reviving it as a great, multi-faceted occasion that was peculiarly Gaelic.

In 1897, Dublin Gaelic enthusiasts founded the *Feis-ceoil* for the encourage-ment of Irish music, and in Ulster the new century brought with it enthusiastic awareness of a cultural heritage that had more sides to it than had previously been appreciated. The bringing together of arts and crafts, spinning and weaving, old agricultural talents, and much music, dancing and poetry appealed to all classes of the community, even if such diversification meant that standards of excellence were not as likely to be achieved as they might be in, say, a purely literary gathering. As with most developments associated with Ireland's cultural reawakening, women were the principal instigators and practitioners. The region known as the Glens of Antrim was especially well-endowed with those who organized and those who participated, and, in 1904, the inaugural Cushendall *feis* was held. Ada McNeill, one of the McNeills of Cushendun, provided the site and was secretary of the organizing committee. Although a first cousin of the convinced unionist who became the first Baron Cushendun, she leaned towards Sinn Féin. Then there was Margaret Dobbs, of Castle Dobbs, who throve on bringing together interesting minds and who played a key role in generating sufficient enthusiasm for the *feis* to ensure its success. Alice Milligan, the poet, Gaelic scholar and playwright, was there, partly in her capacity as Ulster organizing secretary of the Gaelic League. Alice Stopford Green's presence served other purposes than those which brought her there: she cemented her relationship with Roger Casement, who was staying at Cushendun House, and helped to confirm his resolve about the path that his future should take.

Whatever their political complexion, those who participated in the Cushendall *feis* believed in the idea of revival or renaissance. Nearly all the organizers were Protestant; the great unionist Sir Horace Plunkett came over from London to open the event; some two thousand people attended, many of them semi-literate Catholics whose Irish awareness had been sustained by the power of oral tradition. It would be difficult to bridge the wide gulf between this collective approach and the methods favoured by Maud Gonne. Though many present subscribed to the opinion that England's materialism was an evil to be resisted, the message of the *feis* was entirely positive.

Not everything to do with the revival must be attributed to organizations and the exceptional people who founded them. As the Famine receded into the background – though it would never be forgotten – and land reform had begun to relieve widespread pessimism, the atmosphere generally became conducive to creative activity, to use an expression which has since been debased. The commercial development of the late nineteenth century brought with it a healthy spirit of enquiry and restlessness that encouraged individuals, notably women, to become painters. Constance Markievicz had studied art in Paris, as did a host of other women, including Evie Hone, Edith Somerville, and another woman of unionist persuasion, Sarah Purser. Evie Hone and Sarah Purser became the most prominent painters of the time of the revival, while Sarah Purser, now best remembered for her portraits of the famous of her day, provided the opportunity in her stained glass and *opus sectile* co-operative An Tur Gloine (the Tower of Glass) for other women, such as Wilhelmina Geddes, Kitty O'Brien and Ethel Rhind, to develop their talents. Much of the output of the 'Tower' went to beautify churches, Catholic and Protestant, in Ireland and England. To the extent that her glassworks did enable a 'school' to establish itself, Sarah Purser was yet another whose activities fell into the pattern that is typical of the revival; naturally, though, her artists were inclined to go off and develop their special talent in their own way.

Those whose education included time at the Tower did not confine themselves to stained glass and mosaic. But, as a corporate body of artists, in their stained glass work they achieved a true renaissance by reviving the outlook and skills of the medieval artists. Contemporary commercial practice involved sub-division of, say, a chapel window among several workers. Sarah Purser could justly boast that each window which came from the Tower was the work of one artist; all the glass was chosen 'and painted by the same mind and hand that made the design . . . [it] should be a work of free art as much as any other painting or picture'.[39] The work differed from other disciplines because collaboration and support was needed for provision of kilns, cutting, glazing, and the many other, often expensive, essentials of running what resembled a small factory. The creator of this environment was not herself a worker in glass (she made only one small window[40]); her principal virtue lay in recognizing the individual integrity of the artists for whom she provided tutors, raw materials and the facilities integral to an art form which needed a studio that was also a factory. Luckily her own talents were fulfilled in her portraiture.

The most famous practical revivalist of the medieval tradition was Evie Hone, whose largest work was the window of Eton College chapel. Her output was prolific, but she was an artist in her own right before she came to the Tower, and partly because of this her relationship with Sarah Purser was sometimes strained. Of the others who achieved fame not all stayed within the physical constraints of a glassworks. Beatrice Elvery, who became Lady Glenavy, proved to have no great love of working in glass and instead, as is well known, made her name as a painter in oils. Wilhelmina Geddes's artistic outpourings included a wide variety of objects, in addition to stained glass: posters, stamps, book illustrations, book jackets and bookplates. She greatly influenced and sometimes collaborated with Ethel Rhind, with whom she shared Belfast connections. But Ethel Rhind followed the other Tower tradition to become Ireland's foremost artist in *opus sectile*. Another product of the Tower, Kittie O'Shea, had a stained glass style which was more suited to the simple requirements of the small rural church than to the great cathedrals which commissioned windows from some of her associates.

Although artists have traditionally been associated with revolution, the visual arts were the least rebellious part of the cultural revival; here art did transcend the narrowness of politics and eternal values took precedence over transient matters. Naturally it tended to be those of unionist background who could afford to undergo training in Paris or London, and who simply wished to make things of beauty to adorn their native kingdom. Even those artists who were rebels, or sympathized with rebels, tended to have similar origins. For example, Grace Gifford, who married Joseph Plunkett on the eve of his execution, was the grand-niece of the painter Sir Frederick Burton. She had been a pupil of Orpen at Dublin's Metropolitan School of Art and developed her talents as a political cartoonist and caricaturist, her style sometimes resembling that of Aubrey Beardsley.

Sir William Orpen numbered among his students many of Ireland's best women painters, including the sisters Eva and Letitia Hamilton, great-grandchildren of another famous woman artist, Caroline Hamilton. Caroline, who had a talent for satire (especially effective when directed at the short-comings of Dublin society after the Act of Union) was the cousin and benificiary of Llangollen's Sarah Ponsonby. Eva and Letitia studied at a time when well-bred women in the schools of art were not only outnumbering the men but carrying off the prizes. For a while there was tension between the sexes because of the supposed professionalism of the men, who had narrow career prospects in mind, and the apparent amateurism of the women. The outstanding quality of Eva's and Letitia's work will have done little to assuage such jealousy. As time went by, they both moved on from the early effects of Orpen's strong influence to develop styles of their own: Eva eventually moving from portraits to landscapes, Letitia often looking at landscapes and everyday objects through the eyes of an Expressionist. Art brought to them both an independence of mind and spirit, as it did to numerous women whose origins lay in the Ascendancy.

Sarah Purser, who attended the Metropolitan School of Art before studying on the Continent, described herself as a Protestant unionist but she lacked the limitations that some would associate with such a label. She acknowledged that nationalism played its part in the cultural revival and painted the portraits of prominent men and women, regardless of their political allegiance. She also became famous for her Dublin 'salon'. Every second Tuesday in the month she would entertain on a grand scale, her parties providing an interesting contrast to those which Alice Stopford Green was hosting in London. However, though the two hostesses entertained differently – Sarah Purser had the advantage of a sizeable mansion – the party-goers were not so different: the important criterion was to be interesting. At a Purser reception, not only did Catholic and Protestant, nationalist and unionist, meet: literary and artistic women met men on an equal basis. 'Second Tuesdays' survived the Troubles of the period before and after the Treaty. Sarah Purser, like most southern Protestants and unlike most northern Catholics, reluctantly accepted the legitimacy of the new political dispensation, and her house became like Londonderry House at the time of the first Labour government; Cosgrave was her Ramsay MacDonald. It is largely because of her influence that Dublin now has the Hugh Lane Municipal Gallery of Modern Art and, though she did not live to rejoice in the happy compromise which brought the Lane Pictures to Ireland and keeps them there in perpetuity,[41] her agitation, like Lady Gregory's, was not wasted.

Whether as individuals or as groups, many of those who were involved in the revival behaved as though independent, yet inter-dependent, movements were being co-ordinated by some mystic force. Nowhere was this more apparent than in drama, an initial uninspiring stimulus for which was Lady Gregory's and Yeats's realization that if Ireland either would or could not read literature, it might nevertheless listen to it. Drama was the one sphere in which Inghinidhe na hEireann can be said to have achieved genuine success. Maud Gonne persuaded two actors, Frank and Willie Fay, to coach her girls, and this arrangement was doubly fruitful. It produced actresses of the stature of Sara Allgood and Maire nic Shiubhlaigh (née Mary Walker) and, more importantly for Irish theatre, it did as much for the Fays as it did for the Daughters of Erin. Yeats came to rehearsals and was so impressed by the brothers' methods that his belief in the need for Ireland to become self-reliant in drama was translated into realization that the time had come: the necessary talents were only waiting for co-ordination. It was the Fays who staged the first production of *Cathleen ni Houlihan*, and it was 'Mr W. G. Fay's Irish National Dramatic Society' which was to merge with Lady Gregory's and Yeats's Irish Literary Theatre to become the Abbey Theatre Company (the Irish National Theatre Society). From this time forward Irish dramatic traditions, partly thanks to George Bernard Shaw, gave to English theatre more than they received from it. Annie Horniman saw that the Abbey was financially secure; Charlotte Payne-Townshend had done much the same for the 42-year-old Shaw.

Maud Gonne's enthusiasm for acting, and her knack of arousing similar enthusiasm in others, gave Irish drama an injection of energy at exactly the right moment. The framework for the many dramatic successes which followed had been created by Lady Gregory and her friends, who had had a peculiar legal obstacle to overcome: the monopoly of theatrical productions which had been granted to Dublin's two theatres, the Royal and the Gaiety. Only charitable performances could be given elsewhere. Using these theatres was expensive and, in any case, English companies on tour booked them for the most profitable seasons. For native drama to have the chance to flower the law had had to be changed, and luckily Lady Gregory had been able to call on the services of an old friend of her husband, the historian and staunch unionist, William Lecky. Lecky was Member of Parliament for Trinity College and with his help the monopoly was broken. Lady Gregory's place in the Ascendancy, and her early commitment to the Union, valuable as they were to this dimension of the revival, were less important than her contribution to the actual substance of the drama, especially through her influence on other playwrights. It was she to whom Yeats confessed that he had abandoned his plan for an Irish theatre, and it was she who made him change his mind. They came down different political roads (Yeats had become a Home Ruler at an early age) to arrive at a shared concept of Irish identity which allowed them, in drama and in real life, to hold fast to aesthetic standards when many behaved as though the end justified the means. Coole Park, Maud Gonne noticed with some dismay, had the effect of making those who stayed there distance themselves from revolutionary politics. Irish drama benefited greatly from the higher preoccupations of those who were drawn there.

A tribute to the cultural revival as a whole and to the part which drama played in it was to come from an unexpected source. When Augustine Birrell, Chief Secretary for Ireland at the time of the Easter Rising, was called to give evidence to the royal commission appointed to enquire into the rebellion, he spoke of the genuineness of the revival and singled out 'remarkable books and plays, and a school of acting, all characterized by originality and independence of thought and expression, quite divorced from any political party'. He went on to say that the Abbey Theatre 'made merciless fun of mad political enterprise, and lashed with savage satire some historical aspects of the Irish revolutionary'. He was amazed by the 'relentless audacity of the actors and actresses' and felt that, given a little more time 'the new critical temper' would have prevailed; it would not have destroyed 'national sentiment (for that is immortal)', it would have killed 'by ridicule insensate revolt. But this was not to be.'[42] The compliment would have infuriated Maud Gonne; she was furious with Lady Gregory and Yeats merely for accepting police protection when an Abbey production was controversial. Her concept of the patriot rejected any thoughts of the Abbey (which owed its survival mainly to the practical support and creative activity - in authorship and acting - of women), being a force for peaceful devolution. Unlike those who, directly or indirectly, put the pen in place of the sword, she could not appreciate the need for the rebirth of a nation to involve aesthetic appraisal and rational dialogue.

Why were women dominant or predominant in so many areas of the revival? The whole fabric of drama alone was held together by women who were playwrights, actresses, organizers, financers, inspirers and publicists; and in other cultural fields they performed similar functions, to which they added their skills as scholars, and even fulfilled the roles traditionally ascribed to them by those who believe that a woman is to be found behind every successful man. The women who were emerging from Ireland's history at the time of the cultural revival were not the same as contemporary women in England who were also beginning to leave the beaten track. Apparently trivial inventions were having odd repercussions in John Bull's larger island, where the bicycle seemed to give women illusions of freedom of movement that had not occurred to them before. This did, however, owe something to Ireland; riding a bicycle emphasized the need for women to wear 'bifurcated' garments, and a leading campaigner for emancipation in this field was Lady Harberton, a founder and president of the Rational Dress League. She was the wife of an Irish viscount, whose family still has strong links with Belfast.

The difference in Ireland was that, consciously and unconsciously, women were looking for opportunities not so much to gain their freedom as to regain it. It becomes fairly clear, taking a broad view of the cultural revival, that in rediscovering and developing Irish culture women were at the same time rediscovering and liberating themselves. For Irish women, paradise – or its humble mortal equivalent – had been lost more recently than had happened in England. Written records and oral tradition reminded them that they had enjoyed privileges under Brehon law which had survived in parts of Ireland until as late as the seventeenth century. In Ireland the past is never very far away, so the excitements of a new scientific age were bound to make any restrictions on female liberty more incongruous than elsewhere. Gaelic and Catholic ways - and the Protestants had absorbed far more of the latter than they knew - had convinced the people that the identity of their nation was characterized by a sovereign female figure; it was a motherland, and there was nothing servile about motherhood. It was therefore easier for a woman than for a man to identify with the nation – Cathleen ni Houlihan – in her wish to achieve responsibility for her own affairs.

When did the revival end? As with 'Ascendancy', the word may presuppose a decline. Such concepts have no precise boundaries, but it has been generally accepted that the beginning of the Free State saw the end of the literary revival. However, although 1922 was to see the strangulation of feminism as a coherent movement, women writers and writers who owed their inspiration to women continued their work without significant interruption until the Second World War. It is said that in Dublin in 1939 'the dregs of the old Literary Revival were still stirrable',[43] and, stretching time still further, that 'the world of Nora Barnacle had to wait for the fiction of Edna O'Brien'[44] – a sentiment which might have worried Joyce, had he thought that it meant more than the world of girls 'in lonely, desperate and often humiliating situations'[45] that Edna O'Brien chose to portray. Then there is a school of thought which implicitly connects the flood of words which emanates from renewed troubles in Northern Ireland (the best of it rising high above sectarianism) with the same tradition. Where there is tragedy there will always be exceptional writing, and it would be absurd to extend the duration of the literary revival artificially. If we accept that its heyday was the early twentieth century, it is sensible to say that it continued throughout the writing-time of the authors who created it or were its creation. Towards the end of the 1940s this fire had almost burned itself out; only a few embers still glowed, Somerville and Shaw among them.

4

WOMEN'S RIGHTS AND SEPARATISM: TOWARDS A FREE STATE

Historians have found it difficult to disentangle the cultural and political strands of the revival. This difficulty has been caused partly by the widely differing backgrounds – religious, social and political – of participants in Gaelic and Anglo-Irish cultural activity, but it derives also from ambiguities in the organizations founded to encourage the development of various aspects of a nation's cultural identity. These ambiguities proved to be especially confusing when it came to posterity's assessment of the role of Inghinidhe na hEireann. The Daughters' position in Irish history has been pushed to the edge of the stage or even left out altogether. Because the organization was swallowed up by Cumann na mBan, the part, or parts, that it played can easily be forgotten. It really existed on three levels: at its base was a rather sad association of well-meaning women, unexpectedly 'tweedie' in appearance, endeavouring to instil the rudiments of Irish awareness into an unprepossessing collection of pupils; then, by contrast, there were the controversial figures who, from time to time, attracted the limelight; finally, there was the organization's mouthpiece, its journal, *Bean na hEireann* (Woman of Ireland). As the years went by and the most prominent figures either became absorbed by their own domestic problems or devoted their lives to serving a multiplicity of nationalist committees and associations, membership dwindled and the time came when the organization really only existed on the pages of its journal.

The columns of the plethora of often short-lived political broadsheets and journals are not where one would look for a cool statement of facts; they are, however, one of the best sources of information about the opinions and prejudices that reveal the motivation of the group or groups for which they speak. An editorial of *Bean na hEireann*, the first women's paper produced in Ireland, proclaimed that Inghinidhe na hEireann stood for the 'Freedom of Our Nation and the complete removal of all disabilities of our sex',[1] and it was this dual stance, more than anything else, which distinguished the Daughters of Erin from the other rebel traditions. Their belief in violence ('a movement that stops short of shedding blood, and therefore forbids you to make the last sacrifice – that of your life – cannot be taken very seriously, and must end in contempt and ridicule'[2]) meant that they had no patience with the constitutional nationalism of the Irish Party. They collaborated with Sinn Féin in its early days: indeed one of their members, Maire Butler, actually suggested its name (Ourselves Alone). But it was found wanting on several crucial counts. Arthur Griffith, showing that he had more in common with Ascendancy families than he knew, believed, as Helena Moloney, founder of *Bean na hEireann* reminded her readers, in a dual monarchy, after what he understood to be the Hungarian model: 'King, Lords and Commons of Ireland'. It was, though, in the area of women's suffrage that members of Inghinidhe na hEireann found that they had to distance themselves from others who in many respects were their natural allies.

In theory the only dilemma which might face a member of the Irish Parliamentary Party who became a suffragist was to do with the lengths to which she, or he, might go to further the cause; means varied from passive resistance to arson. With Inghinidhe na hEireann it was not so simple. Members felt strongly that women should have the vote, but it was contrary to their most basic beliefs to seek the right to elect to a British parliament. What, then, were they to do? How could they pursue the twin goals of feminism and separatism? Despite the militancy that was to be immortalized in republican mythology by Countess Markievicz posing with her revolver, they adopted a fairly subtle compromise. They infiltrated, as far as men like Griffith (no feminist) would allow, the various nationalist organizations, and sought to ensure that, when a truly separate state – not Home Rule – was achieved, it would bring with it equality of the sexes.

One result of this refusal to join forces with other believers in women's suffrage was a loss of membership. Another, seemingly unforeseen by the doctrinaire hard core, was that by putting the separatist goal before that of the extension of the franchise, women cut themselves off from the possibility of voting for Irish independence. Instead of joining forces with those who shared both of their principal aims (and with unionists who only shared the one), they inadvertently restricted many members to the secondary roles that were so despised. The more powerful personalities among them were able to brazen their way into male preserves; others had little alternative but to join in on terms dictated by the men. But there was another consideration which distanced unionist and separatist suffragists from each other: if women were to have the vote on the same basis as it had been granted to men, in accordance with existing property qualifications, Ascendancy women would be the principal beneficiaries of the reform. Those who had pioneered women's suffrage in England had not sought to widen the franchise by basing electoral eligibility on the local government register, but those Irish suffragists of nationalist conviction who did not try to suppress their feminist activities until the separatist goal had been achieved were quick to seek this additional reform.

The specifically female supportive role that, for the majority, was the outcome of the policy of infiltration, was to earn the organization an unexpected and unwelcome bouquet from a member of the executives of both Sinn Féin and the Irish Republican Brotherhood, P. S. O'Hegarty. Looking back on the period of violence which followed the First World War, he wrote:

> its worst effect was on the women . . . they . . . steadily eliminated from themselves every womanly feeling . . . , . . . Inghinidhe na hEireann . . . never forgot that it could not and should not do men's work. It did such useful, commonplace, and unrhetorical work as looking after children . . . But Cumann na mBhan knew better than that . . . Women's business in the world is with the things of life; but these women busied themselves with nothing but the things of death.[3]

In his view the gunwomen became 'unlovely, destructive-minded, arid begetters of violence'. They were 'unwomanly'.

During the decade before the First World War, however, it was not only the male perception of appropriate 'womanly' behaviour which put obstacles in the way of the feminists; it was divisions within their own ranks. To a certain extent these echoed those of Great Britain, but the issues became confused when the aims and means of the two parts of the United Kingdom appeared to overlap. When the cause began to gather momentum, serious differences about physical force soon arose; more divisive were the political developments which seemed to make the granting of Home Rule inevitable. Although the Irish demand for women's suffrage came of age, as it were, in 1908, when the Irishwomen's Franchise League was founded by Hanna and Francis Sheehy Skeffington, realization of the need for votes for women really dated from the founding, by two Quakers, Anna and Thomas Haslam, of the Irishwomen's Suffrage and Local Government Association in 1876. There were several reasons why this first attempt to mobilize public opinion in support of women's rights made limited headway; it only attracted middle-class members and the climate of opinion at that time was not receptive to radical changes in status that did not have the blessing of the Church. More significantly, in the opinion of the women who had gained self-confidence from the experience or the example of the Ladies' Land League, although the Association continued to exist until its aims were achieved, it did not have much influence on the attainment of franchise reform because it was non-militant.

As invariably happens, despite its statistical absurdity, the arrival of a new century encouraged some minds to abandon old attitudes and to adopt, or at least listen to, new ideas. Some minds, though, fulfilled the active, rather than the passive role in this process. A convenient symbol of *fin de siècle* change is to be found in the union of Francis Skeffington and Hanna Sheehy. The first lay Registrar of University College, Dublin, prefixed his wife's surname to his own on their marriage, and shortly afterwards resigned his post after a dispute about the rights of women to academic status. As well as being a feminist, Sheehy Skeffington was a pacifist, an opponent of the Church's influence in 'this priest-and nun-ridden country',[4] and a supporter of the third Home Rule Bill. In December 1903 he was busy trying to drum up support for votes for women. A letter written on Christmas Eve told of how 'we hope to get up a fairly vigorous campaign in favour of the suffrage in the New Year. There will be a meeting in the Dublin Mansion House in the first week in January, at which I expect to speak, – look out for it.'[5] The male half of this marriage was a match for his wife when it came to sincerity and self-sacrifice; but the record, some of which is to be found in the pages of *Bean na hEireann*, shows that despite the pacifist beliefs which Hanna shared with her husband, she believed in a militancy of approach that was new to the movement. Her first term of imprisonment was the consequence of breaking the windows of Dublin Castle as a protest against the exclusion of women's suffrage from the 1912 Home Rule Bill.

After the founding of the Irishwomen's Franchise League Hanna Sheehy Skeffington launched a convincing attack on the nationalist refusal to regard women's suffrage as integral to the separatist cause. She argued that, although women were prominent in the Gaelic League, that was because children needed mothers who were able to teach them and rear them in Irish ways; similarly, when it came to the industrial revival, women were merely required to be the consumers of Irish goods; and the place of women as perceived by the political parties was likely to continue to reflect the prejudices of a conservative, mainly rural, society. In her view, women had to organize their own independent movement, in order to achieve the 'keystone of citizenship': the vote.[6] Although she was to become ever more committed to the separatist cause (though prevented by her pacifism from joining the Nationalist Party), she was nevertheless expressing arguments which were equally valid for unionists.

Unionist women were faced with a similar dilemma when it came to deciding which should come first: the fight to preserve the United Kingdom or the enfranchisement of women to enable them to struggle more effectively to defeat the Home Rulers. They had one advantage: there was no problem about the legitimacy of the parliamentary system in which they wished to participate. But, in terms of publicity, they were at a distinct disadvantage; the last thing they wanted to do was to undermine the existing constitution by unruly behaviour. Their allies in Great Britain might chain themselves to the railings or, when things reached the point of crisis, sacrifice a life bringing down a horse in the Derby; most unionists sought to distance themselves from militant activity, and preferred to think of suffragism as a non-party cause. Nevertheless it was not easy for the general public to distinguish between one sort of rebel and another.

The proper function of politically aware unionist women in Ireland was summarized at an inaugural meeting in County Tyrone, when, on 13 April 1907, it was unanimously agreed 'to organize the unionist women of North Tyrone into an Association, to help the men's efforts by every means possible and suitable for women';[7] and the minutes went on to record that the Duchess of Abercorn consented to be president. When suffragism reared its head, some women found that while they shared the aims of the unionist men, they might differ over the question of what was, or was not, 'suitable for women'. Suffrage societies were beginning to spring up in various parts of Ireland and these created problems for those whose backgrounds had no tradition of dissident behaviour. In 1911 Louie Bennett, a Protestant who was also responsible for the formation of the Irishwomen's Reform League, joined forces with Helen Chenevix to establish the Irishwomen's Suffrage Federation. Initially there were four constituent groups, including the Reform League. By 1913 membership of this non-militant co-ordinating body had risen to some twenty affiliated societies (fourteen of them in the North).

Louie Bennett, who did not become committed to separatism until the 1916 rebels were martyred, was, like Helen Chenevix, anxious to get much more for women than the vote; both women campaigned for improved conditions for working women, and subsequently, having been full-time organizers for the Irish Women Workers' Union, became presidents of the Irish Trades Union Congress. The declared non-militancy of their federation meant that the Irishwomen's Franchise League went down a different road, drawing attention to the split which was developing between those who were prepared to attack suffragism's arch-enemy, Carson, in public, and what could still be regarded as the mainstream of suffragism. Although, in popular parlance, there was soon to be a simple distinction between 'suffragists', the believers in women's suffrage, and 'suffragettes', who used violent methods to force extension of the franchise, inevitably the 'suffragettes' have been remembered to the exclusion of those who, like Lady Londonderry (Edith, who differed from her mother-in-law, Theresa, in this respect), used oratory and peaceful diplomacy.

During the honeymoon enjoyed by respective supporters of the Pankhurst and Sheehy Skeffington arms of the overall movement, most Irish suffragists regarded the Irish Party as the main obstacle to women's enfranchisement, largely because its leader Redmond was implacably against it; the English, however, although initially brought into the Irish fray to help combat nationalist resistance to giving women the vote, were more disposed to take on the Conservative Party, and therefore were soon at loggerheads with its Irish embodiment, the Unionists. But, as Ulster was a hotbed both of suffragism and unionism – the Whitehead branch of the Irishwomen's Suffrage Federation is said to have concluded its meetings with the singing of the national anthem – the days of wholehearted co-operation between Irish-based and English-based suffrage organizations were numbered. Nevertheless, while the Liberal Home Rulers and the Conservative and Unionist Party were seen to be indistinguishable in their opposition to women's rights, there was a strong basis for collaboration. Solidarity was cemented when, in 1912, the Irish Party decided by 71 votes to 5 not to include female suffrage in its Home Rule requirements. At a mass protest meeting which attracted delegations from nineteen organizations, nationalists and unionists closed ranks to apply pressure on the all-male legislature. Their unity of purpose was illustrated by the opinion expressed by a member of the Armagh Suffrage Society:

> I write from the purely Unionist point of view. But it seems to me imperative that all women, of whatever party, should now stand for a great principle – the principle that no democratic Government can be considered complete which ignores not only a class but a whole sex. It is because I know we are one in standing for this that I would gladly have joined you on your platform tonight.[8]

From the platform Hanna Sheehy Skeffington threatened that if women continued to be excluded from the democratic process 'other ways' would be found to enfranchise women.

The move towards a militant approach can be observed in the life of a minor participant in the movement to achieve votes for women. Margaret Robinson, who was born in 1876, was the daughter of members of Banbridge, County Down's Non-Subscribing Presbyterian Church. She joined the Belfast branch of the Women's Social and Political Union (WSPU) and, in November 1911, responded to a request to convey a women's suffrage appeal to Parliament, taking her instructions from Emmeline Pankhurst *en route*. Among those who influenced her approach to the issue were Dorothy Evans, Honorary Secretary of the Ulster branch of the WSPU, and her colleague, Maud Muir; they believed in attacking property, and she witnessed the cleavage which occurred between them and the northern pacifists as a result of the practical policies which they recommended and practised. Margaret Robinson was persuaded that 'The Englishman's God is property', and was imprisoned for breaking the windows of Swan and Edgar, the London department store. As the years went by and the goal seemed no nearer, she justified the increasing incidence of arson by insisting that activists always made sure that properties were empty before they set fire to them.

Dorothy Evans told the suffragists of Belfast that they were declaring war on Carson, and attacks on property continued until the outbreak of the First World War: Abbeylands, Major-General Sir Hugh McCalmont's County Antrim seat, where Ulster Volunteers drilled, was gutted by fire; there was an attempt to burn down the Castle at Lisburn, and within the next three months four large houses in the Belfast area were similarly attacked. Other inanimate victims were the Bellevue Tea House and a pavilion belonging to Cavehill Bowling and Lawn Tennis Club, and many pillar boxes were destroyed with acid. Dorothy Evans and Maud Muir were indicted, having been found to be in possession of explosives; they broke bail and, after having been rearrested, were imprisoned. They then made use of the Irish convict's strongest weapon, the hunger strike, and were released.

Six months before the burning of Abbeylands, the Northern Committee of the Irishwomen's Suffrage Federation had made two pronouncements that were prompted by the behaviour of extremists: 'The Women's Social and Political Union is an English association, and has no connection with any Irish organization' and 'The Irishwomen's Suffrage Federation is both a non-militant and a non-party organization.'[9] But this last claim did not convince feminists with nationalist sympathies, such as Hanna Sheehy Skeffington. She appreciated that the Liberal government's introduction of a Home Rule Bill had placed the unionist feminist in an awkward position; seen from their standpoint, alliances with nationalists were all very well under certain circumstances, but they should not be permitted to undermine the funda-mental structure of the society to which one owed one's loyalty. Nevertheless, the closing of ranks in Ulster, which had culminated in 'Ulster Day', 28 September 1912, and the signing of the Solemn League and Covenant, had not wholly quenched suffragist zeal. Twelve days before this remarkable event Dawson Bates (the man destined to be Northern Ireland's first Minister for Home Affairs), in his capacity as Secretary of the Ulster Day Committee, was doing his best to answer a testy enquiry from the Women's Unionist Council: 'Are we right in assuming that the wording of the Covenant that the women of Ulster are to sign is prepared by the men, and that we have nothing to do with the matter?' His reply was entirely conciliatory: 'The Women's Unionist Council are, of course, responsible for settling what declaration they wish to issue, and the men have nothing to say to it beyond offering their help'.[10] When the great day came, it was of interest to unionist (and feminist) women of the South as well as of the North, partly because southerners were feeling some disquiet about the sectarianism of Ulster politics. Violet Martin travelled to Coleraine to gain a first-hand impression of the event.

Eighteen months later another dramatic occasion, the Curragh Mutiny, served to focus attention on what was at stake, and after the Ulster Volunteers had imported arms at Larne, and the Irish Volunteers had made their response at Howth and Kilcoole, priorities became clearer. Neither the Nationalist nor the Unionist Parties wanted to allow anything to divert their followers from supporting or opposing Home Rule. In May 1913 a bill proposing to give the vote to women was introduced in the House of Commons. After a two-day debate in which no Ulster MP spoke, only nine of the thirty-one members representing constituencies in the nine counties of Ulster voted. Only the member for Belfast North voted for the motion. Although Craig was in favour of it, he abstained; and although Carson was against it, he abstained. Altogether from the heartland of unionism five Nationalists and four Unionists joined forces and went into the lobbies against the bill.

The unionist leadership was quick to realize that disenchantment on the part of their more politically aware women supporters might cause trouble, but the efforts at conciliation which they made alarmed a few Ascendancy women whose influence might well have carried more weight than the votes which the party stood to gain. On 11 September 1913 Dawson Bates asked the

Secretary of the Ulster Women's Unionist Council, J. M. Hamill, to seek women nominees from its membership to serve on the various committees which would have to assist an emergency administration if the Home Rule Bill were to be passed. At the same time he drew attention to the fact that the articles of the Provisional Government included a provision for granting women the vote on the same conditions as already applied for local government. Five days later the Dowager Marchioness of Dufferin and Ava wrote to the Marchioness of Londonderry, telling her what her advice to the executive of the Women's Unionist Council had been:

> Our association stands for *one* political question only, that on Home Rule we are united, on every other question we are probably divided, and therefore ... it is all-important that we should refrain from any expression of opinion on other policies than that for which we are associated.[11]

She need not have worried on this account, for it soon became common knowledge that, as might have been guessed at once, Dawson Bates had acted without Carson's approval. When Carson's response to general awareness of the contents of draft proposals for the constitution of the Provisional Government became an issue, two deputations went to London to try to pin him down to a definite statement for or against this declaration of support for female enfranchisement. One, led by Dorothy Evans, camped outside his house for several days in the hope of being granted an interview. They were disappointed.

For very different reasons from those expressed by the Dowager Marchioness of Dufferin and Ava, Hanna Sheehy Skeffington was also displeased by Dawson Bates's leaked information. When the Northern Committee of the Irishwomen's Suffrage Federation publicly thanked the unionists for their commitment, she accused them of having done a secret deal with those who, like Sir Edward Carson, had had in mind political goals that were unrelated to the feminist cause. It had come to her knowledge that members of the committee had been aware of the unionists' draft proposals as early as January 1912. But the committee and those for whom they spoke found that they were not without allies elsewhere in the movement. The militant branch of the Women's Social and Political Union launched an attack on the Liberal government and its nationalist allies, and looked as though, rather than lose the unionist concession, it would throw in its lot with those resisting the imposition of Home Rule. However, once war had broken out, unionist suffragists suspended their feminist activities and spared themselves awkward decisions about the tactics of domestic politics. They were not alone in this. In the Munster Women's Franchise League, of which in 1910 Edith Somerville had become president and Violet Martin a vice-president, nationalists and unionists worked happily together for women's rights, and gave unequivocal support to the United Kingdom's war effort. One small price of their loyalty was the resignation of the 'Sea-green Incorruptible', Mary MacSwiney, who was to do so much to divide the Free State after the signing of the Treaty.

Less predictably, though equally effectively, the outbreak of war took the sting out of the suffragist organizations which were not tied to the unionist cause. The Irishwomen's Reform League was not merely against England's war but against all wars, and it retained its anti-nationalist position. The pacifism of the Irishwomen's Franchise League created a wide gulf between its dwindling membership and Redmond's nationalist opponents, whose urge for a blood sacrifice was becoming irreversible. As far as the associations solely devoted to women's suffrage were concerned, the war years brought disaster. True, there were milestones on the road to equality, but they were to be achieved by individuals and by organizations whose members did not chant Hanna Sheehy Skeffington's slogan: 'Suffrage first – before all else'. For the vast majority of Irish women and men, England's difficulty was to be Ireland's difficulty too. For the minority, had it found open expression the war-cry would have been 'Independence first – before all else'.

While the last thirty years of Ireland's move towards independence saw a substantial upsurge in feminist activity, on an individual and to some extent on a group basis, in terms of institutional development the general climate of opinion and attitude was, in purely feminist terms, unaffected. The Ladies' Land League was founded for women to do men's work because the men were temporarily disqualified from doing it; as soon as the men appeared on the scene again the brief period of what Anna Parnell certainly would not have called 'men's work' came to an end. Inghinidhe na hEireann came into existence because women were excluded from all the separatist political organizations of the day. Unlike the Ladies, the Daughters did not achieve the responsibility that can only come with a degree of power over events. Until they became a mere branch of Cumann na mBan their broad-based approach to a woman's place in a separated state – with attainment of the vote a consequence, not a prerequisite, of independence – meant that they might reasonably have claimed to be the mainstream of Irish feminism, despite O'Hegarty's unwelcome and inaccurate compliment. The founding of Cumann na mBan, when it came on 5 April 1914, saw the role of the rebel woman clearly defined as the gunman's helpmeet.

Meanwhile, unionist women had stolen a march on separatists in several fields. When a quarter of a million Ulster Protestants had signed the Solemn League and Covenant, no less than 234,046 Ulster women had signed its feminine equivalent. And signing was not all that they did. They became fundraisers, and they underwent training to be despatch riders and nurses. Ulster had not only imported arms and ammunition for the Ulster Volunteers: it was prepared to use them. Apparently embattled once again, and outnumbered on the island, the Unionist majority was understandably more militant than separatists who thought that they had everything to gain and little to lose. The unionist women, on the defensive as were the men, entered whole-heartedly into the mobilization of forces poised to protect their religion and the constitutional position which, in the main, they accepted; they also relished their new-found status in the province, despite the apparently subordinate roles which they performed. Many must have seen the remark in the *Belfast News-Letter* that they had 'an almost greater appeal to one's imagination than the men'.[12]

Because a significant number of the most influential separatist women sought to remove from their own political tradition what would today be termed 'sexism', whereas the most influential unionist women were less likely to be militant on feminist issues, a sizeable proportion of the separatists were doubly rebellious, and this was not conducive to a united response to the creation, on 25 November 1913, of the Irish Volunteers. Among the women, the most politically conscious rebels believed that their role was integral to nationalist Ireland's answer to the loyalist Ulster Volunteers. But, on the surface at least, that was not to be. Their wish to show that they were 'worthy successors of Brigid, Maeve and Grainne Maol'[13] was almost entirely ignored by the founders of the Irish Volunteers. Those women who attended the inaugural meeting of Cumann na mBan had to observe proceedings from a special gallery (rather like the 'cage' from which Anna Parnell and her friends had had to view the proceedings of the House of Commons), and only once did their feminist ears hear an encouraging phrase – as Patrick Pearse spoke of the need to defend 'the rights common to Irish men and Irish women'. It was clear at once that the granting of equal rights for women was not in any realistic sense on the agenda of the new organization.

The real force for separatism, the secretive Irish Republican Brotherhood, though it had no serious aspirations to combine with a sisterhood, was not pleased to witness the alienation of the more militant women. Its subtle manœuvrings behind the scenes had only one end in mind: the founding of the Republic. It used every means at its disposal, even legal means as in the case of the Irish Volunteers, to achieve this end; it wished to bring people from all walks of life, regardless of gender or social background into a force which, unlike the Ulster Volunteers, was – paradoxically – established in order to support a decision of the imperial parliament. The Brotherhood may have been faceless at the time; it was not voiceless. Its paper, *Irish Freedom*, hastened to declare, in an article by 'Southwoman' (surely an ill-advised acknowledgement of the North–South political divide) that there was 'nothing unwomanly in active patriotism'.[14] But the IRB proved powerless to alter contemporary attitudes to women which, for the most part, it shared. Contrary to the impression gained, and passed on, by Sinn Féiners like P. S. O'Hegarty, most Cumann na mBan members found themselves willingly or dutifully fulfilling a purely supportive role until the time came to decide whether or not to accept the Treaty.

If women were not to enjoy membership of the Irish Volunteers, some might be content to serve in a women's organization that was accountable to it. It was with varying degrees of enthusiasm that Cumann na mBan was founded and its narrow terms of reference spelled out by the first occupant of its chair, one of the more conservative members of the Gaelic League, Agnes O'Farrelly. Apart from the overall aim of seeking independence for Ireland by organizing separatist women, the constitution adopted by the meeting committed members to establishing a 'Defence of Ireland Fund', a decision which reflected the activities of their unionist counterparts. But it was the insistence that Cumann na mBan 'assist' the men, by helping to arm and otherwise equip them for the struggle, which alienated those feminists who chose to hear the inaugural address. In it, Agnes O'Farrelly did more than emphasize the supportive nature of a woman's contribution to what was spoken of as the defence of Ireland; she stressed that women were excluded from policy-making. Men would debate and decide what was to be done, women would help to give them the means to do it. Admittedly, there was talk about arms and ammunition, but the purpose of each cartridge was to 'be a watchdog to fight for the sanctity of the hearth'.[15] She had not grasped that to the more militant women the idea of being shackled to the hearth was every bit as distasteful as being a citizen of the United Kingdom.

Women who wished to be associated in some way with the Irish Volunteers had to accept their subordinate role in Cumann na mBan and make the best of fund-raising, some practical training in first aid, and perhaps a little rifle practice to prepare for the unlikely 'last extremity' of women having to bear arms. If this fell short of their expectations, they had only one realistic alternative: to join Connolly's Irish Citizen Army, where inequality of the sexes was ruled out in principle, but there might be other ideological obstacles. From the feminist point of view Cumann na mBan was a pathetic creation; and yet it evolved in such a way that it is rightly regarded as one of Ireland's most extreme rebel organizations. Because of traditional male attitudes the first members of Cumann na mBan had no alternative but to submit all their narrowly circumscribed activities to the scrutiny of the Volunteers; the four Dublin branches were attached to four Dublin battalions, but were not, of course, part of them. They simply obeyed; which meant for the most part that they got on with the job of collecting money.

Although some women were happy to join on the men's terms because they found no conflict with their own perception of a woman's role in society, many others joined while aware of, but not particularly worried by, their acceptance of a subordinate position; they wanted to contribute to the achievement of the principal goal without further delay. It was, of course, the hard-line suffragist element which was most disappointed with the organization's terms of reference. These amounted to an extra set-back after feminists had been experiencing considerable frustration when it came to getting their message across to the general public. Press coverage of their meetings had been subjected to a peculiar form of censorship: for some time the *Freeman's Journal* and *The Irish Times* had suppressed women's suffrage news in the Dublin area, while the Belfast papers had reported English activities and ignored similar demonstrations in their own city. It was the sort of woman who was prepared to break out of invisible, but strong, constraints in order to demonstrate for a cause, who was most bitter about her actions going unreported, and who felt betrayed by others who meekly accepted rules which seemed to have been devised by wives of leading Volunteers. The Irishwomen's Franchise League sympathized with the political aim of Cumann na mBan, but realized at once that by agreeing to perform secondary tasks it had placed itself in a position that was unacceptable to feminists.

The Ulster Volunteers could count on more wholehearted support from women of all classes. The mood of the time can be savoured in the letters received by Lady Londonderry. On 5 June 1914, Lady Leslie was writing from the family seat, Glaslough, in County Monaghan:

> Here, the Volunteers are very keen – & Jack has now 1800 men in the two Battalions – and 1600 of them are *fully* equipped! They look splendid with their new hats & bandoliers – We had a very impressive out of door service for them – & the Bishop of Clogher preached a fine sermon. I am just finishing the second nursing course for two classes – 43 passed the first examination and now we are going to present colours to the two Battalions. Elsie Kerry and Olive to present them.[16]

Olive was the fourth daughter of Sir John ('Jack') and Lady Leslie, Elsie Kerry was her niece, Elizabeth, the Countess of Kerry. Olive's nephew, Shane, was on the other side of the fence: according to family legend, 'Sir John Leslie trained the Volunteers on Mon. Wed & Fri, & Shane Leslie the Catholics Tues, Thurs & Sat – both used the same weapons!'[17] Olive had married Walter Guthrie, of Torosay Castle on the Isle of Mull, whence she wrote in less serious vein to Lady Londonderry, who always managed to be in possession of inside information, and was well able to sort out meaningful information from idle chit-chat. At this time she wrote quite outrageous gossip about the conduct of those who had been most closely involved in the events at the Curragh. But this did not distort the Londonderry grasp of affairs. Now, more than ever, Theresa, wife of the sixth marquess, felt the need to save what she could of the Union. By virtue of character, personality and connections, she worked tirelessly to achieve a constitutional settlement which did not betray the loyalist principles. That Northern Ireland was able to escape the rule of Dublin, when the rest of the island chose to break its links with London, owed much to her example as a public figure, and to the private pressures which she brought to bear on key individuals. If to exercise charm is to intrigue, then, in that sense of the term, she was an intriguer. But then no orator, diplomat, politician, or even statesman, could succeed without whatever it takes to persuade the listener that he should heed what is said. Logic is not enough.

As will be seen, the aristocratic embrace was to prove to be one of the most effective weapons in the Unionist arsenal. For Ascendancy figures who joined the rebels, evidence of good breeding and privileged background could be distinctly disadvantageous, as was seen when Countess Markievicz breezed into a meeting of Inghinidhe na hÉireann and attempted to donate the tiara she had just been wearing, supposedly at a viceregal ball. She received a cool reception from women who immediately assumed that she was in some way involved in a plot concocted in Dublin Castle; the easy way in which she took off her wet shoes and put them to dry by the fire did nothing to allay fears that her visit might have an ulterior motive. Efforts made by the vicereine, Lady Aberdeen, to bridge gaps between nationalist and unionist, met with even greater distrust or hostility. The last thing the separatist elite wanted was conciliation.

While those feminists whose natural allegiance was to the Union provided an undercurrent of militant or pacifist dissent for orthodox unionists to contend with, it was generally true that within most of Ulster, Protestant women of all classes were content to sink their differences and oppose the separatist threat. Rebellion came more easily to those women who had adopted all or part of an ideology which sought radical change. Some, like Rosamund Jacob, expressed the opinion that Cumann na mBan should insist upon representation on the executive of the Volunteers. After all, if the men were incapable of creating a viable force unless the women found the necessary funds, the women were in a strong bargaining position. But the view which prevailed at this stage in Cumann na mBan's history was that, however desirable it might be for the Volunteers' manifesto to state explicitly that the organization was striving for liberty for both men and women, pragmatism demanded that all settle down and work for the goal which united them, and accept that its achievement would bring with it the emancipation of women. Helena Moloney, a woman who had been drawn into active nationalism by Maud Gonne's eloquence and example, summed up the majority's view: 'there can be no free women in an enslaved nation'.[18] She was among the select band of women who joined the socialist Irish Citizen Army, and was to take part in the attack on Dublin Castle in the Easter Rising.

Helena Moloney's hyperbole did not, however, satisfy the Irishwomen's Franchise League. For a while the argument was bogged down in semantics. The Volunteers had declared that their aim was to 'secure and maintain the rights and liberties common to all the people of Ireland'. 'People' is the plural of 'person' and, as the law stood in so many departments of life, 'person' meant 'male person'. What was the official Volunteers' definition of 'people'? At first there was no answer to this question. Eventually, though, as has happened from the beginning of Irish history, it appears that a wife made her husband try to say what she thought needed to be said. Muriel MacDonagh was a member of the Irishwomen's Franchise League, and it was her husband Thomas, the director of training of the Volunteers, who attempted to reassure the suffragists by stating that when he spoke of 'people' (or 'nation') he meant women and men. Moreover, when this statement had been made at the Volunteer convention it had provoked no dissent – only applause.[19] It was another husband of a feminist, though in this case a feminist in his own right, Francis Sheehy Skeffington, who, as editor of *The Irish Citizen*, allowed others to point out the inadequacy of MacDonagh's reply, before publishing his own considered response to it. MacDonagh was a firm friend of his, but he did not allow this to weaken his argument in any way. In an open letter he gave vent to his objections, as a pacifist and a feminist, to the policies of the Volunteers, declaring that 'when you have found and clearly expressed the reason why women cannot be asked to enrol in this movement, you will be close to the reactionary element in the movement itself'.[20]

Seen in the light of the subsequent bloody history of Cumann na mBan, and of the Volunteers, the respected pacifist's wish to achieve equality of the sexes in this realm of human affairs can seem as absurd as his use of that virtually meaningless term 'reactionary'. But seen against the backdrop of the last year of peace, of imminent Home Rule, and of war as it was to the Irish until the Easter Rising, it can give a different impression. The idea of men and women serving together in a movement which, unlike its Ulster equivalent, was formed to uphold United Kingdom law, was not foolish idealism on the part of one who was not party to the schemes of the Irish Republican Brotherhood. (And one might add that the word 'reactionary' had not yet been debased. There did seem to be an irresistible current of human affairs, running in the direction of greater emancipation, against which there was some futile and apparently obstinate reaction.) However, Sheehy Skeffington's attack on the unequal relationship between the Volunteers and Cumann na mBan did not go down well with some who were as selfless in their devotion to female emancipation and the independence of Ireland as he.

Because of the manner of its birth, Cumann na mBan had at first been dominated by women whose husbands were heavily involved with the Volunteers. Women like Agnes MacNeill, wife of Eoin, might have been expected to accept a secondary role for a sister organization. Only a few echoed Rosamund Jacob's view that pressure should be exerted on the Volunteers to grant women rights in advance of achieving Home Rule. Women of more than one strain of opinion – and of temperament – defended the Women's Council as it stood; the most articulate of them was Mary Colum, wife of the poet, Padraic. In her view,[21] expressed some nine months before Francis Sheehy Skeffington's contrary analysis appeared in print, Cumann na mBan was not a servile follower of the Volunteers: it was an independent body, with its own executive and constitution. She closed her eyes to the limiting features of the constitution. Most members, whatever they may have thought of feminist dissent expressed in *The Irish Citizen*, were anxious to stop arguing and settle down to the work which they thought needed to be done. With Mary MacSwiney and Helena Moloney, they got on with the job. Within eight months of the inaugural meeting a convention had been held and a new role for the organization had been defined: it was now, in theory if not in practice, an autonomous body of nationalist Irishwomen, with its branches (sixty-three by October 1914) taking their orders from its own executive committee.

However, though this proclamation of female independence went some way to reassure the rank and file membership, the executive at this stage in the organization's development had few illusions about the realities of their status. They consoled themselves that the Volunteers made requests, not orders, and they invariably complied with them. Money continued to be collected and handed over; discussion about how it should be spent was scrupulously avoided; and all would have been quiet subservience had it not been for John Redmond's reaction to the outbreak of war with Germany, the great event which most of the manhood of Ireland of the day saw as a threat to Great Britain and Ireland. Only a few saw it through the eyes of the Irish Republican Brotherhood: as England's difficulty, and therefore Ireland's opportunity. The leader of the Irish Party demanded that twenty-five of his nominees be co-opted to the Volunteer Committee, in order that he might keep organized nationalism firmly under his control; and, when the Volunteer executive reluctantly gave in to this demand, it carried Cumann na mBan with it, willy-nilly. One of the few males who welcomed Redmond's having influence over Volunteer policy-making was Roger Casement.[22] The retired British Consul-General believed that the Volunteers would have more influence over Redmond than he would have over them. But the suffragists distrusted Redmond even more than did those who were separatists first and women second.

The Irishwomen's Franchise League, influenced principally by the Irish Party's opposition to suffrage bills in the House of Commons, was appalled by the prospect of a women's organization collaborating with Redmond's men. It called on Cumann na mBan to do everything in its power to resist the betrayal of feminist principles which it considered would be the certain outcome of a pooling of Volunteer and Irish Party ideals. But the more conservative elements of Cumann na mBan accepted the all-male decision. They may have hoped that Roger Casement was right; or, like Mary MacSwiney, they were prepared to accept any road, provided that it led eventually to political separation. Events were to show that Mary MacSwiney's concept of an acceptable political solution to Ireland's problems was subject to some vacillation. At this juncture, she was the only member of Cumann na mBan's executive to respond publicly to Redmond's attempted takeover. She commented that the Irish Party would be unable to stand in the way of the necessary reforms, and in somewhat unconvincing deference to Cumann na mBan's constitution, said that the issue should not be debated in the columns of *The Irish Citizen*. The leadership of the so-called 'independent' nationalist body would have remained silent, had it not been for that paper's refusal to ignore the false position in which the women's organization had placed itself; it had no say in the affairs of its dominant partner. There was really no partnership.

Thanks to Redmond, on whom, despite Katherine O'Shea, Parnell's mantle had come to rest more comfortably, within weeks of the outbreak of war in August the vast majority of the Volunteers had revealed their willingness to enlist in the British army. They were now the National Volunteers and, secure in the knowledge that Home Rule was on the statute book – suspended for the duration of hostilities – there was no need for any conflict between their position as citizens of the United Kingdom and as Irish Nationalists. For the next twenty-one months, most Irish Catholics and Protestants were 'loyal'. Most Protestants wanted to maintain the political status quo; most Irish Catholics were either indifferent to the issue or were looking forward to a degree of devolution, of which the most extreme form would be a dual monarchy: it would be no more true to say that Ireland had an English king than that England had an Irish king. History seemed to have brought the natural geographical entity, the British and Irish Isles, to a common-sense political conclusion. That this did not happen can be attributed mainly to England obliging the rebels with the martyrs that were indispensable to their cause, but also to realization on the part of the Irish Republican Brotherhood that the perfect opportunity for a blood-sacrifice was soon to occur. The IRB had been working towards its separatist goal since its foundation in 1858, and it would not be an exaggeration to say that the Irish Volunteers and Cumann na mBan were manipulated as puppets in what was now to unfold.

A member of its Supreme Council later described how the decision to instigate an insurrection was taken in August 1914,[23] and the loss of 'Redmondite' men and women, whose first priority was now the defence of the kingdom, only meant that those who remained were more susceptible to IRB influence. The male and the female responses to Redmond's policy were very different; while 170,000 men became National Volunteers, leaving only 11,000 Irish Volunteers, the vocal women of Cumann na mBan decided, by 88 votes to 23, that 'to encourage Irish Volunteers to enlist in the British Army cannot, under any circumstances, be regarded as consistent with the work we have set ourselves to do'.[24]

It is conceivable that, had suffragism achieved its principal goal, the wives, sisters and daughters of those whose political affiliation had been to the parliamentary Irish Party would have split in similar proportions to the men. As it was, the politically aware separatist women had twice the excuse – or reason – to rebel, while the unionists had little option but to give maximum support to the men who must fight to defend the realm. Between the autumn of 1914 and Easter 1916, Cumann na mBan's attitudes gradually hardened, as did those of Inghinidhe na hEireann, which survived as a separate entity until it was skilfully merged into Cumann na mBan as one of its branches in May 1915. At first the women busied themselves with the traditional fund-raising events: *tableaux vivants* were popular forms of entertainment at that time, and could be used as effective means of propaganda as well as opportunities to make money. Queen Maeve was a reliable subject for a 'living picture', and a whole host of female characters were reincarnated. But, as time went on and the situation on the Continent generated a climate altogether different from that of recent Edwardian days, the members of Cumann na mBan began training in such things as first aid and stretcher bearing, though the patients that they foresaw were not those to be found on the Somme. Soon there were courses in signalling and much importance was attached to drill. Some women took to rifle practice with enthusiasm, though when it came to the Rising few, even in Connolly's Citizen Army, were entrusted with firearms. However, as was often the case in various aspects of separatist activity, there were notable exceptions. Apart from Countess Markievicz's rather affected use of the revolver, when it came to the Howth gun-running, two women, Molly Childers and Mary Spring-Rice, helped crew the *Asgard*. But this was thought to be small compensation for the exclusion of women from the difficult business of getting 900 guns and 26,000 rounds of ammunition safely ashore. Although many women had helped pay for the cargo, and two had been largely responsible for deceiving the coastguards, some were bitter because women had been denied the prestige accorded to those who actually paraded through the streets with their illicit weapons.

Diametrically opposed interpretations of the part played by women in the Rising can be made on the basis of the available facts. There might be nothing very remarkable in that, were it not the case that there is so little disagreement about what the women actually did. During the winter before the deliberate blood-letting began it was reported that the Inghinidhe na hEireann branch of Cumann na mBan had been 'lucky enough'[25] to find three genuine casualties to attend to when on manœuvres with the Volunteers. This may have been tongue-in-cheek reporting; nevertheless the general atmosphere of war, whether it were England's or Ireland's, led to a rise in tension and preparations for the real thing. By January 1916 each Cumann na mBan branch had been divided into squads of six: one for signalling, the others for first aid and home nursing. There were squad commanders and section leaders, the most important responsibility task of the section leader being rapid mobilization of her section. Kathleen Lynn, the only female doctor with overt nationalist sympathies, gave most of the Dublin first aid classes. Countess Plunkett's youngest daughter, Fiona, was a particularly effective organizer of six units, each attached to a Dublin Volunteer battalion.

When the appointed day came, it was immediately to the women that the male leaders turned in an attempt to sort out the muddle created by Eoin

MacNeill's countermanding of the mobilization order. Trading on the contemporary British – and Irish – assumption that a female at large did not pose a threat to security, the Volunteers used women as couriers as efforts were made, in desperation, to ensure that rebel leaders knew that the Rising, although doomed from the outset (as it always had been, as a military operation), was to go ahead. Philomena Plunkett, one of Fiona's sisters, had carried documents from Ireland to Clan na Gael, the American Fenian organization, as part of the scheme to obtain military aid from Germany, and had brought the replies from New York to Dublin.[26] Now, confusion about whether or not the Rising was called off, or whether it was to be confined to Dublin, meant that couriers had to be despatched to Borris, Coalisland, Cork, Dundalk, Enniscorthy, Tralee and Waterford to try to resolve the confusion and mobilize the rural communities. The nationalist men of Ulster were to assemble at Coalisland before joining their comrades-in-arms in the West; there was to be no Rising in Ulster, which was understandable. Not so understandable to the militant women, whose revolutionary zeal had been steadily mounting for years and who were not chosen as couriers, was the difficulty so many of them experienced in finding an opportunity to make themselves useful. After all their preparation, they found that the men whom they had thought of as comrades-in-rebellion, if not comrades-in-arms, strongly objected to their presence. De Valera was never persuaded to accept their help; only after complaints reached Pearse, Connolly and Clarke in the General Post Office was an order hastily issued that led to most major outposts accepting them.

By the very nature of the Easter Rising, those women who wished to take up arms or, failing that, to assist male rebels, were unrepresentative of their sex. Furthermore, the whole operation was the machination of a minority of men and women who were able to make use of some human rights grievances that had lost their validity. This is not to say that the inhabitants of Ireland had neither the wish nor the right to enjoy all the benefits of devolution or self-determination. What was at risk was the welfare of a majority which had not opted for a violent solution to what could so easily have been a step-by-step approach to a fairly simple constitutional adjustment, not merely revealed by hindsight, but visible then to those who had eyes to see. During Easter Week some sixty citizens of the United Kingdom lost their lives while committing acts of treason, in the furtherance of what they saw to be a higher cause, another sixteen were executed later, and all can be admired for putting a principle before their own survival. But the Rising also cost the lives of 132 policemen and soldiers, and 256 civilians (about 2,000 civilians were wounded). For these reasons one must be cautious when evaluating, for present purposes, the courageous or fanatical behaviour of a comparatively small number of women. Like the men, some wished to preserve an ancient culture which they saw as something quite distinct from that prevalent in other parts of the Union; and yet, when the time came for the same principle to be applied to an equally distinctive and ancient culture, that of Ulster, they applied a double standard. That said, in one sense the rebel women were typical of their period: like most cultures until very recent times the majority could only see history as an inter-racial struggle; apart from the supporters of Connolly, who tried to substitute class for race, they could not grasp the idea that political and social reform could be achieved by evolutionary democratic means. Had they possessed broader vision those who were to support the Treaty would surely not have allowed Ulster to be reduced by three counties (especially when they had an unexpected ally in Carson), nor agitated for the acquisition of more bits and pieces of Northern Ireland. By so doing they abused the principle on which they claimed their own right to self-determination.

The General Post Office in Sackville Street had been chosen as the focal point of the Rising because it was a fine building situated in the acknowledged centre of Dublin. Its position made it a practical senior command-post and gave it some additional symbolic value in the 'triumph of failure'[27] which was about to occur. Triumphant the outcome of the Rising may ultimately have been, in the sense that it destroyed the possibility of a unified Ireland enjoying dominion status within the future Commonwealth, to the more extreme feminists it was seen to be a humiliating week for Irish womanhood. Although the male leadership supported their demands for opportunities to participate, only Connolly seemed to act with much conviction. The Commander-in-Chief, Patrick Pearse, in his second manifesto, read to a hostile crowd of Dubliners, announced that 'there is work for everyone: for the men in the fighting line, and for the women in the provision of food and of first aid'. This emphasis had a depressing effect on republican women who had listened to, or read, the proclamation of the Provisional Government of the Republic, addressed to 'Irishmen and Irishwomen', which guaranteed equal rights and equal opportunities to all citizens, and anticipated 'the establishment of a permanent National Government, representative of the whole people of Ireland and elected by the suffrages of all her men and women'. It is surely a testimony to the fervour of the most dedicated rebel Irishwomen that in 1916, when soldiering was an exclusively male activity in practically every country, the proclamation could be interpreted as entitling women to bear arms. Their reaction may be contrasted with that of Pearse's sister, Mary Brigid, earlier the same morning: 'Come home, Pat, and leave all this foolishness.'[28]

The happenings of that Easter Week have become part of a hypnotic mythology, and in Ireland most of those who were active on the rebel side were soon accorded a form of secular canonization; so it requires quite a strong effort of mind to see the point of view, not so much of the British authorities, whose position is well documented, warts and all, but of the large number of Dublin wives whose husbands were fighting in France. A serious disadvantage of having chosen a post office as headquarters was soon appreciated when long queues of women formed in Sackville Street, to collect their British army separation allowances. Their husbands were fighting on behalf of a government which was committed to granting Ireland Home Rule, in a war which acquired a reputation, however suspect, of defending the rights of small nations. They reacted as was only to be expected when informed by the rebels that the establishment of an Irish Republic meant that payment of separation allowances had ceased. After the unconditional surrender, rebel prisoners needed protection as they were marched away: 'If it weren't for the fact that we were so strongly guarded by British troops, we would have been torn asunder by the soldiers' wives in the area.'[29] The wrath of the Dublin women was as disillusioning for the insurgents as had been the looting by men, women and children, of luxury goods from the shops, and even bicycles from rebel barricades. Connolly's beloved working class might have been forgiven for stealing food; golf clubs and toys were another matter.

After it was all over, when Elizabeth O'Farrell had delivered unconditional surrender instructions to all the commandants, and seventy-seven women had been arrested, many women involved and others who had hovered on the brink seemed unable to come to terms with the part that their sex had played in the Rising. Like Maeve before them, some were to become role models, but for the most part the roles that they had fulfilled had not measured up to preconceived notions. Even the first aiders did not come out of it too well: they 'displayed very slight knowledge, and their methods were very crude'.[30] Again the Ascendancy factor had remained. Not content to cook and nurse, Countess Markievicz had been second-in-command of the contingent which occupied Stephen's Green until it had to retreat to the College of Surgeons. She had discharged her pistol frequently; but then she was Citizen Army, and others of that select band, who were not of her class, also had their moment of glory: ten men and nine women, all armed with revolvers were detailed to attack the virtually undefended symbol of British power, Dublin Castle. The women were given arms 'for self-protection'.[31] Nevertheless, when it came to launching an assault on the Castle, both women and men took part in charging at the gates. But their equality as combatants was short-lived. Having been repulsed, they moved on to the City Hall, where they reverted to the traditional role for women in war: they went to the furthest point from conflict and organized canteen and hospital facilities.

The pattern of female behaviour in the General Post Office and in the Four Courts was much the same, and, now that the activities of the ninety or so women who actively participated in the rebellion (about sixty Cumann na mBan, the rest Irish Citizen Army) can be seen against the background of subsequent feminist thought and experience, one can challenge some of the assumptions of those who were most disappointed by the part that women chose, or were allowed to play, in this time of crisis. There were thirty-four women in the Post Office as the time for surrender approached, either in the kitchen near the top of the building, nursing the wounded, or seeing to the despatches. On the testimony of one of the rebel's prisoners, their appearance at the beginning of the week was reported as being quite dashing: 'The girls serving in the dining room at the Post Office were dressed in the finest clothes, and wore knives and pistols in their belts. They also wore white, green and orange sashes.'[32] This was in stark contrast to the sorry impression they made a few days later. When the final hours came, there was heated opposition to the order that they leave, and after some had reluctantly done so, all but three of the remainder were persuaded to escort most of the wounded men to Jervis Street Hospital. Connolly was supported by Elizabeth O'Farrell and Julia Grenan, two nurses who attended to his fractured leg, by his secretary, Winifred Carney, who refused to leave his side, and (though some serious accounts omit this detail) by British Army Lieutenant Mahony, a prisoner who dressed his wound and accompanied him as he left the building. The most extreme example of instinctive, feminine devotion to the needs of the male warrior was observed in the Four Courts when Eilis ni Rian washed the feet of her commanding officer, Edward Daly, with biblical reverence.

Did Eilis ni Rian's actions – she went on to give Daly fresh socks and much boracic powder – detract from her human dignity, or did they enhance it? Similarly, looking at other aspects of supposed master–servant relationships, as illustrated in Easter Week, one may question the judgement of the feminists who have seen subservience of women as an unfortunate feature of the separatist struggle. Many of the militants' actions, viewed without prejudice, may have been of greater dignity than, say, sniping – an activity to which some of the less cerebral women aspired, and at which some of the men excelled. But such examples, it may be argued, miss the main target: they are confined to comparatively low levels of military or political activity. However, it is when one takes a close look at the higher echelons of the command structure that one begins to doubt whether women were, as at first appears, in short supply when it came to making significant policy decisions. As the Treaty debates were to show, and scores of biographies have revealed, Irish men, nationalist and unionist alike (including those prominent today) have been reasonably or unreasonably influenced or manipulated by the women in their lives. A matriarchal society does not necessarily have to manifest itself in overt domination of the executive and judiciary by women. Why should they get their hands dirty? And in a society with a celibate streak running through it for a millenium, the exercise of power by the female is bound to be a matter of puzzlement to some males. The real sources of policy can easily be overlooked, especially when application of influence is instinctively subtle.

Any suggestion that a society is dominated by women acting as puppeteers can easily be misunderstood; it seemingly calls for a list of examples or some degree of statistical support. Moreover, at first sight it gives the impression that its author wishes to remove all those fundamental rights that were hardwon by the feminists who first found their voices in the latter part of Queen Victoria's reign. The trouble with the list of examples is that it is endless; in desperation one may seek to come at the issue from the opposite angle, by seeking exceptions – those men whose actions were not largely controlled by female forces. One ends up with a few isolated cases, and closer examination reveals that even their actions were not always independent of female control. One man whose behaviour in the furtherance of Irish independence was never subject for long to mistress or master was Michael Collins, but it is instructive to see how he reacted when circumstances brought him into contact with persuasive women, such as one of unionism's strongest prot-agonists: the wife of the seventh Marquess of Londonderry, Edith, daughter of Viscount Chaplin.

While Ireland was being partitioned, a testimonial to the invisible forces which guaranteed self-determination to six of Ulster's counties came from Michael Collins's pencil. Ostensibly Collins was writing about a meeting with Lord Londonderry which took place at the Colonial Office; but reading his words, although one learns a little about the relationship between Collins and the two men whom he found it difficult to name, there is more to be learned about how a man of unsophisticated, rural origins responded to the personality of a well-bred, worldly woman of exceptional intelligence. The letter was written on paper headed 5 Cromwell Place, S. W., the inappropriately named address of Sir John and Lady Lavery, Catholic separatists whose friendships and artistic activities bridged the political divide (Sir John Lavery's portrait of his Irish-American wife was subsequently to appear on Free State bank notes):

> Forgive me. I bitterly regret my outburst about L–. You were very kind to try to arrange the meeting and I am well aware that I was very miserably minded to listen to – [*The eighth Marquess of Londonderry's copy which accompanied the original when it was deposited in the Public Record Office of Northern Ireland in 1950 has* 'w–n' *added here. Despite the use of lower case, there is little doubt that Winston Churchill was the individual concerned.*] and his remark about your 'interest' in L. It is all very well to tell me as you do that he has no 'interest' in you – but how can you expect me to believe that – feeling as you know well I feel – so you must forgive my bitterness, and try to imagine what it means to be a man like myself entirely self made – self educated – without back-ground and endeavouring to cope with a man like Lord L – a man who has had *every* advantage that I lack. This is not self disparagement – a mean quality that I think I do not possess but I cannot help recognizing the fact that you and he speak the same language, an alien one to me – and he understands to perfection all the little superficial things that matter in your particular world. Unimportant things may be but oh! not to be under estimated with a woman like you. I *know* that instinctively.
>
> I feel savage and unhappy and so I blame you for a situation for which I alone am to blame, but I contrast myself with him, my uncouthness with his distinction – my rough speech with his unconscious breeding and the worst of it is I *like* and admire him.
>
> On one point alone I believe myself his superior.[33]

As the letter's recipient was to put it, 'My mother-in-law was the leading spirit in making Londonderry House [Mayfair] the centre of a coterie of Cabinet Ministers and English and Irish politicians',[34] and Carson was one leading figure who 'had been introduced into English politics under my father-in-law's and mother-in-law's aegis'.[35] Edith went on where Theresa had left off, having both the zest and the conviction that made her a strong influence for the salvaging of the north-eastern corner of Ireland. She differed from Theresa in several ways: like Lady Harberton, she was a keen promoter of rational dress for women, and her belief in women's rights led her to recommend that the diplomatic corps – though not the priesthood – be a suitable field for female endeavour, provided that career women 'have no home ties'.[36] But on Irish affairs she was in the Theresa mould, using feminine charms as well as aristocratic attractions to influence allies or opponents. She described London-derry House as 'the centre and boiling point of resistance to the Government's policy of Home Rule'.[37]

It was in the Laverys' house, though, that Collins, now president of the Irish Republican Brotherhood and the dominant member of the team negotiating the Anglo-Irish Treaty, was placed under subtle pressures. Sir John and Lady Lavery, notwithstanding their belief in Home Rule, were both members of Lady Londonderry's exclusive 'Order of the Rainbow' (so named because Londonderry House was called 'The Ark', and all the members had to adopt the names of animals or mythical creatures), and during the Treaty negotiations Lady Lavery (Hazel) calculatedly opened her doors to both sides. The heady social environment into which Collins had been precipitated was rather a lot for a country boy, however ruthless, to contend with. And, to make matters more difficult, Lady Lavery was letting everyone see that she was infatuated with her virile new friend, with whom she shared the bond of Irish descent and who had attracted so much notoriety. According to one account, he telephoned her on the night he signed his 'actual death-warrant', as he put it to Lord Birkenhead, the co-signatory who reckoned he might have signed his own 'political death-warrant', and said, 'I've signed your damned Treaty'.[38]

Shane Leslie believed that the survival of the Free State in the difficult post-Treaty period could be attributed to Hazel Lavery's efforts on Collins's behalf (exerted partly by means of her friendship with Churchill), and one can also see her influence on Collins's resolve, more because of the fascination of her social position than the physical consummation of their relationship. To the extent that although Collins attempted to destroy Northern Ireland he was also instrumental in creating it, Lady Lavery and Lady Londonderry, two women of contrasting political and religious commitment, both tilted him towards satisfying their political aims. It was no easy task, considering that their victim had risen to preside over the secret organization least susceptible to a watering down of republican demands. The colours on the map of Ireland today symbolize the compromise that was latent in his relationship with them.

They did not bring it about, but they showed how 'unconscious breeding' or the power of personality as exercised by exceptional women of a certain level in society had an invisible but real effect at a crucial stage in Irish history. Throughout a long day, Collins and the other negotiators were bemused by Lloyd George, the Welsh Wizard; at night Collins was open to other forms of wizardry and bewitchment. The susceptibility of this example of Irish manhood to the power of the female showed that he was really no more immune to a woman's control than were less strong-minded products of the same culture.

Back on Irish soil, women of very different background from those of Kensington and Mayfair were to join de Valera in massive repudiation of the betrayal of which they accused the republican plenipotentiaries. They did not realize it at the time but they were supporting the man who was turning his back on the best opportunity for the two parts of Ireland to be linked by constitutional means. The Government of Ireland Act, 1920, made provision for a Council of Ireland to be convened, consisting of twenty representatives elected by each parliament. It anticipated 'joint action to terminate partition and to set up one Parliament and one Government for the whole of Ireland'.[39] De Valera would not recognize this possibility, even when the idea of the council survived the alterations which were embodied in the Irish Free State (Agreement) Act, 1921. He and like-minded individuals, such as the militant women of the Cumann na mBan majority and the women deputies of the Dáil, rejected the Treaty as a whole. They did not subscribe to a gradual approach, either to Irish independence or to Irish unity. The anti-Treaty vote led to de Valera and his supporters, who included Erskine Childers, acquiring the nickname 'The women and Childers party'.

5

WOMEN AND THE SOCIAL CONSEQUENCES OF IRISH INDEPENDENCE

The United Kingdom Parliament partially pre-empted the actions of national-ist suffragists by passing the Representation of the People Act on 10 January 1918. This gave the vote to women of 30 and over, provided that they satisfied at least one of three criteria: it applied to married women, householders, and university graduates. Not until 1928 was the age of women electors lowered to 21 and other discriminatory criteria on grounds of sex abolished. A month before the 1918 Act, Sylvia Pankhurst chaired two meetings in London at which Maud Gonne spoke about 'Sinn Féin ideals and personalities'. Maud Gonne had spent the war years in France, where news of the Easter Rising and her husband's execution had taken her completely by surprise; now she was living in Chelsea, forbidden to visit Ireland. In the same year the father of her children died and Maud, having illegally returned to Dublin, hoped that, like the battered belligerents about her, she might enjoy a period of truce and recover from emotional and physical strain. But she was soon deported, to spend five months in Holloway prison, before being released because of a recurrence of tuberculosis. By the end of the year she had been allowed to return to Ireland. Although she found that she had lost touch with the mainstream of republicanism, this did not prevent her from playing an active role in the chaotic Black and Tans period which heralded the Treaty, nor in the civil war which followed it.

These are reputed to have been the great years of Cumann na mBan, but Maud Gonne was not a member. She now pursued her own idiosyncratic path, fortified by her new friendship with a kindred spirit of similar background, Charlotte Despard. Mrs Despard, the widow of a British colonel, was the sister of Sir John French, the viceroy, and had been actively involved in the protection of human rights since the 1890s, when she had become a Poor Law Guardian. Among those who influenced her personally and politically were James Connolly, George Bernard Shaw and Emmeline Pankhurst (Charlotte was co-founder of the Women's Freedom League); because of her commitment to the causes which they espoused she was imprisoned four times. Her interest in Irish affairs dated from the Dublin labour disputes of 1913, when she gave her support to James Larkin, head of the Transport

Workers' Union. After the Rising she, like Maud Gonne, worked for improvement of conditions for Irish rebels in English prisons. It was virtually inevitable that the two women who shared so many ideals and so much experience should make common cause. They met in 1920, when Charlotte was 76 and Maud was (probably) 54. Soon they were touring the martial law areas of the South, enjoying the astonishment on the faces of British soldiers who stopped their car from time to time, when Mrs Despard told them that she was the viceroy's sister.

A few extracts from her diary for 1924,[1] when 'My dear Maud' was often staying with her, may serve to illustrate the attitudes and preoccupations of a privileged woman who had adopted the rebel cause. The first entry (in space, though obviously not in time), under 'NOTES', describes 1924, the third year of independence, as 'perhaps the most disastrous year that our country has ever been through'. As with Maud Gonne, racist motivation is not hard to find: 'I am again reading up the history of Ireland and have begun Kettle's book. It opens with a brilliant analysis of the Eng character – insular – individualistic – dominating. Between there and Ireland quite different racial characteristics.'[2] Another twenty years would have to pass before such generalizations would become discredited, and then only among the intelligentsia. Attribution of moral shortcomings to genetics was not to receive a serious setback until Hitler had pushed his thesis to its logical conclusion. The day after this entry appeared more practical and humane matters demanded attention: 'Maud went to Dublin and rescued a stretcher-case from the military.'[3] In July she recorded that the MacBrides – Maud, Iseulte [sic], Sean, and F. Stuart (Iseult's husband Francis) met de Valera 'The President' – 'it is all so wonderful'.[4] Christmas brought two Ascendancy rebels together: 'Con Markowitz [sic] came to tea in her new car, travelling for the first time by herself. We had a long talk and when she wanted to go the car would not start'.[5]

Cumann na mBan had different priorities during the 'Tan War', when impatient rebels provoked counter-terrorism from British special forces clad in Black and Tan uniforms, and during the period of acceptance and enactment of the Treaty. First they rejoiced in the extended franchise, limited though the extension was, and, as Sinn Féin annihilated the Irish Party at the polls, they were largely responsible for Countess Markievicz's electoral success. Then, as Sinn Féin boycotted Westminster and set up its own rival parliament, Dáil Eireann, they found that they had a dual role to perform. On the one hand they carried on fulfilling much the same tasks as they had done at the time of the Rising, resisting the rule of British law; on the other, after forty-three women had been elected to office in the local elections of January, they did what they could to assist in the establishment of a rival judiciary. An executive member of Cumann na mBan, Aine Ceannt, became arbitrator at a labour court in Clare, having no idea whatsoever of court procedures. On one occasion, when acting with another woman justice, Aine Heron, the joint verdict went against a money lender solely because the two women wished to discourage this legal practice. Their judgement was overruled by the Minister of Home Affairs, Austin Stack. In local government, the Hon. Albinia Brodrick, whose brother was the southern unionists' leader, the Earl of Midleton, found it difficult to reconcile her position of seniority on Kerry County Council with her responsibilities as a nurse. As an economy measure the Dáil had decided to close all workhouses bar one in each county. She resigned for a brief period before accepting the decree of the higher authority.

After the Dáil had agreed by 64 votes to 57 to ratify the Treaty (the six women deputies voting against ratification), Cumann na mBan transformed itself into a much more extreme organization. Both in the bitterness of the speeches and in the statistics of their opposition to the agreement reached between the provisional government and Westminster they gave the impression that, if the franchise were immediately extended to women who had reached the age of 21, the result of a general election might lead to rejection of the Treaty. The executive of Cumann na mBan had lost no time in rejecting it by 24 votes to 2; members who attended the convention held on 5 February 1922 rejected it by 419 votes to 63. But, although Griffith's excuses for leaving extension of the franchise until after the election were certainly influenced by fears that these polls might represent the views of younger women in the country at large, the women who alarmed him were hardly typical of the Catholic nation as a whole. As was being demonstrated in the Soviet Union at this time, political elites could be completely out of touch with the so-called masses they pretended to represent. When the Irishwomen's Franchise League and other suffrage societies petitioned him, Griffiths argued that the Dáil lacked the authority and the time to alter the register, and that the British government would regard an election result arrived at by means other than those existing at the time the Treaty was signed as invalid. Nevertheless the Dáil was forced to face up to the issue. Citing the Proclamation of the Republic Kate O'Callaghan (widow of the Mayor of Limerick killed for a supposed breach of curfew regulations) proposed the motion that women over 21 be given the vote. The motion was defeated by 47 votes to 38.

Following Cumann na mBan's convention decision, there were resignations and a pro-Treaty women's organization, Cumann na Saoirse (Society of Freedom), was formed. Membership included many women who were married to 'Free-Staters', and some of the more intellectual of Cumann na mBan's former membership. Alice Stopford Green was among them. To use the terminology of a later age, the new group was to be cast in the role of an Establishment, that is, when it was not being branded as a coven of traitors. But not all of them were respectable: in a prison demonstration, a Cumann na mBan member 'was stripped of shoes, stockings and dress and beaten with her shoes by Cumann na Saoirse women'.[6] The split narrowed fields of vision. With the draining off of women who, for the most part, now favoured a gradualist approach to a thirty-two county republic, Cumann na mBan became increasingly militant. Henceforth they acted as though they shared the belief which prompted the remark attributed to the man they were to support. De Valera was said to have summed up his attitude to the civil war in one sentence: 'The majority have no right to do wrong'.[7] True enough, when defending persecuted minorities; but de Valera reserved to himself the right to decide what was wrong, and then to rectify things by urging men 'to march over the dead bodies of their own brothers'.[8]

According to their constitution, Cumann na mBan were struggling to regain 'for the women of Ireland the rights that belonged to them under the old Gaelic civilization, where sex was no bar to citizenship',[9] and in one fundamental sense, since glossed over, the end of the civil war brought them 'the freedom to obtain freedom' (an expression often used about the birth of the Free State itself). Five years before the United Kingdom Parliament granted voting rights for women between the ages of 30 and 21, Irish women in this age bracket cast their votes in a Free State election. Even seen against a purely economic background, this was a remarkable step towards recovery of citizenship. Some of the anonymous women who voted on 27 August 1923 were the young working girls of whom George Russell ('AE') had written in 1917:

> there are hundreds & thousands even of girls in Dublin who are expected to support themselves on 4/- 5/- 6/- 7/- shillings a week. Girls in Jacobs factory start at 4/6 now. It was 2/6 some years ago before the labour movement grew strong. I believe girls have been there for years and are earning 6/- or 7/- a week for being boss. If that was her wage what was the wage of those she supervised[?]

(A shilling (or 5p) then was equivalent to about £1.08 in 1992).

He went on to speak of 'dens' where 'rags are sorted, old papers packed and the like and the wage is not enough to pay the rent of a room'. His description of the Dublin of his day may conjure up images of Third World wage structures, but conditions were much the same in the East End of London, or in any English, Scottish or Welsh city environment:

> These women live with their families and the wage is not so much a living wage as a contribution to the wage earned by the head of the family. Rooms in tenement houses cost 2/6 3/- or 3/6 a week and the rooms are unsanitary. Whole families live in these rooms. If one gets a job at 4/- or 5/- shillings a week it pays the rent of the room & the earnings of the rest get tea & bread & fish. If the girls are living in the shops for the years of their apprenticeship they get no money at all often. After three years are up out they go and other apprentices come in to do the shop work cheap. They are supposed to learn a trade. Really they are earning a big profit for the sweating employer.

The achievement of voting rights by these girls would not immediately transform their lives, but it would mean that hereafter would-be rulers had to bear their interests in mind in order to get elected. Russell pointed out that few had given much thought to the girls' welfare:

> It is considered disreputable to be mixed up with labour or poor folk in Dublin. The Churches have lost the spirit of Christ & never denounce the employers. They can only find energy to denounce labour & trades unions & the union leaders & strikes for wages. The Churches in Ireland seem to me to be inspired by the Devil & I could not think of any religion better suited to the Devil than some Irish forms of Christianity.[10]

The recipient of this letter was a Quaker. George Russell knew that his outspokenness would cause no offence with the Society of Friends.

Having lost the civil war, de Valera decided to try to achieve power by constitutional means. He resigned as President of Sinn Féin and he and his supporters founded a new political party, Fianna Fail (Warriors of Fal), into which they hoped to bring Cumann na mBan. They were successful in attracting the leading lights of the women's organization; Countess Markievicz, Margaret Pearse (widow of Patrick), Kathleen Clarke (widow of Tom), and a widow who was famous in her own right, Hanna Sheehy Skeffington, were among the women who served on the first Fianna Fail executive. But again the hard core of the women's organization was adamant in its resistance to any form of compromise, however temporary it might be. To them it was inconceivable that a republican could take the oath of allegiance to the British monarch, which entering the Free State parliament would entail. Not for them de Valera's disclaimer that, as he did not touch the Bible, his oath was meaningless.[11] One's contempt for de Valera's petty reasoning, after so much avoidable shedding of blood, should not, however, blind one to the strange features of the hard-liners' own morality. They did not baulk at the prospect of the unavoidable bloody outcome of unconstitutional activity; and yet to them the thought of Countess Markievicz, had she lived long enough, uttering a lie of this nature was a kind of blasphemy.

Despite the terrorizing of some vulnerable southern Protestants (of comparatively humble background) who, at the hands of exceptionally resentful men, suffered horrifying atrocities, including multiple rape, gouging out of eyes, rooting out of tongues, hanging and disembowelling,[12] there were still those – not only of Protestant persuasion – who displayed the Union flag when they wished to commemorate Armistice Day. The residual membership of Cumann na mBan made sure that rioting disrupted any symbolic gestures which indicated sympathy for, or constitutional links with, the imperial power. Meanwhile, in Northern Ireland, a parallel campaign of terror was waged against working class Catholics. In the early years of partition justice was a rare commodity on both sides of the border; the difference in the South, as the number of Protestants rapidly diminished (by emigration and a disinclination to breed) from around 10 per cent to 5 per cent, was that the real split was between members of the same faith. Cumann na mBan moved from demonstrating on the streets, and in the theatre – as when they disapproved of a revealing portrayal of the Dublin working class by Sean O'Casey, formerly secretary of the Citizen Army, in *The Plough and the Stars* – to intimidation of jurors. The women were disgusted that their male comrades, who since 1919 had been known as Oglaigh na hEireann or the Irish Republican Army (IRA), had not only declared a cease-fire, but were rigidly adhering to it; in the autumn of 1927 the executive complained that 'enough time has been wasted on a drift policy and it is up to our organization to end it by embarking on a campaign to end British influences in this country'.[13]

Cumann na mBan was anticipating the policy of the Provisional IRA as practised from the 1960s until the present day: destabilization. Then the principal target was Cosgrave's pro-Treaty party, Cumann na nGaedheal (Party of the Gaels), which governed the South; today, though both northern and southern governmental structures are in the sights of their heirs, destruction of the six county entity is made out to be the sole objective, and is so in the eyes of young recruits. Then, as now, courts had to be made fearful of convicting those engaged in the struggle. Cumann na mBan printed tens of thousands of copies of leaflets known as 'Ghosts' which gave names and addresses of jurors who, as 'degenerate and slavish citizens', had helped to imprison 'men and women who are carrying out the only practical programme to attain freedom': 'These men are traitors to their country. (Death would be their fate in any free country in the world)'.[14] In 1927 the police raided the houses of many Cumann na mBan members, confiscating copies of 'Ghosts' and similar inflammatory material. Naturally juries were especially worried about convictions made in these cases. Nevertheless some women were put into prison, where they adopted the next tactic: the hunger strike. Inspired by the behaviour of 'the Furies', the IRA shot the foreman of a jury.

Before 16 February 1932 was set as the date for a general election the anti-Treaty women had tried various other means to undermine the state, and they had shown that, while they shared the anti-Treaty men's overall abhorrence of the Irish Free State, they had commitments which the IRA lacked. They soon perceived a need to instil the 'right' ideas in the next generation and were eventually distributing history leaflets to schools on a monthly basis. In 1930, the women initiated a boycott of British goods; in this they were supported by the IRA and violence was used if shopkeepers did not comply. But as times seemed to become less exciting and the public at large, weary of troubles, settled down into a condition of apathy, the ordinary membership of Cumann na mBan reverted to its old fund-raising role. A gap then appeared between the leaders and their followers. The elite were influenced by developments, particularly as they affected a woman's position in society, beyond the shores of Ireland. Most Irish women were ignorant of, or indifferent to, such things.

Charlotte Despard and Hanna Sheehy Skeffington had made an extensive tour of the Soviet Union in 1930 and, unlike visitors of the calibre of Bertrand Russell, had been taken in by aspects of communist propaganda. Charlotte, in addition to her many other offices, held that of secretary of the Friends of Soviet Russia, and with several other senior officials of Cumann na mBan, was heavily involved in 'Women's International Week'. Beginning on International Women's Day, 1931, they gave many lectures, drawing people's attention to 'the enslaved conditions of women in all parts of the capitalist world'. Moreover, they urged women 'to take an active part in the struggle for freedom'.[15] The enslaved condition of the average Soviet woman had completely escaped their notice. At this time the IRA also began to adopt a socialist stance. It did so as its violent methods became more widely known in the world at large and the Roman Catholic Hierarchy, if not all the parish priests, became distinctly hostile to a revolutionary organization which, because of the Treaty, was no longer engaged in a war which some might term 'just'. The IRA leaders were only too aware that Maynooth exerted its influence through some of its former allies, the cabinet ministers of the day. But, although the men of the newly-elected Fianna Fail government were less detestable to the IRA than were their pro-Treaty predecessors, only their first action, the release of prisoners, commended them to their recent comrades-in-arms. Adopting constitutional methods of government, as laid down in the 1922 Constitution, drawn up with the British, was tantamount to accepting the Treaty – or so it seemed to the residual IRA and, more so, to Cumann na mBan.

Shifts to the left, as occurred at the 1933 Cumann na mBan Convention and the Republican Congress of 1934, had the dual effect of reducing female and male membership and bringing the two organizations closer together. One generalization can safely be made about the Irish at this time: they had strong distaste for anything tainted with communism. In the meantime de Valera strengthened his position substantially in the 1933 election, and his renewed policy of imprisoning his old allies embittered those who refused to acknowledge the legitimacy of his rule. In 1935 his government introduced legislation which, according to its opponents, was intended to remove women from the workplace. At that time just under 23 per cent of the Free State's industrial workers were women, and many men were unemployed. Section 16 of the Conditions of Employment Bill gave the Minister for Industry and Commerce powers to prohibit women from working in industry, and to forbid employers to employ more women than men, should he allow their employment in specific industries. After the bill had become law, there was a clearly perceptible hardening of attitudes on both sides. The feminists lost ground because aspects of the bill were popular: it reduced the working week to forty-eight hours, gave a one week holiday entitlement, and curbed the exploitation of young workers. Those who had other views about 'a woman's place' found de Valera's Ireland a bastion of sound traditional values. In 1936 the disillusionment of the more militant women was to lead them to adopt a harder line. On 18 June the IRA was declared an illegal association.

The Civil War had been fought because de Valera and his followers could not accept that the Treaty opened the door to a step-by-step approach to a republic. But, from the moment that he entered the Dáil, he chipped away at the 1922 Constitution to remove 'any form or symbol' which suggested that Ireland was not a sovereign nation: 'Let us remove these forms one by one, so that this state we control may be a Republic in fact'.[16] He was encouraged and greatly helped in this task when, in 1931, the Statute of Westminster gave effective legislative autonomy to British dominions. Further unexpected help was provided by the abdication crisis, which not only provided a useful smoke-screen but also enabled the Free State's 'external association' link with the British Commonwealth to be reduced to a tenuous thread. By 1937 he had chipped away so much (the oath, right of appeal to the Privy Council, and most of the largely symbolic functions of the governor-general) that the 1922 Constitution needed to be replaced. It had been a commendably fair and reasonable document, giving minorities scarcely any cause for alarm, though there was one phrase which might alarm the wary democrat. Article 8 owed something to Article 16 of the Treaty, which promised that neither of the Irish parliaments would 'make any law so as either directly or indirectly to endow any religion or prohibit or restrict the free exercise thereof'. In the constitution the wording had much the same import, with one small addition: 'Freedom of conscience and the free profession and practice of religion are, subject to public order and morality, guaranteed to every citizen.' Few qualms were felt about 'public order'; it seemed unlikely that there would ever be much need for rowdy and disorderly religious demonstrations. But what was meant by 'subject to public ... morality'? Who was to be the arbiter when it came to moral disputes? Fifteen years later the answers to these questions seemed to be quite clear.

When the new constitution appeared in draft form several of the articles worried not only feminists, but all thinking people who took account of natural justice and wished Ireland to be a secular and democratic state. There was an immediate outcry about Articles 16, 40, 41, and 45, as a result of which three changes were made. In Ireland the Women Graduates' Association led the way; abroad George Bernard Shaw made his disapproval widely known. De Valera was castigated for having omitted the words 'without distinction of sex' from the entitlement to membership of the Dáil, and the right to vote, which formed the substance of Article 16. The words omitted were restored and a clause was added positively guaranteeing women's electoral rights. But only one other concession was made to the demands of a united front of women's organizations. Whereas Article 45 originally began by obliging the state to see that 'the inadequate strength of women and the tender age of children shall not be abused', the final version spoke of protecting 'the strength and health of workers, men and women, and the tender age of children' from abuse. The same article had gone on to say that 'women and children shall not be forced by economic necessity to enter avocations unsuited to their sex, age or strength'. In the approved version 'men and women' became 'citizens'.

Having modified two of the four articles about which the feminists complained most loudly – 16 and 45 – de Valera stood firm on other articles and clauses which either worried the more vigilant women of his day or were to become increasingly contentious as time passed. The second sentence of Article 40 remained intact, although some women thought that the use of the words 'physical' and 'social' opened the door to discrimination:

> All citizens shall, as human persons, be held equal before the law. This shall not be held to mean that the state shall not in its enactments have due regard to differences of capacity, physical and moral, and of social function.

It was exceptions such as these that were being used in Germany for frightful National Socialist purposes during the very months in which de Valera was devising his constitution. But de Valera had, in most respects, an exceedingly limited field of vision, and gaping loopholes of this nature did not trouble him. They might prove to be useful. His motives were benevolent, but he wanted the Catholic Hierarchy and himself to decide what was good for Ireland, and especially what was right and proper for the women of Ireland. And that is why he cleverly ensured that that one act of legislation which had proved to be unconstitutional in 1925, should not only become constitutional in 1937, but that it would not even be necessary to present a bill to the Dáil to achieve the required end. Article 41, which prohibited divorce, had no loophole; it applied to all citizens, Catholics and non-Catholics alike.

Luckily for de Valera, feminists concentrated their fire on clauses 2.1 and 2.2 of Article 41:

> In particular, the State recognizes that by her life within the home, woman gives to the State a support without which the common good cannot be achieved.
>
> The State shall, therefore, endeavour to ensure that mothers shall not be obliged by economic necessity to engage in labour to the neglect of their duties in the home.

The role of women reflected by Article 41 was an extension of the philosophy expressed in the general declaration which introduced it:

> The State recognizes the Family as the natural primary and fundamental unit group of Society, and as a moral institution possessing inalienable rights, antecedent and superior to all positive law.

The State, therefore, guarantees to protect the Family in its constitution and authority, as the necessary basis of social order and as indispensable to the welfare of the Nation and the State.

Few would disagree with the overall intention of these pronouncements. Such statements are echoed by the spokesmen of the main United Kingdom political parties during the 1990s; but in 1937 those who were aware of Ireland's old traditions of female equality (to say nothing of periods of female dominance), were suspicious of ambiguous phrases referring to the family. They were especially wary when they thought they could see a papal delineation of their domestic duties. But it has to be said that, in the Catholic Free State, it was a very small minority of psychologically liberated women who reacted vociferously. The majority, had they been greatly interested, would have welcomed such a clear exposition of Catholic values. Why should they worry if the words 'antecedent and superior to all positive law' could be interpreted as meaning in the twenty-six county context that the Roman Catholic concept of the family could not be interfered with by secular lawmakers? The day had not yet dawned when the nuclear family would be seriously challenged by alternative social units.

Article 41, after the clauses about a woman's place 'within the home', went on to deal with marriage: as it was the foundation of the family, the State pledged itself 'to guard it with special care' and 'to protect it against attack'. 'No law shall be enacted providing for the grant of a dissolution of marriage'. Furthermore,

No person whose marriage has been dissolved under the civil law of any other State but is a subsisting valid marriage under the law for the time being in force within the jurisdiction of the Government and Parliament established by this Constitution shall be capable of contracting a valid marriage within that jurisdiction during the lifetime of the other party to the marriage so dissolved.

Protestant dissent on the issue of divorce had come to a head in 1925 when, in defiance of the 1922 Constitution, a serious effort had been made by Cosgrave's government to prohibit introduction of bills legalizing divorce. As things stood after three years of self-government, residual United Kingdom law was permissive; an independent state did not begin with a *tabula rasa*, and the majority of Free State citizens were bound in this respect by the laws of their Church, not by the laws of the state. Those of other faiths, or of no faith, were limited only by the quaint and hypocritical rules and practices which the Free State had inherited from Westminster. The strongest voice raised in defence of the right to divorce was that of Yeats, who took his duties as a senator seriously and now made one of the finest speeches ever heard in the upper chamber. He had the breadth of vision to realize that a greater issue was at stake than loss of opportunity to divorce one's spouse: 'you are to legislate on purely theological grounds and you are to force your theology upon persons who are not of your religion'.[17] He was championing minority rights and he was determined to show that the Protestant minority was as much a part of the new nation as was the overwhelming majority. This was the speech in which he boasted that those for whom he spoke were 'not petty people', and in which he listed great contributors to Irish freedom and culture, including Parnell. He made no mention of the negative role in Irish history played by Katharine O'Shea.

After being approved by the Dáil, a national plebiscite was combined with a general election in order to ensure that a satisfactory number of votes would be cast. Cumann na mBan, as a republican movement, refused to participate in what was in its view a bogus operation carried out by a treacherous regime; old-style nationalism eclipsed feminism and a boycott was preferred to a campaign advocating rejection of the new constitution. In the event, the closing of republican abstentionist ranks, male and female, guaranteed de Valera's victory. Nearly a third of the electorate abstained; 685,105 voted in favour, 526,945 against. It has been argued[18] that, but for the stubborn doctrinaire republicanism of their organization, the feminists of Cumann na mBan could have tipped the scales the other way. As it was, the constitution of the twenty-six counties area, 'pending the reintegration of the national territory', came into effect on 29 December 1937.

There were several reasons why prohibition of divorce did not provoke widespread protest as the new constitution was being debated. Apart from the fact that divorce was already prohibited by the religious beliefs of about 95 per cent of the population, and was proscribed on social grounds by most of the remainder, it was generally seen as an indulgence to male infidelity. The supposition that divorce restrictions protected wives from easy abandonment by their selfish husbands was not limited to modern Ireland (where it ran counter to Brehon tradition). It prevailed on the other side of the Irish Sea, and gained support as legislative changes moved towards divorce on demand. When the present divorce position was defined by the British Parliament, the law was immediately dubbed by women the 'Casanova's Charter'; and that is how it would still be viewed were it not for the tide of liberation which brought varying degrees of acceptance to other hitherto unrecognized relationships. James and Nora Joyce, who were in many respects bourgeois in practice and Bohemian only in theory, were not forced to live outside Ireland because of any laws. Part of the reason that they and a wide assortment of free spirits emigrated was that they found the unwritten moral code stifling. De Valera perceived the essence of it and wrote it down; and by so doing he helped to make sure that it would endure.

Given de Valera's talent for splitting hairs, it is surprising that he did not foresee the anomalies which the 1937 Constitution would create. Provision for civil marriage still existed, and, as with Roman Catholic marriages, such unions would occasionally be nullified. The effects of inconsistencies between pronouncements of civil nullity and church nullity, sometimes leading to unprosecuted bigamous liaisons, brought even more harm to the children than to the wives. As civil nullity delegitimized children, under Irish law it removed all rights to support from the father, and all rights to paternal inheritance. Church annulments deprived women of eligibility for widow's pensions and, with cold logic, returned them to their former status as tax-payers. To make matters worse, the Irish authorities soon earned a reputation for inconsistency in their attitude to divorces obtained abroad. In practice the law of domicile created a double standard which favoured men.

The legal framework which developed after the new constitution was in place had other consequences for women which did not compare favourably with Gaelic traditions. Despite breakdown of a marriage (by 1983 marital breakdown in the Republic affected some 35,000 couples[19]), if the family residence was in the husband's name it remained solely his property. If, however, the parties achieved a judicial separation the judgement might sanction separation *a mensa et thoro*, the circuit court judge mischievously taking this to mean 'from bed and board' in a narrow sense: the spouses were still under an obligation to stay under the same roof. Battered wives fled the country *en masse*, and abandoned legitimate children were either placed in institutions or fostered. A series of Acts placed an absolute bar on their adoption; in this respect alone it might pay to be illegitimate.

Although it is customary to blame de Valera, as the author of the constitution, for this sorry legacy, blanket condemnation of him for avoidable consequences may be unfair. Moreover, it is yet reasonable to ask whether or not he did right to make marriage legally indissoluble. Conventional western wisdom, which is not always riddled with fallacies, still has it that the old-fashioned concept of the family – father, mother and children – is the only one ordained by God, or nature (or both). Alternative life-styles, especially where the decision to be a 'one-parent family' has been taken as a matter of deliberate choice, generally produce offspring who are in some way incomplete or unfulfilled. De Valera devised the articles that have alarmed democrats in general and feminists in particular with little help from politicians; he studied the works of Roman Catholic theologians, read papal encyclicals and was continually advised by high officials of the Church, including the Papal Nuncio, Pascal Robinson. But although acceptance of the constitution as a whole was lukewarm, when the substance of Article 41 (3.2) was put specifically to the Irish people half a century later they endorsed it, and the European Court of Human Rights has found that the divorce prohibition does not violate the European Convention. It may be said that such considerations dodge fundamental issues. Yeats's objections are the ones that count. And so they are, when it comes to the all-important principles of personal liberty, minority rights, and secularism in a democracy. However, are these principles necessarily put at risk by the controversial articles?

Looked at in the wider context, what is the real position of an Irish citizen who wishes to obtain a divorce? If the spouses involved are Roman Catholics they already have no choice. If they have abandoned their faith and have no children, they either use the English courts or simply separate. Where the welfare of children is at stake, again the English judicial system can attempt to sort out this insoluble problem, or the Irish judicial separation procedures can be used to rule on custody – and, by means of separate orders, on other matters, such as maintenance and property rights. Protestants, Jews and others who, despite their different origins, share the Roman Catholic belief in the sanctity of marriage, have similar options open to them. Furthermore, although the 1937 Constitution failed to provide for many eventualities which would surely arise simply because of the diversity of human nature, legislation in the last twenty years has done much to remove confusion and introduce a more humane approach to family problems.

One important reform was made in 1989 when judicial separation, with provision for equitable division of property, became similar to the laws of England and Wales. If the couple agree to seek legal separation, they must first live apart for a year; if they find that they are unable to agree, the period is three years – a provision which only really makes sense in cases of desertion (despite the fact that desertion *per se* is one of the grounds for granting a decree after one year). There are, however, other grounds for the granting of a decree: adultery, intolerable behaviour within the family dwelling, and evidence which shows that there has not been what is deemed to be a normal marital relationship during the year preceding the application. There is, though, another route leading to an Irish alternative to divorce. It is more suited to couples who are either fearful of court proceedings or feel able to negotiate a separation without acrimony.

A couple whose marriage has broken down can choose to settle things out of court, and attempt – more effectively – to minimize the harm being done to their children, by resort to the Legal Separation Agreement. Should they feel able to follow this ostensibly amicable route, practically everything relating to divorce, apart from the right to remarry, is sorted out with the help of an experienced and impartial mediator. When the contract is drawn up, much care is taken to see that recrimination, a chronic feature of divorce proceedings in so many countries, plays no part in decision-taking. Both parties are required to discuss the details of an agreement with the mediator, who advises them on the drawing up of a Separation Deed. The first clause of such a deed is a promise to separate from, and not interfere with, the other spouse. Then any number of clauses are listed, taking into account such matters as maintenance, provision for the children's welfare, ownership and occupation of property, as defined in the Family Home Protection Act of 1976, disposal of personal property and arrangements for settling outstanding debts. Both parents remain guardians of their children, though the everyday care of them will almost invariably be left to the mother. Ideally the parents will continue to share responsibility for their offspring, an arrangement which may contribute towards an eventual reconciliation. With this in mind one of the clauses of a Separation Agreement can stipulate that, should the spouses live together again for a stated period, the agreement will become void. But, contrary to what might be expected in a society which believes that marriage is indissoluble, it is not necessary to initiate legal proceedings for this clause to be struck out.

Such are the ways in which the Republic has striven to overcome the difficulties which have been experienced, mainly by women, since de Valera devised its constitution. Nearly half a century was to elapse before the harsher consequences of Article 41 (3.2) were removed. Although the European Court of Human Rights found that Ireland's prohibition of divorce did not violate the European Convention on Human Rights, in 1986 the court declared that its illegitimacy laws offended against the non-discrimination clause of the Convention.[20] A state which put family values above all else had a confused approach to the idea of children being born outside wedlock, and this was reflected in its laws, principally with regard to rights of succession. One cause of the high number of illegitimate births was the prohibition by Church and state of artificial methods of birth control. But, whatever the ethics of those restrictions, it was eventually accepted that there was no excuse for imposing material and social disadvantages on a party to whom no guilt could be attached. The Status of Children Act of 1987 was devised to do away with the very idea of bastardy. It faced up to complex problems which arise from attempts to establish paternity and it provided means whereby satisfactory arrangements for guardianship and maintenance could be made. Above all it made sure that 'children whose parents have not married each other' would inherit in just the same way as the children of married couples.

Another important reform soon followed. In 1988 the Adoption Act was passed. Now in special cases a legitimate child may be placed for adoption – if, for instance, the child has been in foster care for a year or more and the parents have not made contact. Naturally religion looms large in the criteria used when selecting adoptive parents – on both sides of the border. In the Republic a mother will probably be offered the opportunity of meeting and vetting the prospective parents. In Northern Ireland the persons whose consent is needed may specify the religion in which the child will be brought up.

Unwelcome consequences of identification of state with Church could be disposed of without the help of legislation. It is not beyond the powers of the Church to arrive at a sensible approach to marriage annulment, in order that the blind eye policy with regard to bigamy may never reappear. The simplest method of reform is for a Catholic priest to refuse to marry a Catholic in church if that person is still married to another according to the civil law of any nation. To many Anglicans, as well as Roman Catholics, the only marriage which counts is the one that takes place in church. Nevertheless, it must always have been clear to the Hierarchy that western culture had no traditions that could make the Irish double standard on nullification acceptable at a social or individual level. What de Valera wanted, and it was not so unreasonable, was a society in which the breakdown of marriages, and therefore of families, would be contrary to the national ethos. He had a Utopian view of a contented pastoral country built on family values. He was not forcing people into marriages; that was their decision. Once they had taken it, society should not weaken their resolve by making divorce 'socially acceptable, even fashionable'.[21] Not long before he drafted the constitution, he was consulted as a Commonwealth prime minister on what to do about Mrs Simpson. Adroitly he advised Baldwin that, as divorce was a recognized institution in Great Britain, there was no need for the king to abdicate. But, while the Irish government wished to take a detached view of the crisis, it felt that Mrs Simpson should not become queen. She played her part in Irish history by diverting English attention while de Valera saw that the constitution made no reference to the monarchy.

The rural Protestant community, as a dispersed, dispirited and diminishing minority, was not inclined to protest loudly about the marital implications of the constitution. Urban Protestants, who still commanded a large percentage of influential posts, were inclined to sit tight and await developments with some stoicism; after all they still accounted for 20 to 25 per cent of employers and business executives, 53 per cent of bank officials and 38 per cent of lawyers.[22] The only reaction of much significance was the appearance of a number of pamphlets claiming that the Church of Ireland was the true Christian Church founded by Saint Patrick. The otherwise quiet response was not entirely attributable to the loss of political power which they had sustained. Other less tangible factors were at work. Over the years Protestants in general had unknowingly absorbed similar beliefs to the dominant creed about the family and marriage. Despite latent theological differences (and breeding habits), attitudes to women and a woman's role in society – except among the intelligentsia – were much the same regardless of religious persuasion. However, it should be borne in mind that the view from the North gives a different picture. During a recent interview the Reverend Ian Paisley emphasized that in their approach to women's issues Roman Catholic families embraced 'the ethos of the nunnery – seen and not heard', whereas the Protestant ethos was one of liberty for the female.[23]

The impact of the new constitution on the personal conduct of Irish citizens did not really begin to make itself felt until after the Second World War. De Valera's other constitutional manœuvrings did, though, have a great effect on the nation as a whole; he was able to deny British access to Irish ports, contrary to the original terms of the Treaty, and he had achieved the authority to keep the Free State neutral throughout the hostilities. The separateness of the twenty-six counties from its larger and combatant neighbour was stressed by its calling itself by the Irish word for Ireland: Eire (a word which, as few

British citizens realized, could be used for the contrary purpose of laying claim to the whole island). Throughout the war the Free State's ambivalence remained unaffected by the declaration of neutrality. De Valera, of course, gloried in it, sticking closely to all the protocol that was involved, even signing the book of condolence at the German embassy when he heard of Hitler's death. Republican women chose another course; they provided help and comfort to the influx of German agents who were attracted by Ireland's anti-British reputation. Maud Gonne's daughter Iseult, as Mrs Francis Stuart, was in the thick of this (her husband broadcast for the Nazis). Others were vintage rebels of 1916, such as Cathal Brugha's widow, Caitlin. Their chronicler dubbed them 'the Angry Old Ladies'.[24] At the same time the Irish secret service was working hard for a British victory. As, one by one, German spies were caught, they were subjected to a series of interrogations. Full details of their answers were on the appropriate desk in Whitehall by nine o'clock the following morning.[25]

After the war few could doubt the Free State's independence, but its membership of the British Commonwealth still rankled with some. The year 1948 saw two key developments which put Southern Ireland's constitutional status to the test, one at an international level, the other at a personal and social level. Repeal of the External Relations Act had often been contemplated, but the temptation had been resisted because to indulge it would be to sever the one real link with the North. Irish cabinet papers on the decision-taking process are missing because, according to one cabinet minister without an axe to grind,[26] the then Taoiseach (prime minister), John Costello, took the decision on the spur of the moment. While at a banquet in Ottawa, given in his honour, he felt that he detected an intentional discourtesy to his wife. The insult, whatever it was, was then compounded by a piece of Protestant symbolism in the form of a silver cannon, 'Roaring Meg', a replica of a real piece of artillery used in the siege of Londonderry, being placed on the table in front of the couple. There and then Costello decided to declare a republic. Later he insisted that the decision had been taken unanimously by the Cabinet.

The year of the transition from Free State to Republic also saw the appointment of Dr Noël Browne as the coalition government's Minister of Health, an event which would lead rapidly to the social and personal effects on Irish citizens of the constitution becoming apparent. Browne's short ministerial career is mainly remembered for his 'mother and child scheme', though he could claim the credit for a remarkable hospital building programme and for many reforms, especially in the fight against tuberculosis and cancer. It was soon brought home to him that the Catholic Archbishop of Dublin, Dr John McQuaid, who had been one of de Valera's most constant advisers for the drafting of the constitution, had oblique means of controlling hospital staffing and management within his diocese. Dr McQuaid wore several hats, including that of Chairman of the Board of Directors of several Dublin hospitals, and he annually pronounced it to be a mortal sin for Catholics to attend Trinity College, Dublin, Browne's alma mater. The Catholic Archbishop and the Catholic mortal sinner were soon at loggerheads over legislation which Browne wished to see passed. An immediate bone of contention was the unequal status in hospitals of nuns and lay nurses; Dr Browne declined to exempt the nuns from night duties, and opened the opportunity of promotion to the senior nursing posts to all who had suitable qualifications. For this even-handed measure he was branded a Communist. He was, as he acknowledged, 'a minister who had very clear views about the proper relationships between church and state in a democracy'.[27]

One of many clashes with the Roman Catholic Church occurred when Browne asked the Archbishop if nuns might visit the houses of mothers admitted to sanatoria to be treated for tuberculosis, in order that the children might have proper care. Dr McQuaid's reply was that the sight of nuns entering houses of absent wives 'would give scandal'.[28] Contrary to popular belief, the origins of the genuine scandal that was to cause Browne's downfall were not of his making. In 1947 Fianna Fail introduced a Health Bill, which became law before Dr Browne entered the Dáil. There had been objections from the Hierarchy, but these had been to the principle of compulsory medical examination for schoolchildren. Part 3 of the Act set out proposals for a mother and child health scheme, and there had been no specific complaint about them on the grounds later put forward by the Church. Supporters of the Church's position in this affair could, however, maintain that the objections voiced applied equally to state interference in matters of education or health. Browne now sought to implement existing law, without recourse to a means test. The resultant furore revealed the true balance of power in the Republic, and in so doing made all parties to the dispute clarify their position on a woman's place in the Irish scheme of things.

After accepting his appointment, Browne prepared his ground well. The public speeches which he made in the early months of 1948 brought home to the nation at large the urgent need for reform in the overall approach to maternity care. He pointed out that over the previous five years infant mortality in the Free State had been 55 per cent higher than in England and Wales. While the twenty-six counties had, since the beginning of the century, seen a decline in the number of infants dying during the first year of life, the improvement only lessened the death-toll by 25 per cent. This Browne contrasted with progress elsewhere. Over the same period the survival rate in England and Wales had improved by 67 per cent; in New York State by 71 per cent; and an infant's chances of survival were far greater in the six counties than in the twenty-six. Accordingly he set about introducing a Mother and Child Scheme by means of an amending bill to the previous administration's Health Act. It had three main points: free maternity care to all mothers, child care up to the age of 16, and an education scheme to help reduce maternity problems. Unlike the British National Health Service, which operated on the principle of National Insurance, the Irish scheme was to have been paid for entirely out of general taxation. As with the introduction of the British National Health Service, there were two main sources of opposition. In both countries the medical associations resisted change. The British Medical Association was not happy about socialization of medicine and wished to retain the autonomy of practitioners and consultants; its members were conservative in more ways than one. The eventual compromise was largely a happy one. Most of the remaining resistance was mounted in the House of Commons by the Conservative opposition. The Irish Medical Association's resistance was two-pronged. Like the BMA they did not care for socialism, and like the BMA they were largely united with an organized force for opposition. The difference was that the Irish doctors did not need much political help of a secular nature; they could depend upon the Pope's battalions fighting the battle for them.

On 10 October 1950 Browne was summoned to a meeting at the Archbishop's Palace, where a letter from the Hierarchy was read to him by Dr McQuaid. Addressed to the Taoiseach, it claimed that the powers assumed by the state in order to implement the Mother and Child Scheme were 'in direct opposition to the rights of the family and of the individual and ... liable to very great abuse.'[29] It argued that parents were to be denied their right to provide for the health of their children. Although the state might help 'indigent or neglectful parents' (estimated at 30 per cent), that was no reason to deprive responsible parents of their rights in this sphere. If the powers were to be enshrined in law 'they would constitute a readymade instrument for future totalitarian aggression'. The educational provisions of the proposed health service were the subject of further objections. Physical or health education was inseparable from moral education, and on moral questions 'the Catholic Church has definite teaching'; moreover, education for motherhood would include 'instruction in regard to sex relations, chastity and marriage' and the state had no competence in this field. The Church was specific about which aspects of its teaching it considered to be most threatened: 'Gynaecological care may be ... interpreted to include provision for birth limitation and abortion.'

Browne belonged to that small fraternity who did not necessarily regard concessions or compromises as signs of weakness. But nor was he going to allow the bishops to get away with misrepresentation. He immediately pointed out the false assumptions of the letter – for instance, it spoke of the 'elimination of private medical practitioners by a State-paid service' – and, which at that point came easily to a lifelong Catholic, he subsequently promised to 'provide such safeguards in matters of health education as would meet the requirements of the Hierarchy'.[30] He felt that regardless of cost to his political career to provide this scheme was a moral and social imperative. To get it going he was even prepared to mollify the bishops on what he saw as a fundamental constituent of the scheme: its freedom from the means test; he conceded that a pregnant mother might qualify for all the benefits of health care by an initial payment of ten shillings. As cabinet colleagues and fellow politicians began to shun him as an embarrassing liability to the government, he started taking advice from a Catholic theologian. This mysterious figure, whose identity is still a secret, made Browne realize that there was an important distinction between Catholic moral teaching and Catholic social teaching. For the faithful to disobey Catholic moral edicts would be to sin; Catholic social pronouncements were not binding – they left room for individual conscience. The theologian also expressed puzzlement as to how bishops of the same faith tolerated a health scheme in the North, while they objected to similar provisions being introduced into the South.

Forty years on, the disgraceful circumstances which forced Browne's resignation can be reassessed. At the time the Church was cast as the principal villain in the saga, and there is no doubt that certain bishops, whom Browne has named, behaved in ways that cannot be reconciled with Christian charity. However, the real villains were Costello and his political henchmen, notably Maud Gonne's son, Foreign Minister Sean MacBride. It was their duplicity which handed over the reins of government to the clerical establishment. As a body, the Church can hardly be blamed for giving advice as forcefully as possible to ensure the triumph of truth as it sees it; despite cries of 'render to Caesar', the Church of England frequently does the same today. But in the Republic there is only a thin line between consensus rule and majority tyranny; the obligation on the secular power to protect minority interests – including the 'minority rights' of the female majority – is therefore all the greater. Moreover, the assumption that in the case of the Mother and Child Scheme the nation's spiritual leaders articulated the will of their flock is open to question (they did not actually make the claim, nor did they feel the need to do so); parallels with the banning of divorce and abortion, on which the people's voice has been heard, cannot be sustained. The problem of over-lapping majorities, and of one man's majority being another man's minority, are at the root of Ireland's current Troubles.

The failure of Costello's government to face the consequences of con-frontation with the Hierarchy was inexcusable. For futile reasons of ex-pediency, in an act of political cowardice, they betrayed the electorate as they betrayed Browne. In some ways, though, the Church's apprehensions have since been justified by the effects of Great Britain's Welfare State on the British public. When the Church spoke of 'future totalitarian aggression', it doubtless saw Eastern Europe as the model, with England moving in that direction. The degree to which the British proletariat would be sapped of its sense of responsibility by the state providing everything from the cradle to the grave, may or may not have been appreciated. The Church did seem to be only too aware that rights imply responsibilities; that a mother must not expect to leave decisions about her child's health or education to a state official. Furthermore, although the watered-down health scheme that became official in the Republic in 1953 was a pathetic shadow of Browne's far-sighted plan, means-testing has since been shown in parts of the Republic to be both equitable and humane. It can benefit the poor without humiliating them. The principle, however, conflicts with the socialism of Dr Browne, whose integrity is not in doubt. He recently complained that 'one third of our hospital beds are closed. Only the wealthy have ready access to Health Care ... Dick Turpin's 'Your money or your life' could be said to dominate Irish medical practice'.[31]

The behaviour of the celibate clergy in this issue illuminated the Irish Catholic view of women. The Church reserved to itself the right to implement Rome's decisions about contraception, which should be of equal interest to both parents, and about abortion, which some say is exclusively to do with 'a woman's right to choose'. There are at least two directly opposed ways of responding to official Irish Catholicism's portrayal of womanhood outside the nunnery. (One must carefully distinguish between Roman Catholicism and Irish Catholicism in this context: Church–State relationships in Italy, for example, belong to another world.) Feminists have regarded the social consequences of the 1937 Constitution, Browne's aborted bill and much related legislation on issues such as birth control, as demeaning. A certain ideal type of Irish woman, allegedly submissive to domestic traditions, crystallized in the mid-twentieth century, and rapidly fossilized. But, taking a more charitable view, the Clerical Republic, as its enemies termed it, may be regarded as having placed women on a pedestal. The culture in which they are raised may be stifling in some respects. What culture does not appear repressive to young people in the twentieth century? Having reached adulthood, these women, as the 1986 referendum showed, believe in family ties being reinforced by the laws of both Church and state. Some may see the battered wives who flee to refuges in London, instead of seeking Protection Orders under the Family Law (Protection of Spouses and Children) Act, 1981, as the result of a repressive culture coming apart at the seams; others may take them to be symptoms of contamination from alien cultures. In certain aspects of life the Catholic Church may have screwed the lid down too tightly. But, when seen in comparison with social disintegration elsewhere, the Irish family can still be regarded as an example of what can be achieved by holding fast to the best in western religion and culture. It survives, whilst all around standards are falling. Many of its women freely choose to lead from the hearth, and send their husbands out to win the bread. Their dominance has been symbolized, paradoxically, by the election of a woman as head of state.

Dr Browne's initiative was not wasted, whichever view of Ireland one takes. Irish democrats may not have been happy with the Health (Family Planning) Act, 1979, the so-called 'Irish solution to an Irish problem'. But for all its shortcomings it was a step forward, and it owed much to the modified attitude to clerical interference resulting from Browne's resignation. Browne had not advocated contraception, but he had demonstrated the need for secular justice to be seen to be done. This naturally meant that it might even be done from time to time. Under the 1979 Act contraceptive devices might only be obtained from registered pharmacists if a doctor's prescription was produced; and the Act contained a conscience clause enabling doctors or pharmacists to refuse to co-operate should they have moral or religious objections to such methods of family planning. As with the situation which has always prevailed with regard to divorce, citizens of the twenty-six counties have never had any real difficulty in circumventing birth control regulations. England and Northern Ireland have provided leaks in the dam, or safety valves in the boiler, and, except for the impoverished and the illiterate (a dwindling minority), a limitless supply of contraceptives has always been available by post. Although a Criminal Law Amendment Act passed in 1935 prohibited both sale and importation of contraceptives, the actual use of them was not proscribed and nobody who really wanted them had problems, other than those of conscience.

For many years, despite concessions to changing values, the state tried not to stray too far from the Church. Until recently family planning was mainly regulated by two Acts which amended the legislation of 1979. The Amendment Act of 1985 allowed condoms and non-medical contraceptives to be dispensed to those aged eighteen and over, through approved medical outlets. The 1992 Amendment Act lowered the age restriction to those over seventeen. But, in July 1993, the 1979 Act – which had been for the benefit of married couples – was virtually repealed. To stop the spread of Aids, section 2 of the new Amendment Act altered the definition of 'contraceptive' to exclude condoms. The new law also effectively abolished age limits and legalized vending machines. Nevertheless, Roman Catholic mothers will continue to have large families; and, despite the economic pressures caused by this, the children will certainly have more likelihood of developing normally than the isolated offspring of Europe's increasingly fashionable fatherless families.

It is often said that the Roman Catholic prohibition of artificial contraception is a direct cause of high rates of abortion; and the cynic may ask how this can possibly be so, if abortion is proscribed and hospital ethics committees[32] are vigilant. The Church may answer that its rulings are made in the interests of the unborn child and serve to stabilize the family unit. Marriage is indissoluble, according to Church and state, and under the secular law the only circumstance in which abortion might be contemplated by a parent was the one which brought the Republic into conflict with the European Convention on Human Rights. After the Referendum held in 1983, Article 40 (3.3) was inserted into the constitution: the state acknowledges 'the right to life of the unborn and, with due regard to the equal right of the life of the mother, guarantees in its laws to respect, and, as far as practicable, by its laws to defend and vindicate that right'. But, because the nation's laws owe so much to the Church, in any conflict between the life of the mother and that of the unborn child it is generally accepted that the child's survival has hitherto taken precedence over the mother's. Critics of the Irish Catholic approach to abortion have paid too little attention to one of the principles of the Catholic Code of Ethics as circulated in the Archdiocese of Dublin. In practice the last sentence quoted has not proved to be narrowly restrictive:

> Operations and treatments necessary for the cure of serious organic pathological conditions of the mother, which cannot be postponed until the foetus is viable, are permitted even though the death of the foetus results. This principle applies to extrauterine pregnancies.[33]

In other Roman Catholic countries the problem is not a legal one; individual conscience can overtly play its part. The Republic, though, shares certain features with Islam, to the extent that its founding fathers tried to identify secular and religious law, and nowhere is this more apparent than in its stance on abortion. Again, however, the law has been a dead letter; a few hours away are British National Health or private clinics ready to abort for nothing or for £250. Were it not for the proximity of the United Kingdom's resources, one wonders whether or not the few laws of the Republic which are supposed to discriminate against women would have been repealed years ago. Either that or emigration figures would have been even higher.

As the Republic is more and more closely integrated with Europe, its stand on 'women's issues' (which are only artificially segregated from those of men) and the place of women and the family in society, becomes increasingly difficult to sustain. The challenge of the Single European Act has concentrated minds on matters that seemed to move off the stage when independence was achieved. There have been several psychological and intellectual jolts that can be exemplified by the supposed implications of EEC membership on the border. Initially some rejoiced that European unity would wipe it off the map; euphoria was soon dampened down when it was appreciated that the same political changes, if they ever came about, would remove the frontier between Ireland and the United Kingdom. In much the same way double-sided aspects of international relationships have been reflected in the Republic's approach to the major United Nations treaties on human rights. So far the state's ambivalence has been such that it tends to sign them and put off the evil day of ratification indefinitely. When it joined the European Community in 1973 it attached to itself a body of law in the form of the Community's treaties, and accepted both the compulsory jurisdiction of the European Court of Human Rights and the right of individuals to petition the court.

Because the European Convention is not part of the internal law of member states, and may not be directly pleaded before their courts, when a fundamental human right is at issue, there are at present only two alternatives. Either the state in question amends its legislation or the individuals affected may take the bewildering and expensive step of seeking a judgement from the

European Court. Unfortunately the problem may not end there. Assuming that an Irish citizen gets the ruling that she wants, what happens next? For example, in 1986 the Irish High Court ruled that the Dublin Well Woman Centre Limited, and Open Line Counselling Limited, were in breach of the law when providing counselling and information about obtaining lawful abortions in the United Kingdom.[34] It did so in defiance of a decision of the European Commission of Human Rights, [35] taken in 1980, which began by stating, 'The "life" of the foetus is intimately connected with, and cannot be regarded in isolation from, the life of the pregnant woman.' The Commission went on to state that if protection of the foetus were seen as 'an absolute', abortion would be illegal even if the pregnant mother's life were to be put at risk: this would be 'contrary to the object and purpose of the Convention'. Then, twelve years later, as will be seen, the High Court made another abortion ruling which contravened the European Convention on Human Rights. This was overruled by the Supreme Court judges, whose decision seriously threatened the concordat which had hitherto existed between Church and state in the Republic. In the same year (1992) the European Court found in favour of the Well Woman Centre; it ruled that to deny a woman's right to receive factual information was in breach of Article 10 of the European Convention.

The Catholic Church remains vigilant about the dissemination of birth control information in schools. Education, though, is a sphere in which the Republic, whilst following closely the strictures of its spiritual leaders, is less likely to find itself facing insurmountable difficulties with supra-national law. For this it can thank the provisions which had to be made at the time of independence for the Protestant minority. Although educationally well-endowed, in terms of real estate and scholastic traditions, Protestants no longer posed a political threat, and their separation from the mainstream did not seem to be undesirable. Furthermore, Catholic and Protestant alike, having more of the puritan ethic in common than they knew, favoured the separate education of girls and boys, and resisted progressive trends. For good or ill the birth of the Free State coincided with the failure of British efforts to end denominational teaching in schools. In 1921 the Central Association of Catholic Clerical School Managers had made its position clear, reasserting 'the great fundamental principle that the only satisfactory system of education for Catholics is one wherein Catholic children are taught in Catholic schools by Catholic teachers under Catholic control'.[36] Luckily the converse applied, even to the extent that in 1937 a Protestant cleric could boast that the exchequer was paying for school buses to take Protestant children 'past three or four or five schools to the school of their own denomination'.[37]

Papal law on co-education meant that children were segregated on the basis of sex. This has often meant that in Catholic boys' schools the nucleus or virtually the whole of the staff were celibate priests, while the girls were similarly cared for by celibate women – nuns of one of the teaching orders.

There has been some disquiet about this, but there is no real body of evidence to prove that separation of the sexes at the primary or secondary stage of schooling is harmful to their development. In England today mixed schools are supposed by those who teach in them to encourage development of easy and healthy relationships between boys and girls; though a number of parents, and their daughters, feel that a single-sex environment makes for better attention to scholarship and fewer emotional traumas. In the independent school tradition there is often a compromise whereby girls are admitted to the sixth forms of boys' schools, though naturally this is frowned on by committed co-educationalists. In Ireland it has been the celibate dimension rather than segregation itself which has attracted criticism, mainly from outsiders. For the day school pupil, mixing with a host of siblings for all the out-of-school hours, including weekends, the possibility of emotional imbalance resulting from being temporarily deprived of the company of the other sex seems remote. However, from the strict Irish boarding school tradition there has come a steady stream of anecdotal evidence that celibacy has had its drawbacks, especially when those who practise it were responsible for the administration of corporal punishment.

The effect of segregating girls in schools has done nothing to lower the national perception of the status of women in Irish society. It is not as though girls' education was less resourced or had any stigma attached to it. Church and laity alike can be relied upon to enhance a woman's role, in the light of the faithful's conviction that the family is ordained by God and therefore sacrosanct. If educational segregation on grounds of gender has adverse effects on pupils, it is the boys who are the more obvious losers; the girls then suffer as a result of the boys' lack of awareness. The London parents who said that they wanted co-education for their sons, single-sex schools for their daughters,[38] were not necessarily employing a double standard. Young Catholic girls can benefit from the realization that puberty affects the sexes differently. But that notional advantage has to be offset against another characteristic of the system. In one important department of knowledge the Irish girl may be disadvantaged: the Roman Catholic opinion that sex education can be ignored in schools and may be safely left to parents and priests has had harmful effects. In a secular state a good argument can be made for not making special provision for this particular subject. If the biology mistress knows what she is doing, all the physical aspects of sexual relations, including Aids, will be dealt with as an integral part of a comprehensive course. All the moral aspects will be dealt with by whomsoever is responsible for religious studies, assuming that the ten commandments have not been branded as part of a reactionary tract. But in the celibate environment, interest in sex or ignorance of sex can reach unnatural proportions. The astonishingly high proportion of abortion seekers known to English police and social workers must be partly a reflection of Ireland's failure to face up to this problem, in boys' schools as well as girls' schools.

Drawing attention to the Republic's shortcomings can too easily lead to a distorted impression of its position with regard to women's rights and the place of the mother and the family in society. The popular prejudice that Ireland is always fifty years behind the times is usually based on the assumption that the rest of the civilized world is taking steps in the right direction. There is no reason why Ireland should not be right and the European Community, for example, wrong in some of the disputes which have arisen in recent years. Taking a global view, the Church had been right about the threat of totalitarianism, and the state, unlike other newly independent territories, had no illusions about the consequences of adopting Marxist policies. Church and state saw the extremes of Stalinism for what they were, and observed that, nearer home, socialist England was planning to remove rights and responsibilities from its citizens. The rulers of the Republic may not have been too much impressed by the National Health Service. They had genuine cause for alarm as the United Kingdom came within an inch of abolishing parental choice in education. One wonders what their thoughts were as famous public schools revealed contingency plans to evacuate their premises and move to the Republic.

Between the death of Countess Markievicz in 1927 and that of Maud Gonne in 1953 the nation consciously moved towards Rome. Cosgrave even envisaged a senate as a peculiar theological watchdog, to make sure that the lower house did not stray from the papal path. Nothing came of that, but strict adherence to Catholic rules about marriages with members of other denominations tightened the hold of the dominant faith even more strongly. Hanna Sheehy Skeffington, somewhat tainted by her visit, with Charlotte Despard, to the Soviet Union in 1930, remained politically active until 1943, and died in 1946. Then, after the last of the old-style, high profile nationalist feminists had died and an era seemed to have ended, Ireland enjoyed a brief period of economic development and intellectual stalemate. This ended during the 1960s, when several events occurred which on the surface appeared unconnected with one another but on closer inspection can be seen to have roots in common. Republican celebrations of the fiftieth anniversary of the Easter Rising, civil rights demonstrations in the North, international agitation for women's liberation and the changes inaugurated by the Second Vatican Council had a cumulative effect. When, in 1988, a member of the Official IRA was asked how she had been drawn into the movement, her reply was more meaningful than perhaps she was aware: 'You see, I was a child of the sixties'.[39]

The independent state which witnessed the Second Vatican Council made no explicit attempt to blend the Gaelic concept of the dominant woman with the mother figure of Rome. Brehon divorce practices are hardly reconcilable with the 1937 Constitution. But the Church's wish to define a woman's role in terms of wifely duties and motherhood does not have to be interpreted as making women subservient or inferior. To maintain that they should fulfil the natural role prescribed for them by God does not necessarily demote them from their elevated position in Irish mythology. A new kind of Irish woman would not agree. Her attitude might be summed up in the words of Belfast-born artist Rita Duffy, whose triptych in oils *Emerging from the Shamrock* was on display in Kilmainham Jail during Dublin's year as 'European City of Culture': 'The central picture turned into a sort of self-portrait: Irish women, disillusioned with Republican ideals and the macho heroes of nationalism, step into the twenty-first century. The tableaux left and right represent State and Church, with symbols of death, hypocrisy and empty-headedness'.[40]

6

WOMEN AND THE SOCIAL CONSEQUENCES OF IRISH DEVOLUTION

The wife of the seventh Marquess of Londonderry took up the unionist cause with as much conviction as her mother-in-law had displayed. There had been a time when Theresa 'was supposed to rule England and statesmen used to quail before her',[1] and Edith was to gain her reputation as the last of the great political hostesses. However, Edith had no alternative but to play her Irish political part on a smaller stage. It had not been in the power of the Londonderrys and their friends to prevent partition; now Edith would use her skills to preserve and strengthen what remained. Like other unionists, she was fortified by the moral basis of the new political dispensation, as proclaimed by George V at the opening of the Parliament of Northern Ireland. He hoped that the occasion would be 'the prelude of a day in which the Irish people, North and South, under one Parliament or two, as those Parliaments may decide, shall work in common love for Ireland upon the sure foundation of mutual justice and respect'.[2] The words 'as those Parliaments may decide' removed the ambiguities that Lloyd George was alleged to have used to bring about agreement. Redmond and his dwindling band of supporters had believed that partition would be a temporary expedient, Carson and Carson's Army were convinced that 'Ulster' was a permanent political entity.

As King George and Queen Mary sat on temporary thrones in the council chamber of Belfast City Hall, the boundary which was to separate the Free State from the largely self-governing province had not yet been agreed. The King spoke on 7 June 1921; the boundary did not become a fully-fledged frontier until 3 December 1925. During the intervening years a boundary commission sought to find ways in which Clause XII of the Treaty could be implemented. Its task was to determine a boundary 'in accordance with the wishes of the inhabitants, so far as may be compatible with economic and geographical conditions'. That it finally came up with the decision that Northern Ireland would not have to yield an inch owed much to the friendship which developed between Edith and Prime Minister Ramsay MacDonald. It was the King who brought them together when, shortly after the first Labour government took office, he and the Queen gave a dinner to which he invited the principal members of both government and opposition, with their wives. The Prime Minister was asked to take Lady Londonderry in to dinner, where he sat with the Queen on his right and Edith on his left. Immediately common Gaelic bonds were found between the illegitimate Highland Scot and the Gael of another culture, with the result that the Londonderrys were the first to sign the visitors' book at Chequers at the invitation of the new incumbent.

At once letters began to flow, and MacDonald was soon asking for Edith's help and advice. Another consequence of Lloyd George's wizardry had been that there were two different interpretations of Clause XII. The unionists thought that it referred to minor rectifications, the Free Staters thought in terms of major transfers of territory. A three-man commission was required, one commissioner for the North, one for the South, and a neutral party to act as arbitrator. A South African judge assumed the responsibilities of arbitrator, and the Free State government was only too happy to appoint a commissioner seemingly to negotiate the slicing off of pieces of Ulster. But then, not having been a party to the Treaty, the northern administration refused to appoint a commissioner, and MacDonald was faced with the problem of having to impose one by means of adding a special measure to the Boundary Commission Bill. He needed the co-operation of the opposition if the bill were to succeed, and he knew how to get it. In a private letter to Edith[3] dated 5 August 1924, he said, 'I know that you will do your best to get your friends to meet us reasonably within the period between now and the end of September.' He went on to say that 'This is a thing to settle between friends who wish to be happy rather than squabble over [sic] by dishonest politicians and hard mouthed bigots.' The trouble was that 'apparently the south people had a different pledge from Lloyd George'.

In her reply,[4] Edith treated MacDonald to some of her views on the Irish Question in general and on the rights of the inhabitants of 'Uladh' in particular. She described the southern Irish as 'an inconsequent race'; they were like children: 'when given too much latitude, they get out of hand'. If she was to get her friends to meet him reasonably, he had 'to be reasonable too and keep the faith with Ulster'. She claimed that so far, unlike the southerners, Craig had 'always kept his people under control' (the truth of this, in the light of certain bloody occurrences, rather depended on whom she meant by 'his people'). But there was 'a point beyond which men of Scottish blood will not be led'. That point would be reached when they thought that the British government had 'not kept its word to them, pledged in the 1920 Act . . . Ulster never asked for this form of self-government and when it was reluctantly accepted, it was accepted for a clearly defined territory'. She continued,

The original North-East Ulster (Uladh) was won by a MacDonald who was the first to touch these shores, by cutting off his left hand and throwing it from the boat on to the land which he claimed. Hence the bloody hand of Ulster. Won't you, another MacDonald, extend to us the other hand, the right hand of fellowship and maintenance and throw us the olive branch?

She might have made her argument even stronger had she indicated that the ancient MacDonald was claiming the land which had originally been settled by his forefathers. Instead, she made him consider that, though they were in 'opposite camps', they might yet 'have the same goal in view'. She would help him all she could, provided that he reciprocated. But Ramsay, who recognized the red hand of Ulster, was already on her side on the boundary issue. More than that, the Prime Minister had started along the road that led to his falling in love with Edith. For her part she did not merely like MacDonald because of his position; she developed a genuine affection for the man himself. They had more in common – much of it to do with Gaelic traditions – than the social gulf between them seemed to allow. The relationship, though close, remained entirely chaste.

The Boundary Commission Bill became law on 30 September 1924, initial delays having been caused by the civil war and allied Troubles, and the commissioners worked in secret for a year. By November 1925 various changes had been decided: South Armagh and small parcels of Fermanagh and Tyrone to be ceded to the Free State, a few parts of eastern Donegal to Northern Ireland. But the commission's recommendations were leaked to *The Morning Post*,[5] which published them in some detail, and the prime ministers of all three interested governments, appalled by the prospect of renewed disturbances, hastily met and agreed to leave the border where it was, following the parliamentary boundaries of the six counties. The commission's report was to remain a classified document until 1968.

As Edith knew well, both the principal parties were guilty of allowing their judgement to be coloured by ulterior motives. The Free State wanted as much territory as it could get, regardless of the long-term consequences of wholesale removal from Northern Ireland's electorate of a large proportion of Ulster's Catholic population; Northern Ireland, failing a united Ireland within a United Kingdom, wanted to remove nationalist voters from its territory, regardless of loss of land. The principle of self-determination for a nine-county Ulster had been jettisoned before the Treaty; both sides had moved Northern Ireland's barricades to positions where, depending on one's angle of approach, they might best be attacked or defended.

Ironically, the territory within which the social structures of the island's minority culture were to develop was a product of the very legislation which, before the war, most of Ulster's population had abhorred. Moreover, the Third Home Rule Bill, which had been mildly approved of by the southern population as a whole in the pre-war years, was, as has been seen, vigorously rejected by them when the time came for it to be implemented. Too much had happened during the period in which the statute had been suspended. One can understand nationalist objections to the Government of Ireland Act which provided for the establishment of two parliaments; it is a matter of regret for both traditions that the means to bridge the gap between them – the Council of Ireland – was never given a chance to act as conciliator. From this time forward divergent paths were to be followed and attitudes were to harden. When there was co-operation, it often had to be furtively pursued, lest those who trod that dangerous path be branded traitors.

Even private bonds of friendship were attracting disapproval. After the war, shortly before her death, Theresa had received an anonymous letter which reflected the deeply personal nature of political antipathy.[6] Its author, a woman member of the Primrose League (dedicated to maintenance of 'the imperial ascendancy of Great Britain'), complained that 'our greatest stumbling block in canvassing amongst the Unionist Tradesmen and Workingmen [sic]' was 'the social friendship existing between Mr F. Smith and that Bounder Churchill'. She said that 'Radical workingmen' and unionists were never 'chummy'. Until the doors of all unionists were 'banged in the face of Radicals socially or otherwise as in the days of Beaconsfield and Gladstone' politics would not be 'true and healthy'. 'Shut the door socially against Asquith, Churchill & Grey.' To this 'distressed Ulsterwoman' the idea of cross-party friendships did not conflict with principles of open government that were proclaimed later in the twentieth century. She simply wanted a clear line drawn between friend and foe. The complexity of the Irish Question did not seem to have occurred to her. She was spared the knowledge that so much of the future of South and North had been decided in London at 5 Cromwell Place and Londonderry House, in Ulster at the Londonderrys' residence, Mount Stewart.

Although Northern Ireland, with its border still not finalized, began life sharing most of its laws with the remainder of the United Kingdom, the outcome of their application was different. In local government, for instance, only property owners had the vote, and in 1921 Protestants owned most of the property. This was a no less democratic situation than existed elsewhere in the British Isles, but it meant that the province got off to a poor start psychologically. Women were subject to the limited franchise that dated from 1918, which meant, in effect, that some Protestant women had political rights denied to Catholics of either sex. This imbalance was emphasized in 1922, when the Free State granted the vote to women who had reached the age of 21. In the same year, as nationalists boycotted Belfast-manufactured goods in retaliation against the dismissal of Catholic workers, 'woman the consumer had become woman the activist',[7] though more so south of the border. Cumann na mBan hardened its attitude greatly when news was received that as part of an anti-boycott campaign of terror five members of a publican's family, the Mac-Mahons, had been murdered. Eithne Coyle, one of Cumann na mBan's presidents, reacted by turning highwaywoman and holding up trains at gunpoint, when they stopped at stations to deliver newspapers and goods. She and other members of Cumann na mBan continued this harassment – which was partly in protest against the IRA's inadequacies as they saw them – until the outbreak of the civil war brought the boycott to an end. It had not achieved its object, the reinstatement of the Catholic workers.

As the Free State looked inward at its own contradictions and bloody disagreements, the North slowly began to develop in ways that were neither British nor Irish. While Great Britain extended its education system on the assumption that places would eventually be offered to all comers, and that lack of sufficient intelligence would be the only bar to access to higher levels, the Northern Ireland Education Act (1923), setting up non-denominational schools, was boycotted by Catholics and opposed by Presbyterians. The Roman Catholic tradition that, on the whole, it was better for girls to be taught by nuns, boys by priests, ensured that while sectarianism was entrenched the Catholic concept of the different roles of the sexes was sustained. Protestants also favoured single-sex schools, though their preference was more to do with the Protestant work ethic than with religious conviction. From the outset, both Catholic and Protestant schools taught their own versions of the history of Ireland, and these contained within them justifications of opposing views on women's issues. Sectarian education not only perpetuated the political divide, it consolidated the different stances on divorce, birth control, illegitimacy, mixed marriages and all the moral matters that were to be the subject of constitutional change south of the border.

While inheriting the same body of law, the two 'statelets' (as their opponents called them) were free from their inception to diverge as much as their distinctive cultures inclined them so to do. On the face of it, Northern Ireland had the best of both worlds. As well as being represented at Stormont, its citizens returned MPs to Westminster, and the six counties could adopt a take it or leave it attitude to most matters in which the electorate had a personal or social interest. When it came to issues such as the legalization of certain homosexual acts, both traditions in society were only too happy to dissociate themselves from Westminster's decisions. Increases in unemployment benefit, however, brought forth a different response; the Northern Irish were, in general, satisfied to be underwritten from the start by the financial strength of the largest empire the world had ever known. Education was the most fundamental of all aspects of state influence; as well as having immense potential for benefiting or warping the soul of the nation, it was an ever-increasing burden on the national exchequer. When the power of the churches and the power of the state were combined, the possibility of indoctrination was an alarming prospect, and the founding fathers of Northern Ireland sought to combat misuse of educational resources. In 1921 Lord Londonderry, Edith's husband, accepted the portfolio of education in Sir James Craig's cabinet.

In 1923 the 'Londonderry Act' became law and, in a very different way from the Free State, Northern Ireland did its best to break away from the system which both governments had inherited from Dublin Castle. Under the old regime virtually all the schools were voluntary bodies mostly run by the churches; three departments in Dublin saw to overall administration, dealing direct with many committees of management. Now Lord Londonderry tried to provide a non-sectarian basis for public sector schools and teachers' training colleges, whilst granting sufficient facilities for religious instruction. But by 'religious' he really meant 'moral', and he was more than half a century ahead of his time. Each county or county borough became a local education authority, and administration was placed in the hands of education committees (eighteen of them, at first). Children from age 6 to 14 had to receive elementary education 'literary and moral', based on the three Rs. Londonderry wanted to bring about a non-sectarian state, but one that was 'not secular in the sense that it takes no interest in the moral upbringing of the children'.[8] His Act prohibited the teaching of religious instruction in elementary schools during regular school hours; nor was it permissible for a local education authority, when making an appointment to a school under its control, to take notice of the applicant's religious denomination. Immediately he fell foul of both Protestant and Catholic hierarchies and had to concede an Amending Act permitting 'simple Bible instruction'. His scheme was to suffer a fate similar to that of the McPherson proposals in the South. They represented a last-ditch attempt by the United Kingdom to desegregate education before final British withdrawal, and were easily defeated by the Provisional Government and Rome.

Londonderry believed that 'All the quarrels between Roman Catholics and Protestants arose out of the teaching of the Bible', and he 'wished the children of all denominations to meet in the same schools and grow up in a friendly atmosphere'.[9] But, as was their right, the churches were not prepared to co-operate with what was in their eyes an educational merger that involved a spiritual betrayal. The Protestants were placated by the Amendment; then, after Londonderry's time, the Roman Catholics were given a subsidy of 65 per cent of the cost of new buildings, 65 per cent of their lighting and heating costs, and equal pay for equal qualifications. Funded on the same basis as any denominational school (approximately 97 per cent of total costs from public funds) the Catholic elementary schools went their separate way. The most serious result of this special brand of apartheid – paradoxically derived from perfectly respectable democratic principles – was that the negative features of hostile traditions became institutionalized. Protestants and Catholics were in danger of being brainwashed about the nature of each other's political beliefs and social practices. In practical terms, many Roman Catholic schools were extending into the domain of another jurisdiction the outlook and philosophy of the Free State. This included perpetuating the Catholic perception of the family and the woman's role in society.

Plural segregation – on grounds of both sex and religion – took a heavy toll; as well as basic Protestant and Catholic divergence, there was a male

Protestant view of life, a male Catholic view, and two similarly divided female views. Given a reasonably united culture, without a long history of hostility between traditions, diversification might have enriched society. Unfortunately Northern Ireland's factions were too rigid in their outlook for this type of diversity to contribute to mutual respect. However, although the tensions between the communities were undoubtedly exacerbated by the educational system during the economic difficulties of the 1930s, the intervention of the Second World War briefly sublimated aspects of sectarian antipathy. Then, when England and Wales went ahead by means of the Butler Education Act of 1944 to divide the populace on the basis of intelligence and aptitude, Northern Ireland followed suit with the establishment of its own eleven-plus system. Still further segregation, in accordance with the terms of the Northern Ireland Education Act of 1947, led directly to the present position. As the Act provided for increases in grants for voluntary schools, most of which are Roman Catholic, there were some loud protests. But, in general, Northern Ireland has been happier with selective education than the English and the Welsh, democratizing the system to some degree by allowing parents of eleven-plus successes to opt for independent schools without having to pay twice for choice, as did most of their mainland counterparts.

When Great Britain's socialist landslide of 1945 eventually led to moves towards an educational monopoly in the form of a network of comprehensive schools, Northern Ireland, unconsciously reflecting the fears of the southern Catholic Hierarchy about totalitarianism, would have none of it. The pattern of mainly single-sex Protestant grammar schools and secondary intermediate (equivalent to 'modern') schools, single-sex Roman Catholic schools, and mainly single-sex independent schools, remained. State education meant Protestant education; the Catholic schools came under the management of the Council for Catholic Maintained Schools. By January 1992 there were 696 'controlled' schools, that is to say schools controlled by education and library boards, with all costs paid for by public funds; there were 586 'maintained' schools, mostly under Catholic management, receiving public funding for most or all of their capital and running costs; and 52 'voluntary grammar' schools, under Roman Catholic or non-denominational management, all receiving grants from the Department of Education for Northern Ireland. In addition, there were eighteen independent schools. At both parental and governmental levels there is concern about the sectarian straitjacket into which most children are forced. In 1972 the initiative of two Catholic mothers, Cecil Lenehan and Elizabeth Benton, led to the birth of All Children Together and the establishment of a small number of inter-denominational schools, the prime example being Lagan College, Belfast, founded in 1981. The two Catholics were joined by two Protestant mothers, Thelma Shiel and Margaret Kennedy, and Bill Brown was their first Presbyterian parent. There was considerable Church opposition, including temporarily withholding the sacrament of confirmation from Catholic children educated in integrated schools, and Protestant stonewalling when it appeared sensible to 'integrate' the management structure of existing grant-aided schools which already had a good mixture of pupils from different denominations. But there are now fourteen integrated schools in Northern Ireland, and it is largely thanks to All Children Together that the Education Reform (Northern Ireland) Order, 1989, found its way on to the statute book. This important legislation has made it much easier for Northern Ireland parents to choose integrated education for their children.

However, school hours do not encompass the whole of a child's education. Out of school, girls and boys have ways of absorbing cultural influences, good and bad, which have been denied them in the classroom. Although many years were to elapse before the multiple effects of Women's Liberation and the products of Great Britain's move towards freedom and promiscuity were to penetrate Belfast and other urban centres, the process was bound to begin north of the border. Being part of the United Kingdom meant that British precedents would eventually be followed by a new generation exposed to liberated literature and sexually explicit television; and temporary migration for education or employment would speed up this process. That there was a considerable time-lapse can be attributed to the matriarchal close-knit family life of both religious traditions. As one historian has put it, 'In both states, the twin evils of secular education and sexual licence were ecumenically condemned. The Irish museum of puritanism straddled the border.'[10] It was to be the Protestant matriarch who would change her habits first, as the use of contraception within marriage became acceptable to members of her faith. Eventually younger women, who had begun to rebel against the materialism of the property-based rural marriage market, realized that help towards further emancipation was one consequence of the invention of sophisticated methods of birth control. Their subsequent behaviour was more akin to Gaelic licentiousness than to Victorian puritanism. But, for a brief period, one strand of another Irish culture moved in the opposite direction. While Catholic girls from the South sold their bodies in London, the sexual inhibitions of their co-religionists in the North became more deeply entrenched: among the residual Anglophobic Catholic population 'Victorianism had its last and least predictable efflorescence'.[11]

Educational segregation saw to it that the territories of the ghettos reflected closely delineated states of mind. The irony of the continued existence of ghettos is that in one sense they are consequences of the civil rights movement which helped to eliminate institutionalized discrimination in the province. For the movement, which began peacefully and saw its aims achieved (as far as law and official practice were concerned), inadvertently helped to bring about extremes of confrontation which keep today's barricades intact. The Northern Irish Civil Rights Association (NICRA) began life in the 1960s as a small group of decidedly non-violent people collecting information about discrimination against Catholics in the allocation of accommodation and jobs. It grew rapidly, attracting such moderate activists as Betty Sinclair, a member of the Communist Party of Ireland, whose political philosophy superficially resembled the beliefs of another member who was to become internationally known in a very short time, Bernadette Devlin. However unwelcome it was to some, United Kingdom law, when it applied to Northern Ireland, brought with it measures of personal freedom and protection which steadily increased the unionist vote among middle-class Catholics. That for a sizeable proportion of the Catholic working class it proved to be a dead letter was ultimately to lead to the fall of Stormont.

Though she might well object to the comparison, Bernadette Devlin's life has had too many points in common with Maeve's for the coincidence to be ignored. As a tribute to her mother, Bernadette used for the story of her early life a title which Elizabeth Devlin had chosen for a book that she was never able to write: *The Price of My Soul*. The price was what 'we must all pay to preserve our own integrity';[12] the title as a whole implied that Cathleen ni Houlihan was the preferred model, and that Yeats was the source. If so, the mother's allusion does not transfer comfortably to the daughter. Miss Devlin (now Mrs Micheal McAliskey) was too fiery a warrior to be able to be identified with the much more soulful and sad representation of Ireland that appealed to an older generation. She was gaoled for making petrol bombs during the 'Battle of the Bogside', and even in the chamber of the House of Commons, on the day after 'Bloody Sunday', she could not resist the temptation physically to assault the Home Secretary, Reginald Maudling. One might make something, too, of her ability to lead the Irish hordes in an attack on the heartland of Ulster. She had considerable powers of oratory, and demonstrated personally her disregard for conventions about bearing children within the Church's understanding of the married state. Moreover, like Maeve, she had a pagan god to follow, if not to worship: namely Karl Marx. But that is where the comparison must end.

After attending Saint Patrick's Girls' Academy in Dungannon, Miss Devlin received her higher education in one of the few essentially Northern Irish institutions where the community is wholly undivided on grounds of gender or religion, Queen's University, Belfast. More significant, though, is the time when she read for her degree in psychology. Born in 1947, she attended university during the heady days of student unrest. Naturally Queen's became one of the focal points of the civil rights movement, and, with Bernadette Devlin in the thick of things, the new People's Democracy Party became a viable force for change. Then, as has happened so often in Irish history, the level of support briefly enjoyed by a political phenomenon was no reflection of the fundamental convictions and prejudices of its supporters. Given the opportunity, People's Democracy would have replaced governments supposedly corrupted by capitalism, North and South, by a socialist republic. The citizens of Mid-Ulster who elected a 21-year-old girl to Westminster (the youngest MP ever elected) did not see things in this light. She saw them as the down-trodden working class; they saw her as a likeable Catholic lass who would champion their rights and get things done.

The civil rights movement did achieve its laudable goals, but in terms of the most basic of the old 'four freedoms', 'freedom from fear', the victory was a Pyrrhic one. The method was quite simple: like the blacks in the southern states of the USA the dispossessed would march peacefully through or near districts traditionally forbidden to them. But from the first there was a difference about the actual composition of the group who marched. According to the doctrine of the People's Democracy Party they should have been working class, and of no particular religion. A non-sectarian demonstration should have taken on the bourgeoisie who were keeping the vicious capitalist social and political structures in place. The rank and file of the marchers did not see things like that, nor did those who opposed them. As well as housing and jobs, the Catholics who marched wanted franchise reform and an end to gerrymandering in places like Derry, where a Catholic majority was ruled by a Protestant minority, thanks to cleverly rigged boundaries. The Protestants, who usually called the city Londonderry,[13] feared any loss of power that might jeopardize the survival of the state. Neither denomination was greatly interested in left-wing dogma. Confrontation led to street violence.

Miss Devlin and other members of NICRA organized their marches because laws were inherently unfair, or were not enforced even-handedly. Many of the injustices of the time were especially hard for women to bear and, as the western world was already being subjected to loud calls for women's liberation, feminism was a mainstay of Northern Ireland's civil rights movement. Photographs of civil rights activity often show a preponderance of women and girls, frequently accompanied by young children. Though the marchers' cause was a just one, they failed to appreciate that part of the responsibility for the social shortcomings of life under a parliament with devolved powers lay on the shoulders of those elected to Stormont as nationalists. A logical outcome, and indeed a virtual obligation, of the Treaty, that was at first appreciated by Northern Ireland's nationalist leaders, was to represent the interests of a good third of the people in the creation of domestic legislation. Deterred by bloody events, misbegotten pressures from south of the border, and the difficulties of influencing change in a political situation of which they did not approve, they failed to present their case in a place where it was sure of gaining a wide audience and might have had some influence on modifying laws. Inconsistent policies of abstentionism meant that the case for easing the plight of Catholic communities was not heard at national level. It is no excuse to say that Stormont had a built-in unionist majority that seemed unassailable. All political parties come from small beginnings; the possibility of social or constitutional change – even of establishing a link with Dublin by means of the Council of Ireland – should not have been ruled out by those who had nationalist or Catholic interests at heart.

A policy of peaceful marches combined with acts of civil disobedience was a poor alternative to getting a sound case put across in Stormont or, better still, in the Palace of Westminster; but it was infinitely preferable to terrorism. As it was, however, the IRA, which in recent years had become a moribund and generally invisible organization, was easily able to take advantage of the clashes which arose when the irresistible force of largely nationalist protesters met the immovable object of mainly unionist resistance to reform. The initiative was soon taken from the middle class. Moderate Catholics who had started the movement were soon superseded by radicals like Bernadette Devlin; after that it was an easy matter for the IRA to infiltrate the movement and gain sympathy from those who suffered most from discrimination. The IRA provided stewards for the protest marches and they began to present themselves as a force to attack social iniquities in general: poverty, unemployment, slums – anything for which the political structure could be blamed. Previously their campaign of violence had failed partly for lack of moral justification; now they had ready to hand the means of regaining the confidence of anyone who had a grudge against the housing authority or any government department. As in Dublin in 1916, only a few deaths would be needed to start the process of destabilization; only this time they would be civilian deaths that would occur in front of photographers from Great Britain, the Continent and the United States.

Miss Devlin's election to Westminster as MP for Mid-Ulster came at a time when the Northern premier, Captain Terence O'Neill, was pushing for reform a good deal faster than many of his colleagues found comfortable. It also occurred when the IRA, because of the influence of the socialist rebel Roy Johnston over its leader Cathal Goulding, was adopting a Marxist step-by-step policy that was not far from People's Democracy principles. Abstentionism having failed, those who sought a workers' revolution should try to destroy the existing system from within the 'illegal assemblies', such as Stormont and Leinster House (where the Dáil meets). Having created socialist regimes north and south, the working class of both parts of Ireland would unite and sweep away capitalism and the border. Abandonment of abstentionism was heresy to some republicans, but both Johnston and Goulding were pragmatists now, and the opportunity was not to be missed of defeating the Ulster Unionist candidate when civil rights disturbances had created a resurgence of sympathy for an IRA identified with social justice.

The various anti-unionists of Mid-Ulster needed a compromise candidate: 'they would have voted for the floor mop to save the vote from being split'.[14] Even at the age of 21 Bernadette Devlin had shown some talent for the hustings. An excellent canvasser, she went tirelessly about her prospective constituency preaching a message that made working-class solidarity palatable to non-Marxist voters; their unity could bring the social improvements that O'Neill was finding it difficult to deliver. She was a highly articulate and attractive speaker, and the vote (33,648 to the Unionist's 29,437) showed that she had persuaded about 1,500 Protestants to support a papist. Her lack of years and experience did not count against her. Her unorthodox views about religion were not allowed to lose her the Catholic vote, and both her feminism and her femininity (which could have cancelled each other out), she used to her advantage. Naturally the Church was not at all happy about the prospect of a workers' revolution. Cardinal Conway, Primate of All Ireland, let it be known that socialism, as preached by these Marxists, meant slavery. But 'The Cardinal knew perfectly well the difference between Communists and socialists, and that the Marxist theory propagated in Northern Ireland had been strongly anti-Communist' and, unless it 'dug its heels in', there would be room for the Church in a socialist Ireland. She made it plain that she was 'fighting for the economic rights of underprivileged people, not to win back the Six Counties for Ireland'. The South being economically in a worse state than the North, she hoped that 'as we step up the struggle in Ulster, there will be those in the South who would step up the struggle there'.[15]

The year 1969 saw yet another Irish watershed. Apart from Bernadette Devlin's successful campaign to be elected as Unity MP for Mid-Ulster and the building, amid much bloodshed, of innumerable barricades, matters came to a head in the IRA. After its convention in that year there came the split between the Provisionals (PIRA), who could sometimes make common cause with People's Democracy, and the Officials (OIRA), whose socialism lacked the glamour of those who were suddenly transformed into brave defenders of the oppressed. In the no-go areas behind the barricades it was the Provos who championed civil rights, and the squalid environment seemed of itself to be a justification of their cause. They were learning that at the broad base of society there were many people who lacked true republican motivation but who could do much of the work that seemed to be necessary. Women's clandestine contribution to the 'armed struggle' from within the ranks could now be supplemented by the advantages they enjoyed when publicly demonstrating face to face with the British Army or the Royal Ulster Constabulary. The propaganda potential was limitless, especially when carefully presented to gullible American senators, sentimentally inclined towards shamrocks. And yet, even in 1971, after an ugly incident involving angry Belfast women and some soldiers, the Provisionals were taking a patronizing public stance that would not endear them to the type of woman who otherwise sympathized with them:

> We realize that protest which takes the course of physical force is alien to all women, yet how they proved to be a force to be reckoned with! We are proud of you![16]

Bernadette Devlin's clash with the authorities illustrated the value to Irish republicanism outside Northern Ireland of women in conflict. When she was arrested, Conor Cruise O'Brien recorded in his diary, 'Her arrest had more impact in Dublin and London than in Belfast, which is entirely taken up by its own troubles.'[17] In the same entry he speaks of 'B.D.'s status as *primissima donna*' and attributes local reaction, or lack of it, to her being 'a wee girl from west of the Bann [river]'. As an individual her appeal in Ireland was bound to be short lived, but while it lasted the IRA was one of its beneficiaries. However, while she appreciated the need for international support for the changes that she wished to bring about, on her first visit to the United States she made the mistake of comparing the oppressed Irish with the American negro, and her distaste for capitalism was too heavily emphasized by her refusal to accept the keys of the City of New York. Her failure to use the guile that is integral to Marxist political method was to bring an end to her mainstream public career when, in 1974, the Catholic voters showed that they did not, after all, care for her policies, which in heat and haste, they had enthusiastically misunderstood. The Workers' Republic of a United Ireland had never appealed to them. What most of them had wanted were mundane civil rights; as soon as these were in train there was no apparent need to support this rather daring young woman, colourful though she was.

Miss Devlin's political career was pursued at more than one level before and after her departure from Westminster. Her prime allegiance was to the People's Democracy Party, which collaborated with Provisional Sinn Féin through a grouping it helped to establish, the Northern Resistance Movement (NRM). Because this coalition opposed internment, it could sometimes depend on the support of the Northern Ireland Civil Rights Association. Normally, though, relations with less radical groups were strained, partly because NRM was intent on the abolition of Stormont. The Officials became particularly antipathetic to Bernadette, on one occasion referring to her and others as 'parasitic sub-life'.[18] Offensive though this was, there was a lot of 'sub' activity going on in 1972, when the epithet was used. Presumably the insult hurt less than one used of her by the leader of the Social Democratic and Labour Party (SDLP) the following year. Gerry Fitt called her 'an irrelevancy', to which she replied that the SDLP were 'political gangsters'. Her more considered verdict on Fitt's party, made in response to the SDLP's collaboration with the Sunningdale power-sharing agreement, was that, 'from now on, they are part of the British establishment, enemies of the Irish people'.[19]

During 1974 three events occurred which were to lead Bernadette Devlin to the discreet, more cerebral, position which she holds today. She lost her seat in the general election, she became Mrs McAliskey and she joined, as a founder member, the Irish Republican Socialist Party (IRSP). The IRSP had broken away from Official Sinn Féin, the political wing of the Official IRA, after a row over policy which had been brewing among the 'sub-life' for at least two years. The conflict of conscience which had faced the Mrs McAliskeys of yesteryear had been between feminism and nationalism. Now the Officials wanted nationalism to wipe the class struggle off the agenda. Seamus Costello, a veteran of the IRA's 1956 series of attacks on border posts and military installations (the 'Border Campaign'), led the breakaway group and Bernadette McAliskey was his most eloquent supporter. About eighty delegates walked out of Official Sinn Féin's 1974 convention in Dublin, claiming that national liberation, as they saw it, and socialist revolution must be intertwined. The split encouraged the formation of the Irish National Liberation Army (INLA), among whose victims was Airey Neave, and the tilt towards violence was foreseen by Official Sinn Féin:

> The political development and prospective unity of the IRSP will depend on the extent to which such diverse and personally ambitious characters as Costello and Bernadette McAliskey can staunch the gangster elements and the factionalists who dominate the rank and file.[20]

In 1976 Mrs McAliskey, now a member of the executive committee of 'Irps', as it is called, resigned from the party, and eleven members went with her. There was a dispute about the balance between the two types of war to which the new party was supposed to be dedicated; those who resigned felt that too little attention was being paid to the class war, and they differed on the desirability of using violence as a means to achieve their goals. In April the Relatives Action Committee (RAC), composed almost entirely of women, was formed to try to have special category or 'prisoner-of-war' status restored to republicans serving sentences in Long Kesh. The organization grew and in 1978 the attention of its Coalisland Committee was focused on the H-Blocks (so-called because of their ground-plan) and other matters affecting justice in the province. Bernadette was a leading light in what looked like a revival of the civil rights movement, but there were now far too many splinter groups for concerted action to be made and, in any case, issues were no longer clear-cut. As Conor Cruise O'Brien had once asked, at a public meeting convened to call for the release of Bernadette Devlin, 'what was a political prisoner?'[21] He gave as an example the man who booby-trapped a car 'putting children's lives at risk and killing innocent civilians – if that man were tried, sentenced and imprisoned could he then become one of the political prisoners for whose release we were asked to call?' Nobody attempted to answer his question.

Bernadette McAliskey continued for a few more years to use constitutional means for getting her voice heard, standing unsuccessfully for election to the European Parliament and trying twice to get elected to the Dáil. It was in 1981, while she was spokeswoman for the National H-Block Committee, that she had the frightening experience of being the object of a loyalist assassination attempt; she was also somewhat embarrassed by receiving aid on that occasion from an unwelcome source: a British Army patrol. She is not one to be easily intimidated. By her influence on the causes which she supported she has left an indelible impression on social disposition within the province.

People's Democracy sought changes that, according to Marxist theory, would have altered the status of women in Irish society. Since those noisy days at Queen's University, though, the world has seen that everything the wicked capitalists said about the real position of women in the countries which had based their ideas on Marx was true. Cardinal Conway had a point. Events were to show that there was little to choose between socialist ideology and Communist ideology in left-wing dictatorships. And, far from being eman cipated, women in Marxist states were exploited by men and by the system. Prominent exceptions did nothing to fool most observers. All this was a far cry from Northern Ireland; nevertheless the devolved system of government allowed or encouraged discrimination against women in the workplace, particularly when it became politically more difficult to discriminate against Catholics. Indeed, keeping women away from work and the wage packet in a society crippled by unemployment was a possible, if dishonourable, means of uniting a workforce otherwise divided on sectarian lines. An old-established bond between Catholic and Protestant workmen was the conviction that the single woman should not be allowed to do a job that could be done by a married man. The married woman should, of course, be raising her family.

Another 'dashing'[22] woman who did not accept the assumptions of this tradition, but who was in every other way unlike Bernadette Devlin, indicated how a constitutional road to reform, strictly within the boundaries set by the law, could be found. A Catholic former president of Queen's University Literary and Debating Society, Sheelagh Murnaghan stood as Liberal candidate for Queen's and was elected to Stormont in 1961 (gaining 2,622 votes to the unionist's 2,370). She refused to make use of 'the ancient grievances of the Irish' and promised 'not to do anything which will alter the constitutional position of Northern Ireland unless I am required to do so by the majority of the people of the province'.[23] A barrister who declared herself to be an enemy of Sinn Féin, since it was the political wing of the IRA 'which has plagued us for so long', she presented herself to the electorate as a unionist 'with a small "u"'.[24] While the civil rights movement was succeeding in bringing discrimination on religious grounds to an end in key social areas, what might be taken to be a collaborationist approach to the political and social consequences of devolution was encouraging importation of women's rights from the British mainland. Each in her own way, co-religionists Devlin and Murnaghan illustrated one of the not especially remarkable conclusions of a recent report prepared for Northern Ireland's Equal Opportunities Board that those who attended higher education institutions such as Queen's were the group most amenable to unorthodox thinking.[25] Flexibility of mind took them in opposite directions, but it encouraged both women to use the apparently Protestant electoral system as it stood, although they stood miles apart on fundamental issues. Each one distanced herself from the partition debate, but for very different reasons. Bernadette Devlin believed that the frontier would disappear after more important things had happened: 'Only if it's an all-

Ireland working-class revolution are there enough of us to overthrow the powers that be'.[26] This is not the same as saying, as Sheelagh Murnaghan said, 'Let us try to get to the stage of accepting people as they are, respecting their views and insisting only . . . that the majority opinion of the people is to be the deciding factor . . . on . . . the Border'.[27] Her methods were less exciting than those of men and women who were frequently in the headlines, but then she would not make petrol bombs. Nor would she say of the unionist Government: 'we are witnessing its dying convulsions. And with traditional Irish mercy, when we've got it down we will kick it into the ground'.[28]

Simply going along peacefully with the constitutional status of Northern Ireland brought many changes in the law which affected women's rights. For nationalist women of the political left and centre, as legislation catered to their demands, it was almost embarrassing to observe how in their terms it paid to be citizens of the United Kingdom. Moreover, they could see that although the civil rights movement, hi-jacked by the IRA's propaganda machine, had achieved its ends, it had left the Ulster people a high price to pay in community relations. However, not everyone welcomed the freedoms that originated in Westminster and permeated Northern Ireland society. Educational seg-regation on a sectarian basis served to make the writ of the twenty-six counties run in large areas of the six. What was freedom in one tradition might be licence in another.

Many of those responsible for teaching primary and secondary school children have striven nobly to keep Northern Ireland's special brand of politics out of the classroom (though those teaching history need to try even harder to see the other side's point of view). It is, though, in the moral and social realms that Rome's rule has its greatest impact on the developing girls of the North, and this made its first most obvious appearance in the field of birth control. When the South had banned books promoting contraception and then prohibited importation and sale of contraceptives, the moral effect of such legislation had not been limited to twenty-six counties. Some clerics in the North found it a matter of grave concern that these restrictions placed no legal constraint on Catholics who lived within the part of the island which had settled for internal self-government instead of outright independence. To the priest of nationalist inclination here was another argument for a united Ireland. And yet the practical response of Protestants was not very different from that of the minority faith within the province. After Marie Stopes visited Northern Ireland in 1934 a family planning clinic was opened; but, as the minutes of the Northern Ireland Family Planning Association put it, it 'languished'[29] and then closed after the war. A clinic started by the Northern Ireland Ministry of Health at Belfast's Royal Maternity Hospital in 1940 is also said to have 'languished', but it survived.

In 1973, when Senator Mary Robinson, future President of the Republic, introduced into the Irish Senate a private member's bill which would have legalized, to a limited extent, sale and use of birth control devices, some of the loudest protests came from northern Catholic sources. These became even louder when the Supreme Court of the Republic declared the prohibition of birth control unconstitutional. A priest resident in Northern Ireland, teaching at Saint Patrick's Academy, declared that it was 'a more serious matter for married people to have contraceptives available than for single people who are intent on fornication. It is a blasphemy against the nature of marriage'. He was also worried about the spread of contraceptives to the unmarried: 'Married women could act as agents for them and pass them to single friends.' But his underlying fear was that 'a native Irish government' should contemplate legalizing birth control. Although Northern Ireland had contraception and 'therapeutic' abortion, only 'to some extent' did it suffer from corruption of family life. This was because the community was split: 'the Catholics have contempt for contraceptives as Unionist things'.[30]

Again, one has to stand back from the fray and see whether or not, regardless of religious dogma, the anti-contraceptive lobby had something, perhaps derived from nature rather than theology, to justify its stance on this issue. Mrs Robinson had considerable propaganda to withstand at the time of her bill, none more effective than that provided by Mrs Desmond Broadberry. Mr Broadberry was a vociferous opponent of birth control and felt that he had in some way won the argument when, shortly after he had had a face-to-face debate with the senator, Mrs Broadberry gave birth to her eighteenth child. It may seem laughable, but those who have witnessed the success – in terms of the balanced personalities of the offspring – of even larger Irish families, can be forgiven for gaining the impression that the old natural practice had, and may still have, something to be said for it. The trouble is that it seems only to work in rural communities, and depends on a steady stream of remittances from members of the family who prosper in Boston, Liverpool or New York. Moreover, for a state to impose it on non-believers is hardly reconcilable with the basic tenets of democracy. Such things only happen in theocracies. Northern Ireland did not, and does not, have laws which interfere with the private lives of its minority (unless abortion be regarded as a private matter), and the Supreme Court of the Republic did much to restore the balance of justice south of the border. Nevertheless, when the first Northern Irish Brook Advisory Centre opened in Belfast in September 1992, its twice-weekly sessions were picketed by Catholics and Protestants. The protesters feared that contraceptive services would encourage promiscuity and actually increase the number of unwanted pregnancies.

As time goes by the gap is steadily narrowed between the legal positions, North and South, with regard to contraception. Although Rome stands firm, despite the pickets the people are less inclined to obey; after all, it is not as though a sperm or an unfertilized egg, kept apart, could reasonably be perceived to constitute an independent human life. But once these two constituents are united everything changes. It is not easy for Catholics, or for Protestants, to face up to all the implications when the survival of a foetus is at stake. In Northern Ireland the legal position on abortion is only absolutely clear when the life of the mother is in danger. As in England and Wales, the initial relevant legislation is the Offences Against the Person Act of 1861. This, in sections 58 and 59, made it an offence unlawfully to procure a miscarriage, and offenders could be sentenced to imprisonment for life. In 1929, the law was substantially changed by the British Parliament, but not by Stormont, with the passing of the Infant Life (Preservation) Act, which created the offence of child destruction, and stated that there was no offence if it could be proved that the only intention was to preserve the mother's life. Northern Ireland did not choose to introduce similar legislation at that time; it has, however, been affected in this field since 1938 by case law: 'the essence of the matter is that the preservation of the life of the mother is not construed merely as saving the mother from immediate violent death, but permits the termination of pregnancy where its continuance would make her a physical or mental wreck'.[31]

Northern Ireland's nearest equivalent to Westminster's 1929 Act did not appear until 1945. Then section 25 of the Criminal Justice Act (Northern Ireland) made it an offence wilfully to cause a child, then capable of being born alive – that is to say, having survived for twenty-eight weeks or more – to die before it had an existence independent of its mother. Those found guilty of 'child destruction' were, and are still, liable to be sentenced to life imprisonment. The next stage in English and Welsh movement towards 'abortion on demand' came with the 1967 Abortion Act, which did not impress the Northern Irish. Their general distaste for child destruction, regardless of creed, is not far removed from that of citizens of the Republic who voted against abortion in the 1983 referendum. But, because of a wide interpretation of how a mother's life may be threatened during pregnancy, their position is not clearly defined. Although the law reverses what is popularly understood to be the Pope's preference when a choice has to be made between the life of mother and foetus, decisions about the likelihood of mothers becoming physical or mental wrecks are made in a cloudy area.

The liberal aspect of the Northern Irish position stems from an English case, *Rex* v. *Bourne*, reported in 1938. In other respects Northern Ireland has continued to turn away from United Kingdom legislation in this field of human rights. When Bourne was charged with procuring an abortion for a 13-year-old victim of multiple rape, Justice McNaughton acquitted him. He ruled that as there was reference in the 1861 Act to 'unlawfully' procuring a miscarriage, there was an implication that there could be circumstances in which abortion was lawful. In his judgement the only exception to the prohibition of abortion was a sincere attempt to preserve the life of the mother. More than half a century was to elapse before similar circumstances were to make Irish public opinion and the southern Irish judiciary follow in Justice McNaughton's footsteps. But between 1967 and 1992 the position on the British mainland changed drastically.

Northern Irish anti-abortionists, or impartial jurors, have reasonable grounds to believe that the door stands ajar to permit the eventual entry of unlimited 'social' grounds to abort. The Presbyterian Church has tried to come up with useful guidance for parents and doctors, having seen the massive increase in abortions carried out legally in England since the 1967 Abortion Act was passed. In 1979 in Great Britain over 90 per cent of abortions were allegedly performed because the mental or physical health of the mother or her dependent children was at risk. A few were performed under the clause in the Act permitting destruction of the foetus when 'gross abnormality' was detected in the foetus, and the Presbyterian Church has expressed its concern about the definition of 'gross'. It has stressed that many physically and mentally handicapped people live happily, and some have made a useful contribution to society. The presence of a Downs Syndrome child in a family can be an influence for good, having a bonding effect and compelling parents and siblings to recognize the need for self-sacrifice.

The Presbyterian conclusion made the link with prevention that was not available to like-minded Roman Catholics. Unwanted births should not be avoided by recourse to abortion; prospective parents should adopt 'a more responsible attitude to personal relationships outside marriage, and within marriage, a fuller use of the contraceptive knowledge now available, and a higher degree of personal responsibility and self control'.[32] Devout Roman Catholics could take little comfort from such words. They would share the belief that, while 'a woman's right to choose' applies to aspects of her own life, it does not sanction any action which might harm the one that is nurtured within her; and, should women fall into difficulty, even as a consequence of rape, they would be well-advised to turn to the Irish pregnancy care service: Life. Founded in 1981, this charity has nothing ambiguous in its aims: 'We believe that all human beings have the right to life from the moment of conception', so we offer a service that cares for both you and your child'.[33] Alternatively they could turn to Cura, an organization similar to Life in both aims and methods, but funded by the Catholic Hierarchy. Unfortunately the realities of life are such that the complex moral, or immoral, standards of modern society overlap in Northern Ireland to a degree which drives many to act against the principles of their own faith. Many pregnant girls flee to London, where few questions are asked. Others, to whom contraceptive devices may have been forbidden, join the ever-expanding category of society, made up of those who are called – with no regard for accuracy – 'one-parent families'.

By 1983, 10 per cent of Northern Ireland's 'families' had no visible father, a state of affairs which, seen from the child's perspective, was greatly to be deplored. Presumably it did, however, demonstrate unwillingness to dispose of some of these children on phoney social grounds by means of abortion. To that extent it is a welcome statistic. On the other hand it reflects three other factors which tend to undermine traditional family life in the province, and are partly the consequences of north-east Ireland's altogether different heritage from the rest of the island. Depressed urban living, changing western values and fashions, and the dominance among religious denominations of those which accept the notion of the irretrievable breakdown of marriage, all threaten the family. On the credit side, the unwanted child's lot has been greatly eased in Northern Ireland by a more enlightened approach to adoption than that which existed until recently in the Republic. As well as permitting the adoption of legitimate children who are not orphans, the law enables parental consent to adoption to be dispensed with by a court if the parent has neglected or otherwise abused the child. Adoption procedures were clarified by the 1967 Adoption Act, as a result of which fewer children are likely to be abandoned. The right to stipulate the religion in which the child will be reared is, of course, fully appreciated in a divided society.

Fortunately, attitudes towards the religious upbringing of children of mixed or inter-Church marriages have softened since the Second Vatican Council. In fact the situation is more conducive to good family relations than was the case before the Catholic *Ne Temere* Decree of 1908 was promulgated. That ruling, which was incorporated into the Code of Canon Law in 1918, required that both parties to a mixed marriage commit themselves in writing to bringing up the children as Roman Catholics; before the decree the practice in parts of Ireland had been that sons were reared in the faith of the father, daughters in the faith of the mother. In 1983 new legislation applying to mixed marriages was in accordance with Pope Paul VI's *Matrimonia Mixta* document, whereby only the Catholic partner, who must inform the non-Catholic partner of the position, was obliged to try to bring up the children as Catholics. This made for some improvement in community relations in the Republic, but in Northern Ireland, at a time when every new Catholic child seemed to be a potential enemy of the state, the change was not very enthusiastically received.

The difference between the prevailing views of motherhood in the two Irish states is not as great as some statistics and contrasting legislation might lead one to believe. Despite the existence of religious and political chasms, the two communities have more in common than they know, and distinctions can more sensibly be made between rural and urban Ireland, than between one ideology and another. Northern Ireland may seem to be fifty years ahead of Catholic Ireland in its pursuit of certain democratic goals; nevertheless, the social assumptions of those citizens unmarked by the effects of an indus-trialized environment are remarkably similar. That researchers sometimes come to the opposite conclusion is caused by their understandable tendency to interview members of elite groups instead of living long enough among people who might be regarded as 'ordinary'. Although 'the average woman' does not exist, her views certainly do and, whatever her class or creed, throughout both Irelands she believes for example that abortion for social convenience is a form of murder. By contrast, most of Northern Ireland's political parties are conscious of the need to be seen to have women's sections, and their spokeswomen seem to be largely in favour of abortion on demand, although this is not their party's official line.

There is nothing especially Irish about politically ambitious men and women losing touch with the convictions of the electorate, though occasionally their indiscretions may give the observer pause for thought. The trouble is that they are the articulate ones and it is their views which can too easily be thought of as representative of their community or party membership. For example, a certain political party[34] does not support indiscriminate foetus destruction, but the impression given by the nominally Catholic woman official interviewed was that it had practically no reservations in this field. What she had to say must have been an indiscreet revelation of a personal conviction; but, for all that, it should be taken into account. On the one hand it showed the true feelings of the holder of a responsible post, to the effect that an unborn baby deserved very little consideration; on the other it showed how simple it would be for a foreign observer to come to a completely fallacious opinion about the attitude of the Northern Irish. The official made an even worse impression when she discovered who had sent the interviewer to her door. The unionist Catholic Sir John Biggs-Davison was, she volunteered, 'a traitor to his religion' – a telling remark from within the ranks of a 'non-sectarian' political party, and from one who, despite her own religious persuasion, was an opponent of the Roman Catholic stand on abortion.

It must be a matter of considerable irritation to nationalist feminists that, when they perceive Northern Ireland's laws relating to women's rights to be superior in their terms to the Republic's, they have to concede that this is largely attributable to the existence of the British connection or, more precisely, to the impact of the Welfare State. This tends to be most obvious, as European law becomes a factor to be reckoned with, when there are serious marital problems. The differences between the six and the twenty-six counties with regard to disintegrating marriages was given extensive publicity by means of the New Ireland Forum in 1983. Convened in Dublin in order to try to find a democratic solution to the problems of the island as a whole, the Forum attracted submissions, oral and written, from many groups, including women seeking an end to various forms of discrimination. At that time, under the Republic's law, a married woman's place of domicile was that of her husband. If he were to go to England, after one year's residence there he could obtain a divorce in English law that would be recognized in Ireland; the wife's country of domicile, however, remained Ireland and the courts only recognize divorces granted to those domiciled within the jurisdiction of the foreign court in question. The notion of dependent domicile has since been abandoned and a wife's status now is much the same as it is for Northern Irish wives, and as it was in the province at the time of the Forum: when a married couple separate, a woman's place of residence is where she lives if she has lived there for a year or more.

Then, again, in marked contrast to the Republic's limited arrangements for judicial separation, which were usually restricted to failure to maintain (while adultery might at the court's discretion be a bar to the granting of a separation order), the North offered women greater protection. Since 1980, as laid down in the Domestic Proceedings (Northern Ireland) Order, proceedings may be initiated on grounds of failure to maintain, adultery, desertion and intolerable behaviour – the latter being subject to a wide range of interpretation by the court. Moreover, once a separation order has been granted, the new status of the parties becomes clear, making it possible for either or both to receive whatever social service benefits may be appropriate; the housing authority would, for example, be empowered to assist the woman immediately. Then, if there is a wish for the final step to be taken, separation could be made permanent under the terms of the 1978 Matrimonial Causes Order. A divorce would be granted if evidence were submitted to show that the marriage had broken down irretrievably. To prevent Roman Catholics from entering into bigamous arrangements as has happened in the South when the clerical double standard has been applied (a non-Catholic marriage not having been deemed to be a real marriage), they may not remarry in a church unless they have had a civil divorce. Even in an area as contentious as divorce, though, Northern Ireland has not been prepared to go as far away as possible from the Republic's rigid stance. It may seem little more than a token distancing from England's libertarian position, but the North did not choose to allow the writ of the Matrimonial and Family Proceedings Act, 1984, to run within its territory. Instead the Matrimonial and Family Proceedings (Northern Ireland) Order, 1989, makes a modest gesture towards the permanency of marriage: unlike couples on the British mainland, who may ignore their vows after a year, Northern Irish couples must remain linked by law for twice that period.

Erosion of parents' responsibility for their children's welfare was one of the expressed fears of the Roman Catholic Hierarchy at the time of the Browne affair, and a look around some of the depressed areas of Londonderry and Belfast might confirm that such fears were not entirely unwarranted. Legislation, such as the 1977 Family Law Reform Order, which made illegitimate and legitimate children have equal rights to inherit, has an unreal air about it when one witnesses the plight, physical and emotional, of a large proportion of the increasing number of children born outside wedlock. The sight often seen of young children allowed by their parents to risk life and limb on the barricades of Belfast – even during exchanges of fire – makes one doubt the supposed wisdom of doing anything either to remove the mother from the hearth or the children from her apron strings. Many problems arise in working-class environments because the father is not fulfilling his traditional role and, whatever one's views of the nuclear family, it can only thrive if there is a balance between wife and husband, usually reflected in division of labour. When the husband is dispirited by unemployment, is absent, having emigrated to find work overseas, or, as sometimes happens, has been seduced by the phoney excitement of terrorism, more falls upon the shoulders of the mother than nature or custom intended.

Circumstances of violence amid urban deprivation as found in Northern Ireland are exceptional in United Kingdom terms. But they might make one wonder whether some of the vast sums devoted to 'welfare' in general and to social security benefit schemes in particular are having long-term harmful effects. Are they really encouraging family cohesion and autonomy? Too often the man of the house is undermined by state influences until he abdicates from the position seemingly ordained by tradition for husband and father. The three principles of the United Kingdom's Health Service – universality, comprehensiveness and access unrestricted by means – seem to be taken to apply to too many fields of human responsibility. This does not imply that the entire fabric of the Welfare State should be dismantled; it does suggest that the state should proceed more cautiously, and not risk undermining its basic unit, the family.

But such sentiments would fail to impress the inhabitants of the Catholic ghettos of Belfast. Large tracts of the city are dramatic reminders of what can happen if for a long period the impression is given, however wrongly, that some of the Welfare State's ideals only apply to a defensive majority. In this context it might be regarded as irresponsible to contemplate diminishing the influence of Big Brother, at least until the underprivileged have had opportunities for self-improvement and recognition of social interdependence to come their way. Attempts to ameliorate the lot of the underprivileged can all too easily have harmful social effects which negate the improvements achieved. But much can be done. Now that gerrymandering is a thing of the past (its political effect was exaggerated; its harm to community relations underestimated), the social priority should be the restoration of family pride through provision of employment and a decent physical environment. Like the arid inner-city areas of England, the ghettos are seed-beds of corruption. The conditions give no excuse for crime, but they provide the perfect environment for the criminally disposed to give full play to warped tendencies. In these dark regions one of the results of the corruption of family life is the inversion of its ideal; instead of the mother fulfilling her old-fashioned Gaelic role, she is all too often battered and broken.

Were it not for its failure to prevent the problem from arising, Northern Ireland might take some pride in the way it copes with this form of family breakdown. Social provision for the battered women of the North is infinitely superior to that provided in the Republic, notwithstanding the Family Law (Protection of Spouses and Children) Act, 1981. South of the border women persecuted by their husbands can subsist on supplementary welfare but are seldom given accommodation; many flee to England, where sanctuary is provided by Refuge (oringinally known as Chiswick Women's Aid). Their lot has been said to epitomize all the weaknesses of law and services that affect women who fall off the pedestal on which history and religion have placed them; it 'exposes the hypocrisy of a society which venerates the role of the mother in the home, but cares little if she is beaten or raped within it and offers no support if she seeks escape or assistance'.[35] The Northern Irish fugitive, by comparison, is pampered. If she enters a refuge in the North and is in need, she qualifies for the normal income support allowance and an additional benefit to cover her rent. While living in the residence she can make an application in the normal way to the Housing Executive and, if she opts for separation, she will enjoy some priority over less unfortunate applicants. It is very much to her advantage that Northern Ireland has a single housing authority which can assess need on a provincial, rather than local, basis. The misfortunes of the dependent children are also mitigated by social security benefits. One may try to imagine how much easier life is for them than it is for those who have to flee from the South to London. In one case a woman who arrived at Chiswick Women's Aid Centre, bearing a facial scar held together by thirty-eight stitches, was accompanied by sixteen children.[36]

Unfortunately, looking at individual cases, particularly the most tragic ones, can give a distorted impression of society at large. On the one hand there is a need to penetrate the façade and find the sometimes harsh realities of social conditions as they affect women; on the other hand the importance of making an overall assessment which keeps rights and wrongs in proportion must not be overlooked. When living for any length of time anywhere in Northern Ireland, other than in slums and ghettos, one does not gain an impression that women are the losers. This only seems to happen when some perversion of the natural order of things occurs. Despite the evidence of statistics, a subjective impression – for all its disadvantages – may be gained that in general living conditions range from reasonable to good, and that mothers command respect and control a large share of the family income. Payments from the United Kingdom exchequer and the European Community, and remittances from relatives working overseas, may not be the best means of balancing the province's books, but they do permit many citizens to enjoy a decent standard of living.

Within the body of the employed population who live in suburbs or villages untroubled by sectarian strife, attitudes to women are inevitably consolidated by education and recent research conducted in Northern Ireland has enabled some of its effects to be interpreted. It has been shown that a more 'liberal' attitude to the rights and roles of women is acquired in single-sex schools, and that girls' schools are more liberal than boys'. At first sight this may seem to be surprising, given the reputation that the religious authorities have earned in the past for their abilities in the realms of sex-role stereotyping. The researchers' definition of 'liberal', and their interpretation of its implications, show that they want to hasten the departure of the old 'wife and mother' stereotype. They therefore deplore their discovery that co-educational education, far from lessening the differences between the sexes, actually encourages boys to be boys, and girls to be girls. Moreover, as the attitudes of the principals and staff were much the same in single-sex and mixed schools, they concluded that it was the regime itself, rather than those who manned it, which influenced the outlook of the pupils. They had to allow for the fact that most single-sex schools are Catholic, and this consideration again militated against the idea that 'liberalization' was coming from above. Given that the liberal tendencies of teacher training colleges lead their products to promote co-education, the outlook, however unlikely, is that existing traditions will be reinforced as the number of mixed schools increases.

It is not necessary to share the researchers' despondency as they reluctantly conclude 'that most men and women still see a woman's first commitment as being to her husband and her children'.[37] Although some Irish women have led from the front since before the time of Christ, and the Northern Irish Protestant position on this issue is every bit as conservative as Rome's, Ulster men and women feel that women usually choose to lead from the rear. In this way the fabric of the family is protected, there is less temptation to offload the children on to the state, and prosperity depends on both men and women facing up to domestic responsibilities. Apropos the erosion of traditional attitudes to a woman's role the researchers gloomily end their report with a quotation from Oscar Wilde: 'All women become like their mothers . . . No man does.' Employment statistics justify the gloom only if one believes that a mother's place is in the factory or the office.

7

ATTITUDES AND THEIR OUTCOME: SOUTH AND NORTH

Since the Treaty, women have assumed new responsibilities and roles, some of which have already been mentioned. These have differed in the two parts of Ireland. In a peaceful environment there have been cultural reasons for limiting women's entry into the workplace, and in disturbed areas there have been forces which have involved them all either as victims, spectators or participants. South of the border, a principal contributor to the delineation of a woman's approved area of overt activity made its first appearance in 1929, when the Free State government passed a censorship law which gave a Censorship of Publications Board powers to decide what citizens should be allowed to read. Immediately it could be seen that, though maintenance of Roman Catholic beliefs and standards was the justification given, the banning of books was actually about the role of women in a society which set great store by celibacy. Foreign observers were surprised to see that lists of banned books were not modelled on the Index Librorum Prohibitorum, the official Roman Catholic catalogue of prohibited literature which was eventually abolished in 1966. Far from it; the new clerical state could afford to allow outspoken Protestant publications to appear on the bookshelves. The challenge of sex was another matter.

Eight years later the power of the Censorship Board was greatly strengthened by Article 40 of the new constitution, which made it an offence to publish or utter 'blasphemous, seditious or indecent matter'. Democrats could well be forgiven for focusing their attention on 'blasphemous', since all states prohibit sedition and most citizens either disapprove of pornographic material or feign disapproval of it, even though they cannot agree on a definition of pornography. If they feared that minority rights were at the mercy of Rome's authority, and that the Protestant could no longer protest, they were wrong. It was still permissible to publish the opinion of a Protestant canon that 'the Papacy is the father and mother of totalitarianism ... Hitler merely transferred to the political and social spheres the principles which Rome had developed through centuries of autocracy'.[1] The sexual priority of Irish censorship, over and above what most policemen, social workers or citizens in general would deem to be pornographic, was clarified in the Censorship of

146

Publications Act of 1946. This gave the terms of reference of the five-man Censorship Board, which was to condemn books of three types: those which were indecent or obscene, those which were devoted principally to criminal acts, and those which advocated 'the unnatural prevention of conception or the procurement of abortion or miscarriage or the use of any method, treatment or appliance for the purpose of such prevention or procurement'. Four out of the five members of the Board had to agree for a book to be banned, and much care has been taken over the years either to exclude Protestants altogether or to restrict Protestant representation to one member at a time.

The year 1946 also saw the creation of an Appeal Board, largely because five men, faced with hundreds of books each month, made many blunders. The five censors met and deliberated in secret under the chairmanship of a Catholic priest, and it was not intellectually or even physically possible for them to read all the books which were submitted to them. All that they could do was take notice of allegedly offensive passages underlined by Catholic office employees, or by the Catholic vigilantes who were protesting about something which offended against their moral values. The Appeal Board, another committee of five, at first appeared to be a welcome safety net for the better authors whose work had been condemned out of hand; it lifted the ban on certain works by such writers as Vicki Baum, Pearl Buck, Maura Laverty and Kate O'Brien, and strove to save the land of the cultural revival from becoming the most Philistine country in the western world. But it also was unable to cope with its task. Though it and the Censorship Board shared the same secretary, the two bodies soon fell out – which was no disaster – and the Appeal Board became as autocratic in its way as those whose absurdities it sought to minimize. No appeal could be made against the findings of the Appeal Board, and though its membership liked to encourage the idea that they possessed awareness of literary values, it took them ten years to realize that the moral fibre of the nation was not being threatened by Maura Laverty's *Alone We Embark*.[2]

Failure to ban some books caused almost as much laughter and contempt as did the banning for sixteen years of Shaw's *The Adventures of the Black Girl in her Search for God*. Presumably it was the international fame enjoyed by Joyce's *Ulysses* which made the board ignore several printings, though they kept *Stephen Hero* (the basis of *A Portrait of the Artist as a Young Man*) off the market for a while. But it was books about women, or women's issues, which were most likely to meet with the Irish Goebbels's disapproval. It was wholly in keeping with the Censorship Board's known prejudices, and consistent with its terms of reference, when three works by Marie Stopes were banned: *Birth Control To-day*, *Married Love*, and *Roman Catholic Methods of Birth Control*. And it was not remarkable to find an exclusion order placed on either Havelock Ellis's *Psychology of Sex* or Sigmund Freud's *Collected Papers*. As it developed a routine and a perceptible approach to the ever-increasing torrent of publications, the board seemed most fearful of the substance of serious research and the titles of works of fiction; thus, *Sexual Behaviour in the Human Male* and *Sexual Behaviour in the Human Female*, both by Alfred Kinsey's team, had to go, along with the Church of England's *Threshold of Marriage* and the London *Sunday Chronicle*'s *One Thousand Medical Hints*. Phyllis Bottome's *Under the Skin* sounded *risqué* if not downright pornographic, as did Fannie Hurst's *Anywoman*. Kathleen Winsor's *The Lovers* stood no chance at all, especially as it basked in the reflected glow of the author's better known book, *Forever Amber*. But much of the obscenity proved to be in the mind of the reader. Quite how Monsarrat's *The Cruel Sea* came to be banned in the first place (in October 1951), and then released nine months later has never been satisfactorily explained. In this case the Censorship Board admitted that it had made a mistake. But an error of this type can be rectified in five minutes.

Although use of the board's criteria can be discerned in most of their decisions – if one looks hard enough – it is more difficult to justify their omissions. It used to be said with some humour and a measure of insight that a list of books banned by the Board included all that was worth reading in western literature, and that for an author to be left out was a mark of disgrace. If the number of banned Nobel prizewinners is anything to go by, that seems to be a fair judgement. And yet the greatest contributors to Irish letters have nearly all had an easy ride, despite their commitment to the themes which so disturb the minds of censors. Furthermore, a random sample of recent bannings paints a very different picture from the comparatively rosy one to be seen when the board was lurching hither and thither through its backlog, the cultural heritage of the English-speaking peoples. In the period 1 January 1986 to 11 October 1990, thirty-five books were proscribed, one of them on the ground that it advocated abortion.[3] All the others were said to be 'indecent or obscene', and a number sound as though they are: *Christina's Challenge*, *Christina's Craving*, *Christina's Escapade* and *Christina's Touch*. That prolific author 'Anonymous' is much in evidence, with titles ranging from *Lascivious Scenes* to *More Sexual Positions* and *The Lustful Turk*. The serious observer may still be perturbed, though, to see the number of reputable publishers whose products are damned on these grounds. Thames and Hudson, W. H. Allen, and Hodder and Stoughton are not widely known as purveyors of pornography. None of them was responsible for the list's one serious title, *Kama Sutra* (Illustrated). But Thames and Hudson's one item was entitled *Erotic Art of India*.

Holy Ireland is busy defending womanhood from various threats, real or imagined, and it is pertinent to ask where different sections of the community stand on this form of protection. The Irish intelligentsia, like all articulate beings worldwide who are not fighting on behalf of the Fascist or Bolshevik causes, find the whole apparatus of censorship both annoying and frightening. As the Hierarchy should have realized, at least after the Berlin bonfire of 1933 (where many of the same authors were condemned), the burning and the banning of books is one of the ugliest symptoms of a disease which they have always professed to despise, namely creeping totalitarianism. Things eased to a degree in the new spirit generated by the Second Vatican Council, though some say[4] that the change for the better came about more because Irish diplomats abroad were shamed by their country's reputation for philistinism and Soviet-style intolerance than by an actual change of heart. Whatever the cause, in 1967 the Censorship Act was amended, and, subject to reimposition of a ban, if the board thought fit, books other than those banned for advocating contraception or abortion were reprieved after twelve years of prohibition. Some 5,000 titles were immediately released, and the board tried to save its face a little by rebanning a number of them, including J. P. Donleavy's *The Ginger Man*.

As a group, naturally writers have always objected to censorship. Joyce attacked the idea head-on in much that he wrote. Edna O'Brien wrote regardless of any official strictures and made a public stand on the issue. But then, although those who write often claim to reflect the emotions and opinions of society at large, they are seldom 'ordinary' or 'typical' themselves. However much they steep themselves in their subject-matter, there comes a point when they have to distance themselves from it. Until recently, though the Irish liked to read they were not a book-buying race and, apart from the liberated minds of the few, the beliefs held by anyone willing to serve on a Censorship Board, that is to say his prejudices about women's sexuality, were certainly supported by the rural Irish, and by first generation city-dwellers. The women of Ireland, during the hey-day of the Censorship Board, shared the assumptions of the five men about the burden of guilt which they would carry should they depart from the Church's teaching and behave as women did in the banned books. Commentators are always saying that the Irish are conditioned by history: a tautology if ever there was one. The Censorship Board has been a coherent manifestation of the conditioning process, but has functioned as though history was something which stands still. Although in the sixty years or more of its existence it has been composed almost entirely of men, it has helped an Irish woman's view of Irish womanhood – myth and reality – to perpetuate itself. Apart from this, its sole achievement has been to keep pornography underground; it has changed nothing.

Writing has become one of the occupations in which women enter the market-place with much the same opportunities as men. Nevertheless, as the lists of censored books confirm, fewer women than men fell foul of censorship law. They were not favoured because of their sex; there were fewer of them because of their traditional priorities, and they often approached their subject-matter with more subtlety than male authors were sometimes wont to do. The censors were defending womanhood as they saw it and the sex of the author was of no concern to them. Moreover the work of the board was reinforced by a far more effective and sinister form of censorship, which usually took place in secret. For, though the literate population bought few books one of the good legacies of the Union had been a network of libraries, and these were the people's source of literature. It was here that local officials did their best to counter possible consequences of the constitution's failure to ban anti-Catholic books. In the most famous example of censorship at this additional level, the fears were, in fact, the same as those which the national board reflected: that the woman's role, as defined by Irish Catholicism, would be debased. As the key Inquisitor, the Dean of Tuam, put it, 'The views of Catholics and Protestants, especially of late years, on such subjects as birth control and divorce are at variance'.[5] He therefore challenged the appointment of a Protestant woman as a county librarian at the Carnegie Library in Castlebar, County Mayo.

Among the interesting features of this *cause célèbre* is its timing. Miss Letitia Dunbar-Harrison was appointed by William Cosgrave's government as Librarian in 1931, that is, before the censors' powers were increased by the new constitution and by the 1946 Act. To an impartial observer, she seemed ideally suited for the post; her professional training was appropriate and she was a graduate of Trinity College, Dublin. But Catholic Action lost no time in persuading Mayo County Library Committee to refuse to endorse her appointment, arguing that her knowledge of the Irish language was inadequate, and that Catholic rules about books could not be appreciated by non-Catholics. The matter came to a head when the county council supported its library committee and refused to install the government's appointee. At first the government reacted with admirable fairness and political courage; it abolished Mayo County Council. However, as on many other issues affecting women, politicians stood no chance if they attempted to overrule the decisions of priests. Father Denis O'Connor, chairman of the library com-mittee, stood firmly against the appointment; there were demonstrations and parades, and a county-wide boycott of Carnegie Library books ensued. The government backed down, allowed Mayo to have a Catholic librarian, and Letitia Dunbar-Harrison was given a post at the Military Library in Dublin. A dangerous precedent had been set, and its implication was appreciated too well by the other twenty-five counties.

The censoring of literature served to release the female mind from awareness of supposed and real burdens imposed on Irish women by the Church, and it confirmed Irish men in their ancient perception or misconception of the relationship between the sexes. By eliminating from the library service personnel who might dissent from the national consensus, the priestly caste had found a way to extend censorship to books which offended in ways which were not banned by the state. Now there was nothing to stop full implementation of the Vatican's censorship rules and, when authors had offended against Irish Catholicism's more stringent standards, their books too would be excluded from the shelves. Sources of dissent from a narrowly-prescribed norm were few: a few brave booksellers and *The Irish Times* gave democracy a voice. Otherwise ignorance was fast becoming a basic requirement for a newly-independent member of the international community. For those born and educated within the Free State or the Republic old prejudices masqueraded as received wisdom. But every family had its exile, and it was only a matter of time before democratic influences would be brought in from the outside world. Totalitarianism – as Stalin appreciated – is not compatible with freedom to travel or to emigrate. Nor in the Irish context is it compatible with six Ulster counties enjoying freedoms denied to other Irish citizens. The border was not the Berlin Wall; all manner of truths and falsehoods were bound to penetrate the Republic, by land, sea or via the air waves.

The libraries of independent Ireland have always been one of the major strengths of its adult education, but in the culture which they have purveyed has been buried a hidden curriculum. A comment made about the Church and the schools can be taken to apply in some measure to a censored library service: 'Her control of education ensures a self-perpetuating majority for their [sic] teachings – helped by resort to threats of hell-fire for the dissenter'.[6] Does her resistance to some of the demands of feminism mean that 'In the Republic the woman has had but one role. She is the sow and her farrow ... mere breeding stock'?[7] If there is truth in this indictment, those responsible for unofficial censorship in the libraries must take their share of responsibility for silencing dissenters of past and present, Gael and democrat. It is for the women themselves to weigh up the merits and demerits of the traditions into which they have been born. Their oldest heritage encourages them to play a dominant role in family affairs; Rome places a different emphasis on the duties of a wife and mother. Irish feminism, which has not been well-represented on library shelves, challenges both constituents of Irish culture. By seeking to minimize the influence of the women's liberation movement, the powers-that-be in Ireland have given it the strength that comes to all movements which are driven underground.

What actually appeared on library shelves sometimes made a decidedly pernicious contribution to the moral climate. Diatribes against abortion were understandable; strictures against 'mixed marriages' created attitudes which undermined natural bonds between the sexes and harmed community relations in general. Looking back from the end of the century it is not hard to appreciate the harm done by works such as *The People's Priest*, which appeared in 1951, before its author John C. Heenan had acquired his red hat. The book demonstrated clearly the Church's lack of respect for individual human rights and for civil authority at that time:

If the non-Catholic is especially hostile it will do no harm to inform the Catholic girl in his presence, that if he insists on marriage elsewhere the priest will be prepared later on to marry her to a good Catholic ... [and] ... when it is made clear that the Catholic partner regards the union as no marriage at all the non-Catholic can often be induced to see reason.[8]

The future Cardinal Archbishop was convinced that 'mixed marriages' were unnatural, and did everything in his power to prevent such unions from occurring. In the Irish environment – of Liverpool or the Republic – his views helped to destroy personal relationships. Despite *The People's Priest*'s disrespectful attitude to civil law, it was safely outside the scope of the Censorship Board.

Access to, and conditions at, the workplace are other aspects of women's rights that have differed greatly in the two Irelands. Here, for once, though politics and religion are important factors, they do not eclipse economic and social considerations. As Ulster has been the seat of the island's industrial development for centuries, and women have always outnumbered men in the linen industry, that is where the most effective pioneering activity was carried out by exceptional women. The most significant of these, Saidie Patterson, was different from most of the others of her sex whose efforts have brought social benefits to the province, in that they were either middle or upper class. Saidie Patterson's working-class parents lived in Belfast's Protestant Shankill, where she was born in 1906 and where she lived all her life. It does not appear to be the likeliest locality for an ecumenically-minded pacifist's personality to flower, but then not everything in Northern Ireland fits into the stereotyping that makes for rapid reportage. The Patterson family were Methodists, and their faith sustained them through several crises which occurred during the eldest girl's childhood. Her father, a blacksmith, died at the age of 27, and her mother soon remarried. The new husband, a widower, brought with him five children, to add to the Pattersons' three, and his health rapidly declined until he was made physically helpless by a nervous complaint. It was an over-crowded house with no male breadwinner and heavy responsibilities fell on the mother and the senior daughter. Out-working brought in meagre takings. When conditions were extremely hard after the First World War, Saidie Patterson started work as a weaver in a linen factory.

A combination of her upbringing and her work experience made Saidie Patterson a Christian Socialist for whom an early goal was the achievement for women of the benefits of trade union membership. When Beatrice Webb had visited Belfast, she commented that the male craftsmen of the province were 'contemptuous and indifferent to the women earning miserable wages in the linen factories',[9] and working-class men generally regarded the trade union as a male preserve. The Patterson method of approach to this situation alternated between diplomacy and confrontation. Few dared step out of line in the struggle for improved wages and conditions, lest they lose not only their wage, but the tied factory house in which so many workers lived. There was, therefore, a great need for solidarity; gender divisions as well as sectarian ones had to be removed. Saidie Patterson kept confrontation as the last weapon in the arsenal and set about persuading men to widen the definition of trade unionism in their own interests; the numerical imbalance in the linen industry was sufficient argument for removing barriers, and the point was soon taken. It was harder for her to persuade the management to recognize the equality on the shop floor of the female worker. But, as a shop steward, she was well placed to demand a guaranteed wage structure and the abolition of 'waiting time', whereby, if the work opportunity did not come at once, the woman hung about unpaid until it did.

Looking back on the industrial relations period of her career, it is with some misgivings that one remembers that the main achievements of her life were initiated by what history could interpret as two betrayals. In 1940, when the United Kingdom was facing up to the forces of the Third Reich, and the Free State was basking in its neutrality, she was encouraged by Ernest Bevin to call a strike at her employers, William Ewart and Sons, the vast textile firm. That was a remarkable enough initiative for a member of the loyalist tradition to take, but the reason for striking has also lost favour with democratic socialists: to achieve their long-term aims, the shop steward and her followers were attempting to force the management to adopt a 'closed shop' policy. It was the only time in her life when she became more socialist than Christian, and sacrificed the rights of the individual workers in the interests of the collective good, as she saw it. Although an outcome of current trade union orthodoxy, insistence that Ewart's refuse to employ non-union labour was an undemocratic act. Given her subsequent exemplary record on human rights, it is charitable to put this aberration, which remained integral to trade unionist dogma for many years, down to her lack of a coherent political philosophy. She had the welfare of all workers, especially the unfairly treated female workforce, at heart, and at this stage in her development allowed the end to justify the means. Two thousand women paraded in the streets of Belfast after she had persuaded them to 'tighten their belts and make ends meet somehow',[10] which meant subsisting on twelve shillings a week strike pay.

However, she had reckoned without another who had effective powers of persuasion that made sacrifices sound attractive. At this time Churchill 'consorted with' Ernest Bevin, as he put it.[11] Already the by-no-means-pacifist socialist had obtained trade union permission to become Minister of Labour and National Service. When he consented to join the War Cabinet, it signified the moment when 'the trade unionists cast their slowly-framed, jealously-guarded rules and privileges upon the altar where wealth, rank, privilege, and property had already been laid'.[12] Bevin, seeing the effects of the strike on morale, reversed his position, and a disappointed shop steward had to explain to the women why the strike had to be called off. She reckoned that the strikers had lost a battle, but had won their war: 'Women were now organized and were fully aware that the factories could not work without them, and they were also determined to pursue their cause whatever the cost'.[13] She was right about this other war. Within weeks, negotiations with management led to 'a revolution in working conditions in earning and welfare'.[14] It is probably not naïve to see in the management's response that the motives that had led to an unexpected capitulation were appreciated. As happens when a nation is faced by an external foe, class barriers were lowered. By the end of 1940, the shop steward could report wage increases of 15 per cent, holidays with pay, minimum rates for women on time work, and introduction of sickness benefit funds and accident and legal aid schemes. As a result of her part in these achievements, keenly observed by Bevin, she moved on to a larger stage as the only full-time woman officer of the Transport Union in Ireland.

For the remainder of the Second World War, Saidie Patterson was able to work towards the improvement of working conditions and the welfare of women and children in Great Britain and Ireland. She no longer confined her attention to Belfast but, although her horizons were wide, her principal concern was always for Northern Ireland. Looking to the future, she was involved in many groups which sought changes in the law which would ensure permanent improvements. Co-ordination of the efforts of women's groups was essential if progress was to be made, and to this end in 1943 the Standing Conference of Women's Organizations of Northern Ireland was formed. A federal body, it brought together thirty-five women's groups to press the government for social and civic reforms, anticipating the letter and the spirit of the Beveridge Report. It commissioned investigations into health and welfare amenities, and the published results showed that the figures for infant mortality and for deaths attributable to tuberculosis were far worse than for the rest of the United Kingdom. As soon as the war was over, many of the women of Northern Ireland adopted a similar political commitment to that which was to produce the ill-fated Mother and Child Scheme in the South. This was the time when devolution had some obvious advantages over independence in Ireland. But achievement of social benefits is an integral part of political activity, and politics in this divided community meant that some feared the stabilizing effects of the Welfare State.

At first the specifically political activities of Saidie Patterson were wholly predictable. She worked hard in the 1945 and 1949 elections to try to improve the Northern Ireland Labour Party's representation at Stormont. In 1945 she was mainly responsible for getting its candidate, Bob Getwood, elected for North Belfast; in 1949 he was defeated. Then, in the 1950s, she moved forward into promoting a 'United Ulster', hoping that the Labour Party, of which she was now Treasurer, would come into power as the true non-sectarian voice of the people. In 1956 she became the first woman to be elected Party Chairman. She began to see the same flaws in society which were to be identified by Bernadette Devlin; the orange and green of the province seemed to her to have too much in common with white and black of the southern states of the USA. But, instead of advocating class war, she worked hard to bring together the disparate elements of society. She preached the doctrine of unity, which meant preserving the link with the rest of the United Kingdom on the basis of

Protestant–Catholic unity within the province. At the time this was not an unrealistic approach though, as the province enjoyed a share of the wave of affluence that swept over the British Isles, it was the Unionist Party which attracted some votes that previously had gone to nationalist candidates. Then, as 'you never had it so good' failed to get through to victims of discrimination, the civil rights movement got under way.

In the years that followed, legislative improvement in the field of women's rights in the workplace and elsewhere occurred while community relations declined. The present legal position may not be ideal, but it is much more just than when Saidie Patterson took up the cause. The Equal Pay Act (Northern Ireland), 1970, which was amended in 1984 following infringement proceedings taken against the United Kingdom by the European Commission, had paved the way for the Sex Discrimination (Northern Ireland) Order, 1976, as amended in 1988. This not only makes discrimination on the grounds of sex or marital status unlawful in employment, but covers many other matters, including education, housing, credit facilities, goods and services. The province's watchdog, the Equal Opportunities Commission for Northern Ireland, has a wide and demanding role to fulfil. The commission had been quick to see a serious flaw in the Equal Pay (Northern Ireland) Act, whereby the principle of 'material difference' could be used to reduce a woman's wage in relation to a man's. It therefore lost no time in recommending that an 'equal value' clause find its way on to the statute book, in order to comply with European equality law. When the 1984 amending order was made, fortuitously it brought Northern Ireland into line with existing law in the Republic.

The Republic's more enlightened legislation on women's pay went some way towards detracting from its reputation for dragging its heels on some other aspects of women's welfare. The Anti-Discrimination (Pay) Act, 1974, in addition to its 'equal value' clause, declared that discriminatory collective agreements made since it became law were automatically null and void. The position in Northern Ireland is not so simple; before 1988 anyone wishing to challenge such agreements had to take the employer to the Industrial Court. But, in the Sex Discrimination (Northern Ireland) Order, 1988, the government removed the power of the Industrial Court to review any discriminatory provisions of collective agreements. This amendment, according to the commission, is potentially contrary to European Community law. In addition it must be said that rather too much falls on the shoulders of aggrieved parties in the North. There, as also happens in the South, individual equal pay and sex discrimination cases are pursued through industrial tribunals. In the South, though, the 1974 Act provided for the appointment of equality officers with powers to investigate. Unfortunately this merit of southern provision was offset by the fact that the decisions of the Republic's tribunals did not set precedents; with each case being judged in isolation the

WE ARE BUT WOMEN

door was open to anomalies and discrepancies. The legislation of both regimes is marred by a considerable flaw: a woman seeking equal pay cannot make comparisons with employed men other than those on the pay roll of her own or an associated employer.

While it is essential to have a sound framework of legislation to guarantee their fair treatment when economic necessity or free choice takes women into the workplace, the actual decision to go there brings its own problems. In each individual case these are likely to bring to the fore the tensions which arise when there is conflict between roles traditionally accepted by and for women in the different Irish cultures. In Ireland social attitudes have always carried more weight than law, and liberalizing influences from outside have sometimes led to a re-examination of the duties of mothers and wives. There are certain parallels here with the abortion issue. For instance, just as it is generally assumed that the majority European stance on the foetus must be right, it seems to be assumed by many supporters of equal rights in the workplace that the needs of children are secondary. It can be agreed without much difficulty that once a woman is at work, she should enjoy every right enjoyed by an equivalent male worker. But are there obligations which should take precedence over her aims or ambitions as a worker? The weight of emphasis in a survey can tell as much about the researchers as about their subject. Thus, one's suspicion that 'the facilities for the care of children of working mothers are poor'[15] can be read to mean that it would be better if far more mothers worked, is confirmed when one finds the words 'disappointing' and 'encouraging' elsewhere in summaries and conclusions.

It has been found that in Northern Ireland 'the younger male population do not seem to be as imbued with the spirit of liberalism as their female counterparts'[16] and, as previously noted, researchers do not hide their disappointment that they can scarcely find any 'decrease in traditional values'. Sometimes there are clues as to what may be meant by 'liberal', as when 'Women's marital status influences scores on the attitude scales, with single and divorced/separated women being significantly more liberal than either married women or widows'.[17] The same report says that Catholics appear to be 'somewhat more liberal' than Protestants, and comments on the widespread agreement across professional groups that having children 'will severely disrupt a woman's career'.[18] A questionnaire had been sent to male and female members of these groups, and in their replies many of those selected indicated that they felt 'women should invariably place child rearing, and often looking after their husbands, ahead of any other commitments'.[19] Nevertheless, it was confidently asserted that 'Women professionals are far more liberal than their male counterparts.'[20]

For present purposes the significance of the report lies in its overall conclusion that traditional attitudes are not greatly threatened, at least not amongst the law-abiding majority. If one feels that family stability lies at the centre of a well-ordered community, and that divorce, abortion and single parents are numbered among the threats, then one may be relieved. If, on the other hand, one believes that a woman's self-esteem is enhanced by the liberalizing effect of casting off some of the responsibilities of motherhood, one may feel frustrated. Unfortunately, though, the law-abiding majority, who have never had any reason to be complacent about their traditional values – which have sometimes led them to deny basic freedoms to others – are under more serious threat. The Irish way of life, a complex web of traditions, is under continual attack from those who believe in imposing their scheme of things by violent means. The role of women in their organizations has become increasingly important in recent years.

Within organizations committed to the violent overthrow of existing power structures in Ireland, there have been changes of roles and attitudes which date from the split between the Officials and the Provisionals in 1970. As the Provisionals became the main vehicle for what was increasingly termed the 'armed struggle', they found it necessary not only to accommodate women as activists but to come to terms with ideas and issues dear to the hearts of the sort of woman who is prepared to use Semtex or a gun. She is not made in the mould of the first members of Cumann na mBan, although the women who share her ideals and meet regularly are still nominally members of the same rebel association. She is 'liberalized', and some of the older members of the IRA have found it difficult to face up to the implications of her membership. When Seamus Twomey, commander of PIRA's Belfast brigade, was arrested by the Irish police in 1977, he had with him a so-called staff report which showed that the Provisionals intended to try to adopt a new attitude to women. The document urged that Cumann na mBan should be disbanded and that its 'best' women be inducted into PIRA. 'Best' can be assumed to include suitability for membership of 'active service units' and, as events in Gibraltar were to show, ability to take command in the field.

Changes in attitude and policy were brought about after 1970 by complaints from women who had absorbed many ideas about womanhood which had surfaced in the 1960s. The Officials had disbanded that part of Cumann na mBan which opted to face the future under their auspices; and these women, who were supposedly fully integrated members of this part of the republican movement had found that their training was not as thorough as that given to men, that they were far less likely to gain promotion, and that many men were openly hostile to their being employed in any responsible capacity. Those who went into the Provisionals made up a separate formation under the direct command of PIRA's Army Council, and they felt from the start that they were kept well away from the decision-making process. Although some saw active service 'they were not part of the IRA but merely useful adjuncts'.[21] While a few exceptional women became leaders, most had 'to combine their political commitments with domestic concerns'.[22] Disillusioned Provisional women began to feel that they were a token presence. As long as they were known to exist, the Provisionals' failure to adopt a positive and coherent approach to women's issues could be glossed over.

There has never been much open debate in republican journals. Correspondents are not encouraged to contribute items presenting the case for anything other than the party line; consequently it is reasonably easy to make sure that few indiscretions occur. However, in 1974 a small item appeared in *Republican News* condemning a proposal to change the rules governing the sale of contraceptives in Ireland. It was argued that no matter whether such reforms emanated from Dublin or Westminster they were part of an attempt to seduce young Provisionals from their duties 'with a surfeit of drink, drugs, fags and sex'.[23] Such a sentiment could only alienate 'liberal' women who would seek to combine their feminism with their nationalism. It also went against the groundswell of opinion that was coming to see contraception as the solution to the problem of abortion. At its conference in 1979, Sinn Féin began to come to grips with the dilemmas inherent in showing its hand on such matters. Though the IRA had long been proscribed by the Roman Catholic Church, it remained conscious that most of its members had come from Catholic families, and that parts of its nationalist aims were shared by Northern Ireland's minority faith. It therefore tried to do something for which it has always lacked talent: it attempted to compromise. The outcome was not very successful. Although it decided to look into the possibility of Sinn Féin establishing a women's department, when the birth control issue was put to the vote, the decision was that Sinn Féin stood for contraception on demand 'under community control'.[24]

A year later the women's department was established, and Sinn Féin's Commission on Women's Affairs drew up a policy document on abortion. *Women in the New Ireland*, as originally drafted by the commission, managed to face both ways quite well. It took the line: 'we recognize that it is an indictment of society that any woman should feel the need to avail herself of abortion ... we are ... opposed to the attitudes and forces in society that impel women to have abortions'.[25] But the Sinn Féin leadership was becoming more pragmatic than it had been for decades, and the sympathy of the Catholics in general had become more important to it than appeasement of its feminist activists. It insisted on insertion of an unequivocal 'We are opposed to abortion'. Its wisdom was to be acknowledged at Sinn Féin's 1980 conference, when the majority endorsed amendment of the text to read 'We are totally opposed to abortion'. Thus the new generation of IRA feminists found themselves facing a similar choice to their predecessors' in the movement: which comes first, nationalism or feminism? Like Maud Gonne, they chose nationalism. But the day was soon to dawn when, on this issue, no choice would have to be made.

Sinn Féin had to reckon with the uncomfortable truth that the feminists within its ranks were being outflanked on the abortion and sex discrimination front by the Northern Ireland Women's Rights Movement (NIWRM). A largely middle-class group, it pursued its feminist aims by means wholly unacceptable to republicans: it demanded parity of rights with the rest of the United Kingdom, thus recognizing the legitimacy of partition. This was going too far even for those grown accustomed to the end justifying the means. The nationalist radicals who had been fellow travellers for a time soon broke away to found another organization, the Socialist Women's Group. The crunch came when the NIWRM's leaders committed two heretical acts; they supported the Peace People and they criticized the Troops Out Movement. But organizations incorporating 'Socialist' in their title often attract idealists, and the Socialist Women's Group was no exception. It spawned yet another group, the Belfast Women's Collective, which left the academics behind as it plunged into the ghettos demanding improved child-care facilities, employment opportunities and an end to all forms of discrimination against women. It identified the British connection as the source of all ills, and soon begat Women Against Imperialism. The circle was now almost complete; for these anti-imperialists had been whittled down to women with much the same beliefs as the feminist Provisionals. They were socialist, anti-sexist, and anti-British. They differed from the Collective only to the extent that they did not share the parent organization's fear that nationalism might swallow up feminist yearnings. They laboured, and still labour, to educate republican men, even going so far as to picket republican public houses which sometimes exclude females. High on their agenda is improvement in the conditions of imprisoned nationalist women.

The seemingly endless proliferation of women's groups started with the renewed troubles which arose from the civil rights demonstrations and counter-demonstrations. Then, after the IRA had achieved the first of its two principal aims, the suspension of Stormont, the pace quickened. The imposition of direct rule in 1972 had given the impression, quite correctly, that the IRA was calling the tune. The Provisionals had always regarded the failure of the devolved legislature as the essential precursor to their ultimate victory; when it happened minds were concentrated, each shade of opinion led to a search for allies, and some means of voicing fears and aspirations was needed by all who were sufficiently worried about the future to want to influence events. The rebels had many subdivisions, and so had those who favoured the British connection, and those who simply wanted peace. Increased sectarian polarization which followed the closure of the local parliament made it necessary for the peace-seeking organizations to redouble their efforts, and one of them, Women Together, invited Saidie Patterson (who had retired from her trade union work) to become its chairman.

Women Together had been founded in 1970 by Ruth Agnew, a Protestant cleaner in Belfast Gas Works, who was joined by Monica Patterson (no relation), a Roman Catholic English woman with much experience of administration. The organization became a movement which rapidly gained momentum. It was fundamentally working class and ecumenical in outlook, and its early success lay in the common bond between women who were the main victims of violence. The middle classes had never found any difficulty in bridging ideological gaps; strife in Northern Ireland is traditionally a matter for the workers, many of whom felt that they had nothing to lose and much to gain from the collapse of the status quo. The working-class women formulated a few deceptively simple aims which, but for the acceleration of the troubles that was caused by Stormont's dissolution, were practical enough to have stabilized society. The first two really summarized Women Together's *raison d'être*: 'To bring together women who believe that violence with all its heartbreaks must be banished from Northern Ireland' and 'To give them the corporate strength to resist undesirable pressures and to use their influence for peace in their homes, their street and their neighbourhood'.[26] Often their activities have been little more than informal gatherings of Catholic and Protestant fellow sufferers seeking reassurance, and in this respect they have differed little from Women of the Cross, whose members have been widowed in the Troubles. But Women Together has a far broader appeal to those who have so far been able to survive the degradations of ghetto life.

Saidie Patterson remained chairman of Women Together until 1976, when she became its vice-president. While she was in the chair the organization co-existed with a host of small Christian organizations, each striving in its own way to achieve much the same goal. All found, until one particular tragedy occurred, that the prestige attaching to the Provisionals' elimination of Northern Ireland's legislature, and the PIRA's physical grip on substantial portions of territory, made dissipation of fears and hatreds a difficult task. In August 1976, though, three Catholic children were killed in West Belfast, and their aunt Mairead Corrigan (now Maguire) soon found herself preaching peace in the Catholic districts of the city. She was joined in her crusade by Betty Williams, and there was a wave of sympathy from Protestants as well as Catholics that went a long way towards creating the united society that others were fighting so hard to destroy. The Peace Women, as they were called until the organization they inspired was officially designated the Peace People, gave birth to Northern Ireland's greatest peace initiative, as all the existing women's organizations rallied to its support. Characteristically Saidie Patterson, regarded as a peace veteran in her own right, responded to the call, and the contribution she was called upon to make was, with one exception, the most famous happening of the short-lived time of peace.

It was hoped to begin the destruction of centuries-old illusions and prejudices in a manner peculiar to Ulster. In the season of marches and ill will, when bellicose gestures are made, Catholics of the Falls Road were to parade by invitation in the Protestant Shankill. Saidie Patterson canvassed the

Shankill Protestants personally, and she persuaded the Catholics not to carry banners; she also arranged for children to lay wreaths at spots on the route where people had been killed. On a hot day in August, thousands of Catholics, led by Mairead Corrigan and Betty Williams, ventured into the Shankill Road, where thousands of Protestants awaited them. A bloodbath did not ensue; instead some 50,000 people, most of them women, behaved as though they were all part of one united community. Participation by nuns and priests may have helped to allay some fears, on both sides, but subsequent events were to show that a clerical presence does not guarantee peace, even in Holy Ireland.

Today Northern Irish commentators well placed to know the truth say that the award of the Nobel Peace Prize to the Peace Women, in their personal capacity, destroyed the movement which they founded. This is an easy judgement to make in the light of certain apparent consequences; it is not, though, altogether fair. By the time that the Shankill Protestants had decided to make a return march up the Falls Road, the Provisionals had already realized that their efforts to destabilize what they perceived to be an illegitimate statelet were being undermined by a collection of amateurs. The ringleaders of this spearhead of the peace movement, Corrigan and Williams, had had no previous experience of public affairs, and yet their presence moved people to discard mental and physical barricades. Their sincerity was doing more harm to the violent arm of the republican cause than the British security forces could hope to achieve. So, when the Shankill Protestants arrived in the Falls Road, they found that the Provisionals would not be caught off their guard a second time. One error was understandable: who would have thought that Saidie Patterson's precautions would prevent a bloody reception being given to those who trod outside jealously guarded territories? This time Provisional intervention managed to sever the fragile bonds which had been made between the two communities. Among the injured were Roman Catholic and Protestant clergy; Saidie Patterson, whose life was saved by a group of Catholic women, suffered a spinal injury.

Another organization dedicated to creating a united community owes its existence to the initiative of an exceptional woman. Women Caring Trust was created in 1972 by Lady Fisher, an Ulster Protestant (formerly Patricia Ford) who, as Unionist MP for North Down from 1953 to 1955, had been the first woman to represent Northern Ireland at Westminster. As with the Peace Women, the spark which ignited Women Caring was a specific tragedy, though one which was not especially different from many others in the year that Northern Ireland lost its autonomy. The death of an innocent bystander, the widowed mother of several children, led to a peace meeting being convened in Ballymurphy, a well-known IRA stronghold. Lady Fisher contacted the meeting's convenor, a Mrs Fagin, and was encouraged to attend, despite her different religious and political affiliations. She took no account of the serious risk to her life caused as much by her presence in the locality as by her participation in a controversial act of protest. When the gathering was broken up by IRA women, some protesters fled to Mrs Fagin's house, where discussion of the main issue, the welfare of ghetto children in Ballymurphy and throughout Northern Ireland, moved Lady Fisher to take decisive action. She immediately began to agitate for funds to help save the most vulnerable of the innocent victims of the Troubles, and asked her friend Lady Tilney to join her in the setting up of a fund-raising trust. Lady Tilney agreed at a stage in her life which made her of even greater value to Women Caring; she was in the process of converting to Roman Catholicism. From the beginning the trust has always had a Catholic and a Protestant as co-Chairmen.

Although Lady Fisher was a politician, her achievements in this new field were, in universal terms, wholly non-political. The trust serves humanitarian ideals, it is ecumenical, its beneficiaries are selected only on the basis of individual or communal need. Nevertheless it is remarkable that its work has been so successful in Northern Ireland, for its projects are calculated to heal the injured minds of the young and to protect them from the effects of violence, including social deprivation. As an instrument of reconciliation it is an agent for the stabilization of Northern Ireland, and as such it can only work against the interests of organizations which want the social infra-structure of the province to collapse. Voluntary Service Belfast vets the schemes, which have ranged from provision of mobile playrooms in the form of specially-equipped buses to supporting integrated education, by helping to found Lagan College, or by providing integrated holidays at Glebe House, near the Mountains of Mourne. Unlike politicized organizations which wax and wane, and sometimes die, the trust is built on such solid rock that it should outlive future constitutional changes, whether they be for better or for worse.

In the unsettled period before Women Caring Trust was founded outside the political framework, other women were at the centre of the realignment of politics in the North that preceded the suspension of Stormont. In 1967 Dr Ian Paisley's wife, Eileen, had been elected to Belfast City Council as a Protestant Unionist, and by 1971 the Protestant Unionists had five seats. Their party was the product of Protestant fears of a Unionist and Westminster betrayal of Irish loyalists, but its sectarian title was unfortunate. Despite the heat of the rhetoric that was generated by official Unionist 'appeasement',[27] it was a cool decision by Dr Paisley 'that the needs of the country were greater than the needs of any political party'[28] which led to the disbandment of the Protestant Unionist Party and the formation in its place of the Democratic Unionist Party. In the brief period of full-blooded devolution which remained the DUP was to become the official opposition at Stormont, and when direct rule led to an attempt at power-sharing by means of an assembly with seats and cabinet posts guaranteed to minorities who agreed to participate, the executive was brought down by the DUP's support of the loyalist strike of 1974. Another attempt at power-sharing, the result of the Constitutional Convention of 1975, despite built-in safeguards for minorities, was defeated by the Social Democratic and Labour Party's insistence on retaining the quota system which had been central to the functioning of the Assembly. Eileen Paisley served in the Assembly and in the Convention.

As Dr Paisley's name has been associated with the constitutional hard-line approach of Protestant loyalists, it is worth enquiring where members of his party, particularly female members, stand on the women's issues that embarrass so many of those who accept 'Rome Rule' in Ireland. It has already been noted that in general the political parties of Northern Ireland, whether out of conviction or expediency, have seen fit to form their own women's sections. The Democratic Unionist Party has not followed this trend. Its view is that women should be fully integrated, and not treated as a separate species. In 1987, though, Rhonda Paisley, the party leader's daughter, asked if she might create the post of 'Spokesperson for Women's Issues' and was allowed to do so. Her attitudes and opinions, which formerly found expression on the environmental front and are increasingly heard on matters relating to the arts as well as women's rights, do not indicate any of the bigotry and narrowness that biased coverage of events has caused to be associated with the men and women of the Ulster majority. Nevertheless, one republican woman[29] made it plain that merely to interview Paisley's daughter was to cast doubt on one's integrity as a researcher into Irish affairs. She provided a classic illustration of the extent to which Northern Ireland's tragedies are the result of a refusal to listen to, let alone respect, alternative ideas. (In private conversation the same woman, a widely respected contributor to the Irish debate, objected to political killings in Northern Ireland being described as acts of murder; in her vocabulary they were 'executions'.)

Rhonda Paisley's personal opinions, because of her background, tell us more about Northern Ireland today than do her utterances as a party spokeswoman or her electioneering activities. To those who prejudge individuals and groups, she should be the product of quintessentially 'dour' Protestantism, to use an epithet commonly tagged to Scots and Ulstermen by outsiders. As with all of unionist persuasion, one political issue – the province's survival as an autonomous or semi-autonomous entity – is bound to eclipse all others, and her views on it might be assumed to be predictable; her opinions on other matters could too easily go unappreciated, partly because the assessments of so many commentators are based upon preconceived false notions: about Presbyterians and about women in Ulster. One preconception, based on a false perception of her upbringing, might be that Rhonda Paisley would be a narrow conformist. But even on the main political and religious issues which confront the Democratic Unionist Party, Miss Paisley has her own reservations about the way ahead. Whilst recognizing that one of the slogans of her father's party (and of the Official Unionist Party) '"Ulster is British" is not a lip cry from the majority – it is the heart beat of the people',[30] she hankers after something different. 'My political ideal for Ulster is not as part of the Union, but as an independent state'.[31] This 'immature political dream', as she calls it, would be realized not by means of the military coup, which some Protestant extremists favour, but by negotiations with Westminster. In this she is not to be confused with the 'illogical political nonentities' currently engaged in this quest; she is not a campaigner for independence. 'I believe in the ballot box and in Ulster the ballot box makes no indication as yet to our leadership that [the electors] desire any status other than British within the Union.'[32] But she has not been alone in contemplating the day when Northern Ireland might sever its remaining links with the rest of the United Kingdom. At least one former Labour Party cabinet minister at Stormont[33] has voiced his conviction that complete independence is an economically viable proposition, and one which would find support among the province's pacifist loyalists.

Although she is her father's most loyal supporter, Rhonda Paisley owes as much if not more of her decision to be involved in Northern Ireland's politics to her mother's example. She feels that the renewed Troubles have restricted the scope that women theoretically enjoy, which is certainly the case, despite the broadening of scope that has occurred in the illegal, paramilitary field. She is not averse to the idea that men and women have different roles to play in society, attributing part of the blame for current security problems to male aggression. Women, she says, are more constructive in their attitudes, and more practical in their approach to day-to-day issues. In her opinion both Roman Catholicism and 'the very fundamentalist strain in Protestantism in the North'[34] tend to muzzle women. Nevertheless women are, to use her word, gaining 'credibility'; they play an equal role in policy-making and in the practicalities of politics, although their representation in parliament is nil and their county council representation is minimal. Her own contribution to public life and to social welfare has been 'credible' enough. In 1985, at the age of 25, she was elected councillor for the Laganbank area of Belfast, and the following year became the city's Lady Mayoress. Her most valuable social work has been the running of a drop-in centre for the young unemployed and drug addicts. She has also done something to disabuse some citizens of the Irish Republic of their prejudices about northern attitudes; her acceptance of an invitation to host a Dublin-transmitted television programme enabled her to reveal aspects of Paisleyism hitherto unsuspected.

A summary of Rhonda Paisley's views[35] on some of the ways to heal Northern Ireland's wounds does not reveal any evidence of bigotry. Like her father, she has some distaste for Roman Catholicism; she has none for the individual Roman Catholic. She believes that there should be no denominational schooling in state education. At the same time she respects the wishes of those who object to integrated education: their needs should be met by the independent sector. Purveying religion is not in her view a legitimate function of schools; responsibility for religious upbringing lies 'with the Church and with the home'. She agrees that one of the bonds connecting rival traditions – a tragic one – is widowhood; and sympathy can develop between those who are temporarily widowed, as it were, by the imprisonment of their husbands, even when – as was brought home to her mother – prisoners' wives may be on opposite sides. In these cases, as with many examples of unemployment that may be unconnected with politics, women come to the fore as bread-winners; the men either fulfil a supportive role, or are dispossessed altogether. The quest for improvement in women's rights has, she believes, 'never taken off in Northern Ireland' because of the prior need to repel terrorist attacks. Abortion is one of the basic issues that her party has discussed, but the subject has not achieved anything like the degree of attention or interest that such matters obtain in England. As a spokeswoman and as an individual she expresses the view that 'abortion is murder', though she argues the need for compromise on 'a woman's right to choose'. When challenged about how two such different perceptions could be reconciled, she expressed sympathy with the efforts of David Alton, MP, to reduce the number of weeks beyond which abortion became legal. She might feel that abortion on social grounds was never justified; but she had to accept that others might not agree. She extended a similar spirit of compromise to the principle of divorce (though she felt that the Church exerted unreasonable social pressures to achieve its ends) and, unexpectedly, to the Anglo-Irish Agreement of 1985. She hopes that a different Stormont will arise, one with built-in safeguards for minorities, including minorities within the unionist community. Then, she foresees, there will come a time when Northern Ireland will have 'good neighbourly relations' with 'a foreign government . . . our closest neighbours'.

Rhonda Paisley, despite or because of her Protestant antecedents on the one hand, and her concessions to late-twentieth-century liberalism on the other, is very much the embodiment of the Gael. Her less than reverent remarks about the Orange Order recall the attitudes of famous rebels: 'the orange sashes and King Billy's white horse that decks many a fluttering banner make me turn in disgust when I see how weak-minded and feeble-kneed and self-seeking some of the bowler-hatted, white-gloved "leaders" among them turn out to be'.[36] Unlike the Maud Gonnes, though, she respects their right to parade until they are 'blue in the face'. But, although the lessons of Ulster's history have taught her that the British connection cannot always be relied upon for loyal support, she is definitely one of the stabilizers of Northern Ireland. In this she is wholly unlike the women of the Ulster Defence Association (UDA), and its main military wing, the latter-day Ulster Volunteer Force (UVF). The paramilitary Protestants, like their rebel counterparts, undermine their own cause with every sectarian killing.

The UDA's Women's Rights Department has concerned itself with a wide range of issues peculiar to Northern Ireland, and to some which have universal relevance. In some ways, at least until the UDA's banning on 10 August 1992, it was a mirror image of Sinn Féin's women's section. The plight of prisoners' wives has always featured prominently on the agenda, and a large amount of space in the documentation is devoted to anti-British diatribes. It would be a simple task, especially when such topics as fair employment and equal pay are discussed, to change the acronyms and issue UDA propaganda material over the signature of Gerry Adams. The result of any such forgery would easily pass muster as the product of the Sinn Féin office, which still enjoys the protection of the law. The new UVF was formed in 1966 partly as a result of fears about the United Kingdom government's intentions with regard to Northern Ireland. In common with some unlikely bedfellows, it has foreseen a time when the province will have no alternative but to reject London in much the same terms as its majority has always rejected Dublin. As with the Provisional IRA, its professed aims are easy to understand; a good case can be made for them, citing historical events and democratic principles. Law-abiding citizens part company with both organizations because each is committed to violence and, to a lesser degree, because too often each throws up maverick individuals whose actions defy explanation or excuse.

Information received from a female source[37] within the loyalist paramilitary ranks confirms one's worst fears. Asked about how decisions are taken before arrangements are made for a sectarian killing, the woman described how the proposed victim would be tried in his absence. If his judge and jury were satisfied that he was 'guilty', the sentence of death was passed at once and carried out without delay; otherwise another candidate would be put forward and his suitability for what was usually a tit-for-tat killing would be considered. The same woman gratuitously alleged that officials of her organization embezzled much of the funds that they had managed to extract from the community. Without actually saying so, she gave the impression that all the undesirable behaviour of certain sections of the loyalist community could be ascribed to the frustrations of a society which had lost its autonomy. Having lost the right to legislate for themselves, they had lost all respect for the law. Her genuine feeling for the less fortunate citizens of Northern Ireland – especially the children of the ghettos – came through, as did her disillusionment with practitioners of the cause she had espoused.

Naturally the suspension of Stormont did not cast the same gloom over the Roman Catholic working-class community as it did over the Protestants. When the Troubles brought special problems to the women of the nationalist minority, unlike Protestants they did not instinctively look to the Northern Ireland government for redress. Nor did they fall back on Westminster as a poor second best. Those who did not place their trust in the social manifestos of illegal organizations looked to their own resources for a number of amenities, such as crèches, and this led to an inverted form of apparent discrimination. Because of this resort to self-help, more public money has been directed – legitimately – to Catholic schemes for improving social welfare than to equivalent enterprises in depressed areas where a case for giving help to Protestants could be made. But this tilting of aid in the direction of those who formerly lacked civil rights can only have a stabilizing effect on the province. Organizations which seek to destabilize Northern Ireland cannot afford to be seen to deplore improvements in social welfare; they may subvert them discreetly, they may provide alternatives for which republicanism can gain the credit, or they may choose simply to disregard them. The logic of this has been lost on loyalist extremists, whose violent responses play into the hands of their opponents They help the destabilization process.

There are two main approaches to the question of a woman's role today in the key organization devoted to the overthrow of the political structures of Ireland. What is the attitude of Provisional IRA men to the women Provisionals? What is the woman Provisional's perception of the 'armed struggle'? A senior male Provisional who has served prison sentences in Ireland and England stated recently that although recruitment of women, and attitudes to them, was subject to much variation on a geographical basis, everything really depended on the depth of republican commitment in particular families. The same could be said of the importance, or lack of it, attached to things Gaelic. He did not say so, but one was left with the impression that old-style republicans had changed little in these respects since 1916. He was, though, at pains to say that women enjoy equal rights within the PIRA. As with the men, some women are drawn into 'the Republican Movement', as this Provisional preferred to speak of the PIRA. One of the problems of an organization arranged and run on a cell basis is that the left hand must not know what the right hand is doing; overall strategy is kept in the minimum number of minds, but mistakes are inevitably more frequently made than in a more openly co-ordinated system. This means that occasionally fringe groups develop and the 'wrong' sort of recruit is attracted, usually by a misguided belief that the boredom of unemployment will be replaced by a life of excitement. Poor co-ordination also means, he added, that the wrong target is sometimes selected. He personally dissociated himself from the bombing of Enniskillen on Remembrance Sunday, 1987.

The 'right' sort of female recruit, in the opinion of this man (though not of a PIRA woman who was seen shortly after this interview), was not surprisingly inspired to join more by the example of the hunger-strikers of 1981 than by the ideals and aims of Countess Markievicz or Maud Gonne. In Ireland suicide is regarded as sinful but hunger-striking to the death is considered an honourable way of pursuing an illegal cause. It inspires simply by the example of sacrifice: a compelling example – compelling the witness to study and perhaps espouse the cause for which the life was 'sacrificed'. It is easy to understand how such behaviour, especially when young, would give a boost to recruitment; though quite why it should inspire some to put innocent lives at risk is harder to appreciate. As Mrs Thatcher pointed out at the time, Bobby Sands MP had a choice; and he was also subject to a command structure which could have called off his fast before its sixty-sixth day. According to the male Provisional interviewee, the deaths of hunger-strikers led to increased recruitment among the young nationalists, especially girls. Understandably, he declined to talk about their functions. From other sources we know that these extend from doing the chores associated with traditional female activity to bomb-making and to taking command of an 'active service unit'. The grapevine has it, rightly or wrongly, that female influence is found at the very centre of PIRA intelligence. At the end of the interview, a passing reference was made to the way in which the Anglo-Irish Treaty of 1921 was decisively rejected by women. '*And* they'll reject the next one', volunteered the Provisional.

The testimony of a woman Provisional put a different slant on some aspects of PIRA practice. She said that although women were moving into more positions of responsibility there was still male resistance to this development. Despite its valuable precedents for feminists, the Gaelic dimension was of minimal interest to present PIRA membership, though one of its prominent advocates, Countess Markievicz, was mentioned early on in the discussion as contributing to the strength of female motivation today. Her personal example, not her romantic attachment to ancient and peculiarly Irish – or Scottish – women's rights, was the inspiration. Another departure from the habits of some republicans was to be seen behind the claim that within the ranks of the Provisionals religion was an irrelevance. Not-withstanding tit-for-tat sectarian killings and the behaviour of a few renegade Roman Catholic priests, this is not too difficult to accept. While sympath-izing with republican aims, the Church has managed to distance itself from the violent methods used to achieve them. Denunciation by Rome has annoyed the Provisionals not so much because it cuts some of them off from their own roots but because they rely on community support. This they continue to receive, by one means or another, from the nationalist working-class Catholic communities.

At the outset of this interview the Provisional made a statement to the effect that women activists were more dispassionate than the men, and her sub-sequent remarks showed that she had thought through her own position. Her reply to the question, 'How do you justify the violence when the required result might eventually be obtained by use of the ballot box?' was, 'To speed up the process'. In her opinion a war was taking place and the British soldiers, whom she saw as an army of occupation, had to be defeated. If they could be persuaded to withdraw by any other means, all well and good. If politicians would not defer to Troops Out demands, it was up to the Provisionals to liberate the British colony. She spoke as though this might be achieved by force of arms, but she seemed to realize that if her side prevailed it would be by wearing down public opinion until the point came when the British lost the will to sustain hostilities. Discussion then moved on to the aftermath of a hypothetical withdrawal of British forces. She was quite unequivocal about this. As had happened in the South, there would be civil war. This, she argued, was desirable. It was the only way in which all the latent problems could be resolved. At this point the interview was concluded.

Discussing matters with Provisionals helps to bring out the logic that pervades the apparently illogical statements and actions of men and women involved in the day-to-day conduct of a spasmodic guerrilla war. To make sense of the contradictions one has to remember the injections of Marxism which the republican movement has received from time to time and, more importantly, that destabilization of society is the prime goal. There is no point in asking why, if, as the Provisionals claim a war is being waged, loud cries of protest go up when the British are suspected of resorting to a 'shoot to kill' policy. The inconsistency of the protest is irrelevant: it is just another means of hampering the enemy. Similarly it is an understandable part of rebel strategy that legal and illegal means of combating the foe are used in tandem. The wives of Provisionals, as well as shouldering more than their share of the burdens of everyday family survival, may undertake such humanitarian activities as monitoring police procedures, including the strip searching of women. The one great advantage enjoyed by the rebel seeking to undermine a democratic society is that the system can be used for its own destruction. Nobody, loyalist or nationalist, denies that the security forces must be carefully observed to see that no humiliating or otherwise cruel methods of interrogation occur. If or when offences occur, particularly against women in custody, opportunities will arise for achieving more for a cause than is ever likely to be achieved by an explosion in a shopping precinct. Most female prisoners are Roman Catholic; most of those who search them are Protestant. In Armagh Women's Prison can be found 'a marvellous propaganda vehicle for those in and outside Northern Ireland who have used the incidents of strip-searching to add to the political and social tensions within the six counties'.[38]

The attitude of the more militant Irish feminists has hardened as they have observed the granting of rights and freedoms to Northern Irish women while, during the same period of history, the twenty-six county state has moved in the opposite direction. In the opinion of a contributor to a republican magazine, 'the conservative and essentially anti-woman ideology that shaped the contours of the Free State have always been part of Irish nationalism'.[39] Naturally this does not make her satisfied with the situation in the North. She insists that 'Partition has given us two weak and fragile states which have secured their existence through political and social repression' and that 'Demands for social and economic change in the South and political reform in the North have been viewed as threatening the very existence of those states'.[40] She writes as though their existence were not threatened, despite the fact that after her article come details of the latest executions of members of the Royal Ulster Constabulary and other victims of the 'Sustained Guerrilla Campaign'. Apart from political restructuring of the entire island, which is hardly a concise feminist demand, she only proposes that women should acquire power through independent organizations so that they may play 'a central part in the radical republican tradition'.[41] As she troubles to spell out the social shortcomings only of the South, one is left with the impression that her objections to the position in Northern Ireland may have more to do with sovereignty than with women's rights. That she makes them as a feminist could be seen to be purely coincidental. Would she welcome a feminist's Utopia in the six counties if it were to help stabilize Northern Ireland?

8

EMANCIPATION
AND UNITY

The Treaty on European Union created a conflict of interest in the Republic. The great financial attractions of being a member state – Ireland receives six pounds from the Community for every pound it subscribes to it – are to an important extent offset by the moral dilemma which membership creates. To eliminate the possibility of European Community treaties (including the Maastricht Treaty) undermining Ireland's constitutional abortion restrictions, Ireland negotiated a protocol, that is to say a protection clause, with the twelve member states, to safeguard its right to retain Article 40 (3.3). Protocol 17 provides that:

> Nothing in the Treaty on European Union, or in the Treaties establishing the European Communities, or in the Treaties or Acts modifying or supplementing those Treaties, shall affect the application in Ireland of Article 40.3.3 of the Constitution of Ireland.[1]

But ten days after the signing of the Maastricht Treaty on 7 February 1992 a decision was taken that may well lead to the removal of one of a series of troublesome barriers between the two Irelands. When the High Court of the Republic ruled that a pregnant 14-year-old rape victim was forbidden to leave the country to have an abortion it set in motion a process which, regardless of the moral implications of the case, would eventually help to diminish the misgivings northerners feel about Church–state relationships in the South. Northern and southern feminists, and many individuals to whom the abortion issue is seldom a matter of particular interest, were united in their protestations. They were to find themselves united again, seventeen days later, when they rejoiced as the Supreme Court, having considered a case which brought to mind that of *Rex* v. *Bourne*, overruled the High Court's decision.

The importance of this reversal, apart from its consequences for girls who are faced with such a problem, has far wider significance than is shown by its effect on abortion law. The Irish government took the view that the words 'in Ireland' in the protocol meant that freedom to leave the country of their nationality was not denied to Irish citizens; nor was a denial of right of access to information about abortion facilities in other member states intended.

Nevertheless, as it was not feasible to modify or to delete the Protocol before Maastricht, a 'Solemn Declaration' was made, agreed with all member states, and annexed to the European treaties. All the 'High Contracting Parties' to the Treaty on European Union agreed a legal interpretation of Protocol 17:

> that it was and is their intention that the Protocol shall not limit freedom either to travel between member States or . . . to obtain in Ireland or make available in Ireland information relating to services lawfully available in member States.[2]

Apart from acknowledging that states have no right to prevent their citizens from leaving the country of their nationality, and that citizens have rights of access to information, the decision of an Irish court which made necessary the Solemn Declaration has again shown that the Republic's judges are not in thrall to Rome. For all that, though, history may prove that Rome was right to stress that most abortions amount to infanticide: since the constitutional amendment of 1983 there has been an annual exodus of from 3,500 to 4,000 Irish women to Great Britain to have unwanted foetuses removed (4,152 in 1991). Now Ireland, in joining other European countries, may have made a moral and spiritual mistake. However, those who think she has, can console themselves by considering that some good will have come from the whole sordid matter. One of the greatest impediments preventing the establishment of a concordat between North and South has been the subservience of the ostensible bastions of democracy to clerical interest. The Supreme Court's ruling played its part in eroding this obstacle. As Michael Davitt, founder of the Land League, said in reply to a clerical attack on him for praising the American system of universal secular education, 'Make no mistake about it, my Lord Bishop of Limerick, Democracy is going to rule in these countries.'[3]

The furore which followed the High Court's ruling in the 'X' case, as it was popularly termed, did not die down. Indignation or unease, not only among militant feminists, led to calls for change. But on the other hand many who believed that human life began at the moment of conception were fearful of any change that would do more than tilt the balance in favour of a mother's survival. The issue appeared to be beyond the ability of the Dáil to resolve; and so a coalition of mainstream political parties once again passed to the electorate the power to alter the constitution. On 25 November 1992 the people decided to amend Article 40 (3.3) by the addition of new subsections to allow freedom 'to travel between the State and another state' and freedom of access, 'subject to such conditions as may be laid down by law', to 'information relating to services lawfully available in another state'. On the fundamental issue of the relative rights of the mother and the foetus, the wording of the referendum alienated both supporters and opponents of change:

> It shall be unlawful to terminate the life of an unborn unless such termination is necessary to save the life, as distinct from the health, of the

mother where there is an illness or disorder of the mother giving rise to
a real and substantial risk to her life, not being a risk of self-destruction.

Some argued that, because of the Supreme Court's February ruling, the
practical effect of the amendment's wording would be to hold back a pro-
abortion process already in motion. Others were convinced that such a change
in the constitution was tantamount to legalizing a form of murder. In fact,
little would have changed. For Roman Catholics, that is to say practically the
entire population, nothing should have changed. There would, perhaps, have
been fewer allegations about supposedly sinister decisions made by the ethics
committees in Irish hospitals, when difficult choices have to be made. But,
then, any harm they may have done has been in the field of birth control, not
foetus protection. Provided that the mother does not delay too long, abortion,
virtually on demand, continues to be readily available after a brief journey.
Irish mothers may, if they wish, continue to treat the foetus within them as a
disposable chattel. Nevertheless the state still strives to protect the unborn by
discouraging its citizens from adopting a 'European' attitude to pregnancy.
Most importantly, abortion for social convenience is forbidden on Irish soil –
as it would still have been had the people voted 'Yes'. As referendum follows
referendum, and the permanency of marriage is threatened, Ireland will be
hard-pressed to withstand the pressures brought to bear on it by Community
membership. In its resistance, however, it will find that more and more
support comes from the Northern Irish.

Objections to abortion on social grounds are, despite misconceptions about
actual practice of Roman Catholic doctors, an influence for inter-community
concord. Another unifying influence has been promoted by the Catholic
Hierarchy in the spirit of ecumenism. Today it is even possible for a senior
Catholic cleric to make light of abandoned attitudes to inter-church marriages:
'in the not too distant past it was a capital offence for a priest to assist at a
mixed marriage!'[4] And it must be something of a shock for those brought up
on the attitudes of *The People's Priest* to learn of an official admission that 'in
some Mixed Marriages the members have indeed found an enriched sense of
mutual respect and responsibility which has strengthened rather than weak-
ened personal faith and the Church allegiance of each party'.[5] As if to
underline this new tolerance, which can only fortify the bonds of marriage and
improve the relationship between the faithful of two cultures, in 1992 a new
pre-nuptial enquiry form was introduced by the Catholic Church in Ireland.
It has to be completed by all Catholics contemplating marriage and its
important feature is that there is no difference in the questions asked of those
marrying Catholics and those asked of persons entering a mixed marriage.

The trend towards a closing of gaps is, though, by no means constant. In
education it has been the history lesson which has created barricades between
the sexes, the Irish cultures and the nations of the British Isles. Ancient
examples of female leadership and dominance have always featured in the

subject-matter of national school lessons. But there has been the apparent need to tread carefully, to stress heroic elements and to omit references to the morality of the old Gaelic times. A woman's place, as far as most women were concerned, was until recently delineated by the precepts of the Church. Among the few women allowed to deviate from the religious ideal were the famous rebels. It was left to a woman from another Gaelic culture to indicate the common heritage of Great Britain and Ireland. She did so in Edwardian times, when it was not too difficult for a calm and reasonable assessment of the political disposition of the British and Irish islands to be made. But few drew the logical conclusion when the Hon. Louisa Farqharson reminded Scottish Gaels that both the English and the Irish nations were the victims of the Normans: 'The great Strongbow, de Courcy, de Burgo, de Braose, raised their wonderful castles to intimidate the Irish, as shortly before they had intimidated the Anglo-Saxon conquerors of Celtic Britain.'[6]

Had the Irish school curriculum of that time stressed that the English had suffered the same fate as the Irish, several generations would not have been deceived into believing in, and purveying, a racist interpretation of history. 'Putting down the rebellion in Ireland', an expression which appears in too many English history books, would have been best understood as heavy-handed central government either quelling provincial unrest, or coping with class evolution that sometimes manifested itself – in Ireland, Scotland, Wales and England – as revolution. It is not necessary to be a Marxist to see uprisings in terms of turbulence directed against unsympathetic central authority, representative of a ruling class which, though as Irish as anybody could be, often had the outward appearance of another race. But the myth took over. Both sides came to believe in the roles in which ignorance had cast them. A social revolution, aided and abetted by renewed awareness of a fascinating cultural heritage, was mistaken for a national one. Historians, as victims of their own cultures, have unwittingly added respectability to a narrowly racist interpretation of relationships between the two islands.

For women the social revolution brought several exciting possibilities. Some were stimulated by the cultural revival to try to break away from the traditions into which, according to their class, secular and religious influences had placed or confined them. Others were attracted by the idea of separate nationhood. Renewed awareness of the heritage of Brehon law provided inspiration for all. To the women of the educated classes, who felt the first breezes of a wind of change that came with the death of the old queen and the birth of the new century, reminders of the ancient Irish legal system conjured up the spirit of Grania O'Malley. She was the last great example of the dominant female of legendary stature. After her time overt, flamboyant female leadership was rarely to be seen until Ascendancy women, often influenced by a period of study on the Continent, channelled their energies into such causes as suffragism. Some combined the pursuit of women's rights with nationalism, others combined it with an equal desire to preserve the Union. An apolitical-

love of things Irish could be enough for those for whom art was a consuming passion. To many others regeneration of a wide spectrum of artistic traditions in music, drama, literature and arts and crafts was what nationalism was all about: these were the constituents of the essential Ireland. Women were the key organizers of the *feiseanna* which concentrated the attention of whole communities on the joys of celebrating the national identity; and women were prominent as poets, painters and playwrights. Their contribution to drama led to a theatrical tradition with influence that extended far beyond the shores of Ireland.

The Gaelic League was one organization which, but for its infiltration by the Irish Republican Brotherhood, could conceivably have seized Ireland's opportunities without jeopardizing the integrity of the Union. But Ireland's twentieth-century history is the story of a series of manipulations by one elite or another. The single-mindedness of such women as Maud Gonne meant that Gaelic culture was turned to narrow nationalist aims in Inghinidhe na hEireann. Her cultural as well as her feminist aims were subordinated to the quest for Irish independence. Her initiative, as with that of the founders of Cumann na mBan, was running counter to that of the silent majority of both sexes, and continued to do so until the Easter Rising executions shifted the national prejudice. Inevitably the women who actually participated in the Rising were creatures of two worlds. As the children of Victorian parents, they could not shed all the innate predispositions that clung to them from the previous century. They would not have been involved in Pearse's calculated blood sacrifice if they had not been peculiar in some way. And yet the way in which they behaved can be instructive. In some respects they stayed of their own volition within the traditional stereotype that is associated with the hearth. They did not show much resentment when fulfilling the customary duties of womanhood; indeed, they seemed to relish the opportunities to behave in ways which latter-day feminists have thought servile. However, they did remonstrate, with some fervour, whenever they were denied the right to enter fully into the fray. In this they were giving a useful insight into the nature of Irish feminism. Their example, though, was to be hidden behind the more sensational features of that week and was not to have much relevance in Catholic Ireland again for another seventy years. The need to reconcile the demands of traditional duties with natural rights, or traditional rights with natural duties, is at the heart of today's disputes concerning the mother and the wife.

After the Treaty the unity which had existed between feminists of opposing political camps became an anachronism. As devolved government steadily emancipated women, though in very different ways from those of the British mainland, de Valera saw to it that the Catholic concept of the woman and the family prevailed in independent Ireland. The pace of emancipation of British-Irish women, except in the extension of the franchise to women aged from 21 to 30, was much faster than was experienced by the women who had opted for secession from the United Kingdom. The true picture of the restrictions placed on women in independent Ireland was most fully displayed at the sessions of the New Ireland Forum, though it is to be deplored that important submissions, including much testimony concerning women's rights, did not find their way into the official report. Those who were present in Dublin Castle were made aware of some uncomfortable truths; a combination of legislation which fed on its own contradictions with attitudes which had been warped by censorship had led to an extraordinary exhibition of anomalies. As has been seen, these were centred on the unborn child: the birth control ban increased the number of unwanted pregnancies, the ban on the adoption of legitimate babies reduced the options open to one category of mother, discrimination against illegitimate children put pressure on the unmarried mother. And, as if this confusion were not enough, family tensions which harmed women and children while the male bread-winner lived out his life in England or the United States, existed against a background of religious intolerance and inconsistency. The ban on divorce hardly affected men. Irresponsible priests contributed to the domestic tragedies that arise within bigamous liaisons. The mixed marriage rules undermined community relations. And, to confuse matters still further, Roman Catholic dogma also applied to one-third of Northern Ireland's population.

For half a century Ireland's two principal cultures were prised apart by a succession of laws concerning, directly or indirectly, women's rights. During this period, influenced by the Westminster parliament, Northern Ireland enacted or accepted law after law which found favour with the feminist lobby until, at the time of the New Ireland Forum, the difference between the two societies was most embarrassing for nationalists. But, while women of the North had prospered as women, those who belonged to the province's minority faith had suffered considerable discrimination in such secular matters as housing. Although the civil rights movement was not initiated with the aim of redressing the balance between the sexes, Roman Catholic wives and mothers had suffered most under the one-sided system that has now, happily, disappeared.

Since the revelations of the New Ireland Forum the Republic's law-makers, helped by the spirit of the Second Vatican Council, and under the compulsion that has come increasingly from membership of the European Community, have done much to democratize their society. Neither feminists nor Northern Irish critics have been lavish with praise. That is not their habit. But both the accomplishments and the trend must meet with their approval. As each obstacle falls, and as modern methods of communication make each society better informed about the nature of its closest neighbour, the possibility of some form of union between the two territories is more likely to move on to the agenda of those within reach of the levers of power. For the feminists, or simply for democrats, the strongest remaining barrier which stands in the way of achievement of their aims is not a legislative one. In many areas, North and

South, a woman may be the victim not so much of a specific act of discrimination as of the general climate of opinion. Pressure to conform comes from the community at large. In the long term only education is likely to bring full achievement of women's rights. One may doubt whether segregated education will or can ever do so.

Enlightened education also has an important part to play in helping to find an enduring solution to the Troubles in Northern Ireland. During the troublesome years before the suspension of Stormont it was not true to say, though it was often said, that the province had a political problem. All the ills of those days, and of today, are attributable to a psychological problem and a security problem – facts that seem only to be appreciated by the network of independent women's organizations striving to achieve social stability. If the Official IRA women who now call the tune in the Workers' Party can understand the value of the democratic process in the furtherance of their republican aims, there is no logical reason why others from other traditions should not see that political change, if needed, can be achieved at the drop of a vote. But, while the schools fail to show pupils that there are valid historical, economic and social arguments to justify either a united Ireland, a United Kingdom of Great Britain and Northern Ireland, an independent Northern Ireland, or even some form of union between Great Britain and Ireland as a whole, minds will remain closed. And while the psychological blockage remains – the failure to concede that for a group to be a 'culture' it has only to believe that it is one – the intellectually stunted will always turn to violence to achieve their aims. Those who take up the armalite have no excuse for doing so in the Irish situation – their deprived upbringing which apologists sometimes mention is no justification for acts of violence; nevertheless recruitment of terrorists would undoubtedly be more difficult if schools found ways of removing misconceptions about members of other groups. The concept of any culture having the moral and legal right to decide its policy by majority vote is sometimes difficult for uneducated, unemployed, socially deprived individuals of a rival culture to grasp. Moreover, some women members of the cultural minority are excusably disposed to feel doubly dispossessed because of their sex.

Women's organizations, though, provide the best hope of reconciliation within the province, and of its stabilization. Not necessarily connected to politics in the narrow sense or to the Troubles, and often ignoring the border, they have multiplied at a remarkable rate. In February 1992, the Maastricht month, when the President of the Irish Republic visited Belfast, the first item on her itinerary was a meeting with ninety representatives of women's groups in Northern Ireland. 'A woman's place' has always been at the heart of the Irish Question. Today the energy which is devoted to social activities needs a means of legitimate political expression within the province. So long as it is not

possible for women like Sheelagh Murnaghan to speak the language of
moderation at Stormont, her sex will feel locally disfranchised, and Northern
Ireland will continue to give the impression to the gullible and the ill-informed
that it is a British colony. Although the same local disfranchisement applies to
male electors, the disability is not quite so marked; 'a man's place' being what
it is the road to Westminster is not fraught with so many difficulties for him as
it is for a would-be woman MP domiciled in Ulster. Bernadette Devlins are
few and far between. Remarkably, though, women have not been deterred by
the restraints that history has placed upon them. The heirs to Saidie Patterson
are still capable of closing the gap between the Shankill and the Falls Road. In
one respect they enjoy a privilege – one that they might repudiate: despite all
the carnage, it is still unacceptable deliberately to kill a priest or a woman.

Attempts to reconcile the communities in Northern Ireland have in recent
years been helped by changes within the Republic which bring within the
bounds of possibility the idea of reconciliation with the North. These
continue to involve modification of legislation concerning women's rights
and, as the process accelerates, there is a danger that something integral to
Irish culture will be lost. It was easy to say that in the interests of Irish unity,
the twenty-six counties should scrap the bans on divorce and abortion, just as
it was easy to ask the six counties to relinquish their special freedoms. Apart
from the fact that the Northern Irish majority values above all else its freedom
to take its own decisions on the rights of all its citizens, the Irish concept of
womanhood is not to be rejected out of hand. By tradition, although there has
been some fluctuation over the centuries, Irish women in all the provinces
have enjoyed considerable power. True, because of the manner in which they
have wielded it, their legal rights (except those enjoyed under Brehon law)
were minimal and have only improved in recent years. This lack of rights only
seemed important when they stepped outside the parameters prescribed by
tradition. When they did this, women became very vulnerable indeed.

The disadvantages endured by Irish women who strayed from the accepted
norms of behaviour may appear to be little different from those of their
contemporaries elsewhere in western civilization. But in psychological terms,
and when they tried to venture into public life, their plight has often been
worse. If only because of the nature of Gaelic culture, of which as individuals
they may have been only instinctively aware, their endeavours to exercise
their individuality have frequently been frustrating and frustrated. They once
had real power; they lost its legal justification and support; they have had to
face strong opposition in their efforts to rise to a point where they may enjoy
equality of opportunity with men. Now the women of the two Irelands, in the
context of the European Community and its values, are faced with difficult
choices. Are they to abandon altogether the concept of the family that de
Valera sought to protect? Will they eventually outnumber men in the
workplace and in the legislature? Are these extremes plausible or desirable?
Interaction between the cultures of the British and Irish islands should enable

them to enjoy the best of several worlds. The Irish woman can reasonably hope to retain the positive dimension of her traditional role while the doors are opened to all the opportunities enjoyed by men. The strength of her cultural heritage should enable her to strike a balance between enjoying the responsibilities of family life and coping with the demands and temptations of the wider world.

The removal of obstacles which inhibit *rapprochement* between North and South is largely the result of feminist agitation for changes in the law. If the Republic ceases to be a theocracy and becomes a pluralist society, Northern Ireland will look more benignly on the prospect of a link with it. As de Valera appreciated, the greatest obstacle to this was created by the Republic's departure from the Commonwealth, and he even tried secretly to engineer readmission.[7] It is difficult to imagine the present generation coming to terms with an apparent renunciation of all that they have been brought up to believe about 'the English'. Nevertheless there is a growing acceptance in the Republic that whatever constitutional changes are to occur must not be made in disregard of the wishes of the majority of Northern Ireland's citizens. The British Army is now less often described, except by ardent propagandists, as an 'army of occupation'. And the opponents of democracy have even had to take into account the fact that one of their favourite *bêtes noires*, the Ulster Defence Regiment, numbered among its recruits 700 women. Known as Greenfinches, and now members of the Royal Irish Regiment, they were operationally integrated before all other women serving in the British Army.

It would be foolish to predict in precise terms the future of the whole island while a slow but steady process of emancipation makes the legislative framework and the social attitudes of the two Irish states resemble each other ever more closely. The stage will eventually be reached when only the terrorists make the border mean more than a line that runs across the map. Until the men and women who believe in the armed struggle can be persuaded that the border, as a national barricade, is largely their own creation, real links between the different cultures of the British and Irish islands cannot be forged. Genuine unity, as is appreciated by the members of Women Together and many other women's organizations, will have to involve first a British and Irish consensus recognizing the democratic rights of all parties, then a commitment to power-sharing and extensive devolution. The Council of Ireland, which for so long has been waiting in the wings, must surely play its part in creating a unity which does not deny diversity. Were it to be convened, the Republic would find itself associated with the Commonwealth and Northern Ireland would have close links with Dublin, while retaining no less autonomy than it enjoyed before the suspension of Stormont. To reassure the smaller political unit, a mechanism would have to be found whereby a united Ireland could only sever the British connection, principally embodied in the monarchy, if separate majorities of northern and southern representatives were both agreed that such a step should be taken.

To initiate moves towards reconciliation a meeting between two heads of state[8] would set the right tone for wholehearted co-operation and be of great symbolic value. As it happens, in 1993 both incumbents are women. It is inconceivable that in the last decade of the twentieth century they, or the women over whom they preside, will be heard to say, 'We are but women'.

NOTES

ABBREVIATIONS

NLI   National Library of Ireland
PRO CO   Public Record Office: Colonial Office
PRO DO   Public Record Office: Dominions Office and Commonwealth Relations
          Office
PRO T   Public Record Office: Treasury
PRONI   Public Record Office of Northern Ireland (D. denotes original document;
          T. denotes transcript or photocopy)
RS   Material in possession of the author

1   FROM THE BEGINNING

1 R. A. S. Macalister (ed. and tr.), *Lebor Gabala Erenn*, Dublin, Hodges, Figgis,
   1938–56; cited by A. Rees and B. Rees in *Celtic Heritage: Ancient Tradition in
   Ireland and Wales*, London, Thames & Hudson, 1961, repr. 1978, p. 115.
2 For ease and peace I have used the popular, modern, usually phonetic, spellings for
   the names of those characters who are mentioned most frequently.
3 J. Rhys, *Celtic Folklore, Welsh and Manx*, Oxford, Clarendon Press, 1901, pp. 661
   and 671.
4 T. Kinsella (tr.), *The Tain*, translation of *Tain Bo Cuailnge*, Dublin and Oxford,
   Oxford University Press, 1970, p. 169.
5 See T. O'Maille in *Zeitschrift fur Celtische Philologie*, Halle, Max Niemeyer
   Verlag, 1928, XVII, p. 129; also T. O. Raithbheartagih (ed. and tr.), *Genealogical
   Tracts*, Dublin, Irish Manuscripts Commission, 1932, I, p. 148.
6 S. J. O'Grady, *History of Ireland: the Heroic Period*, London, Sampson Low,
   Searle, Marston & Rivington, and Dublin, E. Ponsonby, 1878, vol. 1 (of 2 vols).
7 Quoted by Kinsella, op. cit., p. xiv.
8 J. Vendryes, *Revue Celtique*, XXXIX, p. 366; cited by S. O'Faolain, *The Irish: A
   Character Study*, New York, Devin-Adair, 1949, pp. 16–17.
9 S. Gwynn, *The History of Ireland*, London, Macmillan, and Dublin, Talbot Press,
   1923, pp. 6–7.
10 A. N. Jeffares, *W. B. Yeats: a New Biography*, London, Hutchinson, 1988, p. 36.
11 S. Ferguson, *Lays of the Red Branch* (New Irish Library), London, T. Fisher
   Unwin, and Dublin, Sealy, Bryers & Walker, 1897, p. xviii. From the introduction
   by Lady Ferguson.
12 ibid., p. 142.
13 ibid., p. xix.

14 ibid., p. 37.

15 Kinsella, op. cit., p. 12.

16 S. Ferguson, op. cit., pp. 58–9.

17 L. Duncan (ed. and tr.), *Eriu*, XI, p. 124; quoted by Rees and Rees, op. cit., p. 18.

18 A. Bugge (ed. and tr.), *Caithrein Cellachain Caisil: the Victorious Career of Cellachan of Cashel*, Christiania (Oslo), Norsk Historisk Kjeldeskriftinstitutt, 1905, pp. 59–61.

19 Lambeth Palace Library Carew MS 1535, 26 July.

20 ibid., 1544, 9 October.

21 ibid., 1550, 11 March.

22 W. Knowler (ed.), *The Earl of Strafforde's Letters and Dispatches*, Dublin, R. Reilly for R. Owen, 1739–40, vol. 2 (of 2 vols), p. 19.

23 D. H. Farmer, *The Oxford Dictionary of Saints*, Oxford, Clarendon Press, 1978, p. 267.

24 Cited as an 'Extravagance' in *The Catholic Encyclopedia*, London, The Catholic Encyclopedia, 1912, vol. XV, p. 77–8.

25 A. Chambers, *Granuaile: the Life and Times of Grace O'Malley*, Dublin, Wolfhound Press, 1979, pp. 77–8.

26 K. Nicholls, *Gaelic and Gaelicised Ireland in the Middle Ages*, Dublin, Gill & Macmillan, 1972, p. 73.

27 Aylmer Papers at Nunwell House, Brading, Isle of Wight: Louis Spears, unpublished MS, a history of the Aylmer family. The ring is now at Nunwell.

28 Colclough Papers at Cuffsborough, County Laois; and personal correspondence: RS: Richard Colclough to author, 1990.

29 *Burke's Irish Family Records*, London, Burke's Peerage, 1976, p. 256 (cp. p. 254).

30 RS: Colclough to author, 12 December 1990. Richard Colclough explained how the errors in Burke (*Landed Gentry* and *Irish Family Records*) are a mixture of deliberate attempts to omit the ancestry of rival claimants to the Colclough estates and genuine mistakes on the part of a family employee.

31 J. Carson of Kilpike, near Banbridge, County Down, in J. Hawthorne (ed.), *Two Centuries of Irish History*, London, British Broadcasting Corporation, 1976, p. 55.

32 La Tocnaye, Bougrenet de (tr. J. Stevenson), *A Frenchman's Walk through Ireland, 1796–7*, Belfast, McCaw, Stevenson & Orr, and Dublin, Hodges, Figgis, 1917. Quoted in F. O'Connor (ed.), *A Book of Ireland*, London, Collins, 1959, p. 128.

33 Sir Philip Sidney to the Queen's private secretary, Sir Francis Walsingham, in a summary of his services in Ireland written in 1583. Chambers, op. cit., p. 85.

2   IN THE ASCENDANT

1 W. McCormack, *Ascendancy and Tradition in Anglo-Irish Literary History from 1789 to 1939*, Oxford, Clarendon Press, 1985, p. 237.

2 M. Bence-Jones, *Twilight of the Ascendancy*, London, Constable, 1987, p. 22.

3 *Burke's Irish Family Records*, London, Burke's Peerage, 1976, p. 652 (Kavanagh), p. 962 (Ponsonby).

4 L. Pine (ed.), *Burke's Genealogical and Heraldic History of the Peerage, Baronetage and Knightage*, London, Burke's Peerage (102nd edn), 1959, p. 1730 (Ormonde).

5 In the late twentieth century magnanimous Casements boldly revealed that the traitor/patriot Roger had been, for several editions of *Burke's Landed Gentry of Ireland*, concealed behind the phrase 'with other issue'. He now enjoys some prominence. Not so in *Who Was Who 1916–1928*, though. Its compilers set a dangerous precedent by pretending that his *Who's Who* entries had never existed. Roger became the first 'non-person' of the western world.

6 E. Mavor, *The Ladies of Llangollen: a Study in Romantic Friendship*, London, Michael Joseph, 1971, pp. 27–8.
7 NLI MS 4811: Wicklow Papers, Caroline Hamilton's Journal.
8 G. H. Bell (ed.), *The Hamwood Papers of the Ladies of Llangollen and Caroline Hamilton*, London, Macmillan, 1930, p. 12.
9 Tina McMorrough-Kavanagh, in conversation with the author, September 1990.
10 *The General Evening Post*, 20–2 July 1790 (8862).
11 Mavor, op. cit., p. 83.
12 Prince Puckler Muskaus to 'Julia', July 1828: E. Mavor (ed.), *Life with the Ladies of Llangollen*, London, Viking, 1984, pp. 142–3.
13 Charles Mathews to his wife, 4 September 1820, in Mavor, op. cit., p. 178.
14 John Lockhart to his wife, 24 August 1825, in Mavor, op. cit., p. 162.
15 Hamwood Papers, County Meath, Eleanor Butler's Journal, 4 October 1790.
16 ibid., 13 March 1788.
17 ibid., 19 April 1789.
18 ibid., 20 March 1789.
19 ibid., 28 March 1789.
20 ibid., 10 March 1789.
21 Lady Lonsdale to Lady Louisa Stuart; cited in Alice (Mrs Godfrey) Clark (ed.), *Gleanings from an Old Portfolio*, containing some correspondence between Lady Louisa Stuart and her sister Caroline, Countess of Portarlington, and also friends and relations; 3 vols, privately printed for David Douglas, Edinburgh, 1895–8, vol. III, p. 159.
22 Llangollen Town Council (Plas Newydd Papers), Sarah Ponsonby, Account Book, entries for 2 and 3 July 1800.
23 The Duke of Wellington to Sarah Ponsonby, 17 July 1829; quoted in full in Bell, op. cit., p. 381.
24 S. Butler, a review of Mavor's *The Ladies of Llangollen*, in the *Journal of the Butler Society*, Butler Society, 1971, vol. I, no. 3, p. 214.
25 Mavor, op. cit., p. 9.
26 S. Butler, op. cit., p. 214.
27 C. Woodham-Smith, *The Great Hunger: Ireland 1845–1849*, London, Hamish Hamilton, 1962, p. 299.
28 M. F. Young (ed.), *The Letters of a Noble Woman (Mrs La Touche of Harristown)*, London, George Allen & Sons, 1908, p. 17.
29 RS: Aideen Gore-Booth to author, 22 November 1990.
30 A. Marreco, *The Rebel Countess: the Life and Times of Constance Markievicz*, Philadelphia, PA., Chilton Books, 1967, p. 7.
31 J. Beckett, *The Anglo-Irish Tradition*, London, Faber & Faber, 1976, p. 93.
32 *Hansard*, House of Lords, 30 March 1846, vol. 85, p. 273.
33 Woodham-Smith, op. cit., p. 31.
34 See especially, A. Young, *Tour in Ireland*, Dublin, T. Cadell & J. Dodsley, 1780, vol. II, sect. VI, p. 33.
35 *Report of Geo. Nicholls, Esq., to His Majesty's Principal Secretary of State for the Home Department on Poor Laws, Ireland*, 1837 (690) LI, p. 230.
36 Woodham-Smith, op. cit., p. 30.
37 A. O'Connor, 'Women in Irish folklore: the testimony regarding illegitimacy, abortion and infanticide', in M. MacCurtain and M. O'Dowd (eds), *Women in Early Modern Ireland*, Edinburgh, Edinburgh University Press, 1991.
38 Dr McGilligan, Evidence, *The First Report for His Majesty's Commissioners for Inquiring into the Condition of the Poorer Classes in Ireland*, 1835 (369) XXXII, p. 274. There is some doubt about which are more reliable: oral submissions (and the impressions of famous travellers, like Arthur Young), or the statistics of the 1841

Census, which may have been reasonably reliable as far as overall patterns of behaviour were concerned.

39 D. A. C. G. Campbell to Sir Randolph Routh, 14 November 1846. *Correspondence from July 1846 to January 1847 Relating to the Measures Adopted for the Relief of the Distress in Ireland: Commissariat Series*, H C, 1847 (761) LI, p. 298.

40 PRO T 64/362 B: Captain Waller Report, 28 November 1846; Lieutenant Downman Report, 5 December 1846.

41 RS: J. A. Aylmer to author, 13 November 1990.

42 As recently as 1992 the author was still meeting Irish men and women who believed that Queen Victoria's contribution to Irish famine relief was £5. In fact the queen's personal donation heads the original subscription list preserved in the National Library of Ireland. She gave £2,000 (the second donation on the list, from Rothschild's, was £1,000). A genuine cause for complaint was the rate-in-aid imposed in 1850 to cope with problems arising from the Famine. This was levied only in Ireland. Believers in the United Kingdom as a political entity should have insisted that the burden be distributed evenly throughout the realm.

43 *Belfast News-Letter*, 1 May 1854.

44 Woodham-Smith, op. cit., p. 299.

45 Bence-Jones, op. cit., pp. 63–4.

46 *Leinster Express*, 30 December 1905.

47 C. Clear, *Nuns in Nineteenth-Century Ireland*, Dublin, Gill & Macmillan, 1987, p. 141.

48 H. Martineau, 'Modern domestic service', *Edinburgh Review*, 1862, vol. 15, p. 421.

49 M. M. Colum, *Life and the Dream*, London, Macmillan, 1947, p. 211.

50 Clear, op. cit., pp. 31–2.

51 Quoted in M. S. Daly, *The Church and the Second Sex*, London, Chapman, 1968, p. 66.

52 Marreco, op. cit., p. 297.

53 Constance Markievicz to Stanislaus Dunin-Markiewicz, 14 January 1926 in Marreco, op. cit., p. 296.

54 Marreco, op. cit., pp. 81–2.

55 ibid., p. 124.

56 E. Gore-Booth, 'The triumph of Maeve', in *Poems of Eva Gore-Booth*, London, New York and Toronto, Longman's, Green, 1929, pp. 312–13.

57 E. Coxhead, *Daughters of Erin: Five Women of the Irish Renascence*, London, Secker & Warburg, 1965, p. 87.

58 Maud Gonne MacBride to Count Stanislas Dunin-Markiewicz, 14 May 1931, in Marreco, op. cit., p. 125.

59 Frederick, Second Earl of Birkenhead, *F. E. The Life of the First Earl of Birkenhead*, London, Eyre & Spottiswoode, 1959, p. 133.

60 H. Nicolson, *Lord Carnock, a Study in the Old Diplomacy*, London, Constable, 1930, p. 28.

61 R. Foster, *Modern Ireland 1600–1972*, London, Allen Lane, Penguin Press, 1988, p. 412.

3 IRISH CULTURAL REVIVAL

1 R. Foster, *Modern Ireland 1600–1972*, London, Allen Lane, Penguin Press, 1988, p. 446.

2 Notably by Katie Donovan in *Irish Women Writers (Marginalized by Whom?)*, Dublin, Raven Arts Press (Letters from the New Ireland series), 1988.

3 M. Edgeworth, *Castle Rackrent, an Hibernian Tale: taken from the Facts and from the Manners of the Irish Squires, before the year 1782*, London, Joseph Johnson, 1800, Preface.

4 ibid.

5 ibid.

6 See H. J. Butler and H. E. Butler (eds), *The Black Book of Edgeworthstown and Other Edgeworth Memories 1585–1817*, London, Faber & Gwyer, 1927.

7 Edgeworth, *Castle Rackrent* and *The Absentee*, London, J. M. Dent (Everyman's Library), [1910] repr. 1952, p. 67.

8 Donovan, op. cit., p. 9.

9 Edgeworth, *Castle Rackrent* and *The Absentee*, p. 67.

10 ibid., p. 12, footnote.

11 ibid., p. 346.

12 E. Somerville and M. Ross, *Irish Memories*, London, Longman's, Green, 1917; quoted by G. Lewis in *Somerville and Ross: The World of the Irish R.M.*, London, Viking, 1985, pp. 14–15.

13 In M. Collis, *Somerville and Ross: A Biography*, London, Faber & Faber, 1968, esp. pp. 36–8.

14 Lewis, op. cit., pp. 233–8.

15 E. Somerville and M. Ross, *Beggars on Horseback*, Edinburgh and London, Blackwood, 1895; quoted by Lewis, op. cit., p. 208.

16 Lewis, op. cit., p. 208.

17 Collis, op. cit., pp. 32, 36, 37, 38, 96.

18 Lewis, op. cit., p. 206.

19 ibid., p. 103.

20 M. Gonne MacBride, *A Servant of the Queen*, London, Gollancz, 1938.

21 *Irish Figaro*, 7 April 1900.

22 W. B. Yeats, 'Easter, 1916', in *Collected Poems*, London, Macmillan, 2nd edn, 1950, pp. 202–3.

23 Maud Gonne MacBride to Count Stanislas Dunin-Markiewicz, 14 May 1931: A. Marreco, *The Rebel Countess: the Life and Times of Constance Markievicz*, Philadelphia, PA., Chilton Books, 1967, p. 125.

24 S. Levenson, *Maud Gonne*, London, Cassell, 1976, p. 369.

25 Yeats, *The Countess Cathleen*, London, T. Fisher Unwin, 1892, scene v.

26 *An Claidheamh Soluis*, 18 July 1903; quoted by Ruth Dudley Edwards, in *Patrick Pearse: the Triumph of Failure*, Swords, Poolbeg Press, 1990, p. 78.

27 B. Maddox, *Nora, a Biography of Nora Joyce*, London, Hamish Hamilton, 1988, p. 171.

28 C. MacCabe, 'James Joyce: concepts of race and nation', address to the Tenth International James Joyce Symposium, Copenhagen, June 1986; quoted in Maddox, op. cit., p. 501.

29 J. Joyce, 'The Holy Office', in *Pomes Penyeach*, London, Faber & Faber, 1968.

30 Maddox, op. cit., p. 496.

31 Yeats, 'The Lady's Second Song', in *Collected Poems*, p. 344.

32 ibid.

33 NLI 13088: Casement's brief to Counsel. Because of her experiences in Ireland, Louisa Farquharson was asked to address the Gaelic Society of London. This she did on 18 May 1905. Her lecture, entitled 'Ireland's ideal', was published as Gaelic League Pamphlet no. 31.

34 E. Boyd, *Ireland's Literary Renaissance*, Dublin, Figgis [1916], 3rd edn, 1968, p. 59.

35 Lady Wilde ('Speranza'), *Ancient Legends, Mystic Charms, and Superstitions of Ireland*, London, Ward & Downey, 1888, p. xi.

36 ibid., p. xii.

37 A. S. Green, with subsequent additions by Roger Casement and Bulmer Hobson, *Irishmen and the English Army*, published anonymously. It was circulated by the Dungannon Clubs, which had been founded by Hobson and Denis McCullough to bring about a regeneration of Irish traditions by material and physical means.
38 A. S. Green, *The Making of Ireland and its Undoing*, London, Macmillan, 1908, p. 345.
39 E. Coxhead, *Daughters of Erin: Five Women of the Irish Renascence*, London, Secker & Warburg, 1965, p. 142; from Sarah Purser's speech at the jubilee celebrations of An Tur Gloine, 19 January 1928.
40 In the porch of Loughrea Cathedral.
41 Sir Hugh Lane's presentation of his art collection to Dublin Corporation had been bedevilled by mismanagement and misunderstanding. His gift had been conditional on the corporation providing adequate premises for display. Dublin reacted without gratitude; so Lane gave the paintings to the Tate Gallery instead and altered his will. Later there was a reconciliation and Lane wrote a codicil to his will. As this was not witnessed, when Lane died in the *Lusitania* the collection stayed where it was while Lady Gregory and Sarah Purser agitated for its return. Using her influence with Cosgrave, Sarah Purser was able to obtain a worthy building, Charlemont House, as the Dublin, now the Hugh Lane, Municipal Gallery of Modern Art. Unfortunately neither she nor Lady Gregory lived to enjoy the benefits of the permanent loan arrangement.
42 *Report of the Royal Commission on the Rebellion in Ireland, Minutes and Appendix*, 1916 (Cd 8311), XI, p. 185. Augustine Birrell gave his evidence on 19 May.
43 P. Kavanagh, *Collected Pruse*, London, MacGibbon & Kee, 1967, p. 225.
44 F. Tuohy, quoted by Katie Donovan, op. cit., p. 26.
45 P. Roth, 'A conversation with Edna O'Brien', *New York Times Book Review*, 18 November 1984.

4 WOMEN'S RIGHTS AND SEPARATISM: TOWARDS A FREE STATE

1 *Bean na hEireann*, April 1909.
2 ibid., September 1909.
3 P. S. O'Hegarty, *The Victory of Sinn Féin*, Dublin, Talbot Press, 1924, pp. 56–7.
4 PRONI D.3074/1/1. Francis Sheehy Skeffington to 'my Dear Annie', 24 December 1903.
5 ibid.
6 *Bean na hEireann*, November 1909, Hanna Sheehy Skeffington, 'Sinn Féin and Irish women'.
7 PRONI D.1098/2/1/2. Minute Book, North Tyrone Women's Unionist Association, 13 April 1907.
8 *The Irish Citizen*, 15 June 1912.
9 PRONI T.2125/32/2a. The Northern Committee of the Irishwomen's Suffrage Federation represented Ballymoney, Belfast, Bushmills, Coleraine, Holywood, Larne, Lisburn, Londonderry, Portrush, Warrenpoint and Whitehead. Their pronouncements appeared in *The Irish Citizen*, 27 September and 18 October 1913.
10 PRONI D.1098/2/3. R. Dawson Bates to Mrs Wheeler, 13 September 1912.
11 PRONI D.2846/8/23. Dowager Marchioness of Dufferin and Ava to the Marchioness of Londonderry, 16 September 1913.
12 *Belfast News-Letter*, 21 January 1914.
13 C. M. Doyle, *Women in Ancient and Modern Ireland*, Dublin, Kilkenny Press,

1917, p. 4. Chrissie Doyle wrote as a member of Cumann na mBan and a former member of Inghinidhe na hEireann.

14 *Irish Freedom*, November 1913.

15 *The Irish Volunteer*, 18 April 1914.

16 PRONI D.2846/1/9/27. Lady Leslie to the Marchioness of Londonderry, 5 June 1914.

17 RS: Jaquetta James, widow of David Guthrie-James, to author, 2 August 1991.

18 *The Irish Citizen*, 25 July 1914.

19 ibid., 7 November 1914.

20 ibid., 22 May 1915.

21 *Irish Freedom*, September 1914.

22 A bizarre and tragic consequence of Casement's commitment to Irish separatism was a psychiatrist's decision that, according to the contemporary concept of homosexuality, he was 'a "woman" or pathic'. This diagnosis dissuaded the British Cabinet from granting a reprieve, although the offence of homosexuality had no legal connection with the charge of high treason, of which Casement had been found guilty. Influential persons had already refused to sign petitions calling for mercy, as they had been shown copies of Casement's 'Black Diaries', which revealed his propensities. See *Hansard*, House of Commons, 3 May 1956, adjournment debate: H. Montgomery Hyde: 'A Copy of the Memorandum of 17th July, 1916, [Sir Ernley Blackwell, the Home Office's legal adviser, to the Cabinet] has come into my possession.'

23 O'Hegarty, op. cit., p. 15.

24 *The Irish Volunteer*, 17 October 1914.

25 ibid., 1 January 1916.

26 RS: F. O'Donoghue, 'Kerry in the Easter Rising, 1916', typescript, pp. 24, 33, 42, 93.

27 D. Ryan, *The Rising: the Complete Story of Easter Week*, Dublin, Golden Eagle Books, 1949, p. 257.

28 R. Dudley Edwards, *Patrick Pearse: the Triumph of Failure*, Swords, Poolbeg Press, 1990, p. 277.

29 Department of the Taoiseach, Leinster House, Dublin: Frank Thornton memoir (classified document).

30 *Sinn Féin Rebellion Handbook*, Dublin, *The Irish Times*, 1917, p. 14. The newspaper based this part of its account on the observations of Second Lieutenant A. D. Chalmers, 14th Royal Irish Fusiliers.

31 M. Ward, *Unmanageable Revolutionaries: Women and Irish Nationalism*, London, Pluto Press, 1983, p. 111. Margaret Ward cites Helena Moloney in a wireless interview: no date given; issued by Ceirnini Cladaigh (Claddagh Records) in 1966.

32 *Sinn Féin Rebellion Handbook*, p. 15.

33 PRONI D.3099/3/15/52B. Michael Collins (unsigned) to Lady Londonderry, April 1922.

34 Marchioness of Londonderry [Edith], *Retrospect*, London, Frederick Muller, 1938, p. 73.

35 ibid., p. 75.

36 ibid., p. 145.

37 ibid., p. 173.

38 T. P. Coogan, *Michael Collins, a Biography*, London, Hutchinson, 1990, p. 293.

39 Explanatory Memorandum to the Government of Ireland Bill: 'Although at the beginning there are to be two Parliaments and two Governments in Ireland, the Act contemplates and affords every facility for union between North and South and empowers the two Parliaments by mutual agreement and joint action to terminate partition and to set up one Parliament and one Government for the whole of

Ireland. With a view to the eventual establishment of a single Parliament, and to bringing about harmonious action between the two Parliaments and Governments, there is created a bond of union in the meantime by means of a Council of Ireland, which is to consist of 20 representatives elected by each Parliament and a President nominated by the Lord Lieutenant. It will fall to the members of this body to initiate proposals for united action on the part of the two Parliaments and to bring forward these proposals in the respective Parliaments.' PRO CO 739/15 gives some indication of the initial all-Ireland powers of the Council. According to a communication of 17 October 1922, from the Law Officers of the Crown to the Secretary to the Cabinet Committee on Irish Affairs, the Act of 1920 simply gave the Council 'legislative and administrative powers with respect to three matters, viz., railways, fisheries and the contagious diseases of animals, to the exclusion of either of the Irish Parliaments' (i.e. of both). But no legislative boundaries seem to have been envisaged. The future belonged to Irish men and women regardless of the county of their birth or domicile.

5 WOMEN AND THE SOCIAL CONSEQUENCES OF IRISH INDEPENDENCE

1 PRONI D.2479/1/8. Charlotte Despard, Diary for 1924.
2 ibid., entry for 3 January. The book which Charlotte Despard had been reading was Thomas Kettle's *The Open Secret of Ireland*, London, Ham-Smith, 1912. In Chapter I, 'An exercise in humility', Kettle expresses the hope (on p. 10) that 'sinister pageants of race hatred shall not be suffered to dissolve without leaving some wrack of wisdom behind'.
3 ibid., entry for 4 January.
4 ibid., entry for 17 July.
5 ibid., entry for 28 December.
6 *Eire: The Irish Nation*, 19 May 1923; cited by M. Ward, *Unmanageable Revolutionaries: Women and Irish Nationalism*, London, Pluto Press, 1983, p. 194.
7 J. T. O'Farrell in the Senate, *Seanad Reports*, 20, 1876; quoted by Donal O'Sullivan, *The Irish Free State and its Senate*, London, Faber & Faber, 1940, p. 19.
8 *Irish Independent*, Dublin, 20 March 1922.
9 L. Conlon ('Lil'), *Cumann na mBan and the Women of Ireland 1913–25*, Kilkenny, *Kilkenny People*, 1969, p. 300.
10 All extracts are from RS: George Russell (AE) to Mrs Hobson, 1 September 1917.
11 De Valera is said to have given this explanation on a visit to the Carmelite Convent in Dublin: Tim Pat Coogan in *Michael Collins, a Biography*, London, Hutchinson, 1990, p. 427. The source seems to have been the daughter of the rebel Batt O'Connor, Sister Margaret Mary, who was interviewed by Coogan on his visit to the enclosed order.
12 PRO CO 739/14/15/16 Irish Free State, original correspondence; and RS: personal testimony from a family source.
13 *Irish Freedom*, November 1927.
14 Specimen leaflet quoted by Ward in op. cit., p. 207.
15 *Irish Worker's Voice*, 21 March 1931.
16 *Irish Press* (the de Valera family's own newspaper), 24 April 1933.
17 D. R. Pearce (ed.), *The Senate Speeches of W. B. Yeats*, London, Faber & Faber, 1961, p. 99.
18 Ward, op. cit., pp. 244–5.
19 New Ireland Forum submission: C. Clark and E. Evason, 'Women and social policy North and South', Dublin, typescript dated September 1983, p. 10.

20 S. D. Bailey (ed.), *Human Rights and Responsibilities in Britain and Ireland: a Christian Perspective*, London, Macmillan, 1988, p. 113: *Johnson and Others* v. *Ireland*, judgement delivered on 18 December 1986.
21 Bailey (ed.), op. cit., p. 123.
22 R. F. Foster, *Modern Ireland 1600–1972*, London, Allen Lane, Penguin Press, 1988, p. 534. Foster also points out that in 1926, 28 per cent of farmers with holdings of over 200 acres were Protestant. At this time Protestants were 8.4 per cent of the Free State's population. By 1936, in addition to the influential positions cited, 39 per cent of commercial representatives were Protestant.
23 RS: The Revd Ian Paisley in tape-recorded interview, 26 May 1988.
24 E. Stephan, *Geheimauftrag Irland*, Hamburg, Gerhard Stalling Verlag, 1961, ch. 14.
25 RS: statement by former member of Irish secret service ('HG').
26 N. Browne, *Against the Tide*, Dublin, Gill & Macmillan, 1986, p. 132.
27 ibid., p. 142.
28 ibid., p. 146.
29 ibid., pp. 158–9.
30 P. Blanshard, *The Irish and Catholic Power: an American Interpretation*, London, Derek Verschole, 1954, p. 78.
31 RS: Browne to author, 12 November 1991.
32 Catholic Code of Ethics, the Archdiocese of Dublin, (February 1978); quoted by Denis F. O'Callaghan in 'The value of unborn life', an essay in *Abortion Now*, Dublin, Life Education and Research Network (LEARN), 1983, p. 62.
33 All hospitals have ethics committees which decide what medical research will be undertaken, but there are others in hospitals, especially those controlled by the Roman Catholic Church, which mainly deal with sexual matters. Although membership of committees is predominantly Catholic, some Protestants, preferably Church of Ireland ministers, are invited to serve. A number of committee members are social workers.
34 *The Attorney General at the relation of the Society for the Protection of the Unborn Child* v. *Dublin Well Woman Centre Ltd and Open Line Counselling Ltd*, High Court decision, unreported, 19 December 1986.
35 *Application Number 8416/78, Paton* v. *United Kingdom*, decision of the European Court of Human Rights, 13 May 1980.
36 E. B. Titley, *Church, State and the Control of Schooling in Ireland 1900–1944*, Dublin, Gill & Macmillan, 1983, p. 84.
37 Blanshard, op. cit., p. 128.
38 Bailey (ed.), op. cit., p. 129.
39 RS: from discussion with current member of Official IRA (Belfast).
40 Quoted by Ralf Sotscheck, *The Guardian*, 21 June 1991.

6 WOMEN AND THE SOCIAL CONSEQUENCES OF IRISH DEVOLUTION

1 Elizabeth, Countess of Fingall, Memories of (told to Pamela Hickson), in *Seventy Years Young* [first published by Collins in 1937], Dublin, Lilliput Press in association with Carty/Lynch, 1991, p. 163.
2 Drafts for the speech had been written by Smuts, Balfour and Craig. The final version was written by Edward Grigg, Lloyd George's speech-writer.
3 PRONI D.3099/3/20/5 (archive closed): Ramsay MacDonald to Lady Londonderry, 5 August 1924.
4 H. Montgomery Hyde, *The Londonderrys: a Family Portrait*, London, Hamish

Hamilton, 1979, p. 160. Lady Londonderry wrote from Mount Stewart on 12 August 1924.

5 *Morning Post*, 7 November 1925.
6 PRONI D.2846/1/9/1. 'A Warden, also a distressed Ulsterwoman' to Lady Londonderry, no date. Someone has pencilled '1919' on the original document.
7 M. Ward, *Unmanageable Revolutionaries: Women and Irish Nationalism*, London, Pluto Press, 1983, p. 186.
8 Montgomery Hyde, op. cit., p. 154.
9 ibid., p. 155.
10 D. FitzPatrick, 'Ireland since 1870', in R. Foster (ed.), *The Oxford Illustrated History of Ireland*, Oxford, Oxford University Press, 1991, p. 265.
11 ibid., p. 264.
12 B. Devlin, *The Price of My Soul*, London, André Deutsch, 1969, Foreword.
13 The substance of a PhD thesis is probably to be found in a thorough analysis of the usage of 'Derry' and 'Londonderry' in Irish history, and in contemporary society. Since the siege of the Protestant city by Roman Catholics in 1649 its name has denoted much more than the title of a place. Most Roman Catholics call it 'Derry' (links with London lacking favour); most Protestants of the middle and lower classes insist on 'Londonderry', but adhere steadfastly to the expression 'Apprentice (or Protestant) Boys of Derry'; upper-class (Anglo-Irish) Protestants prefer 'Derry'. Members of the Ulster Volunteer Force (an illegal paramilitary loyalist working-class organization) claim that in the city itself all true loyalists, by which they mean extremists, say 'Derry' to distance themselves from mainstream unionists who use 'Londonderry' for effect. There is also an age factor at work, which leads old people to cross boundaries; perhaps this means no more than a sentimental attachment to 'The Londonderry Air' (though this can always be called 'Danny Boy'). Outsiders, anxiously addressing letters to inhabitants of the city, sometimes try to play safe with 'L/Derry'; their caution may well earn them disapproval from all sides. In general, women seem to be less obsessive than men with regard to this example of Ulster's peculiar vocabulary.
14 Devlin, op. cit., p. 166.
15 ibid., p. 158.
16 *Republican News*, Provisional Sinn Féin, January–February 1971.
17 Conor Cruise O'Brien, diary entry for 28 June 1970. Reproduced in O'Brien's *States of Ireland*, London, Hutchinson, 1972, p. 225.
18 K. Kelley, *The Longest War: Northern Ireland and the IRA*, London, Zed Books, 1982, p. 161.
19 ibid., p. 207.
20 *United Irishman*, published by Official Sinn Féin, January 1975.
21 O'Brien, op. cit., p. 266.
22 J. Biggs-Davison and G. Chowdharay-Best, *The Cross of Saint Patrick: the Catholic Unionist Tradition in Ireland*, Bourne End, Kensal Press, 1984, p. 374.
23 *Belfast News-Letter*, 2 October 1959.
24 ibid., 7 October 1959.
25 J. M. D. Kremer and C. A. Curry, *Attitudes Towards Women in Northern Ireland*, a report prepared for the Equal Opportunities Commission for Northern Ireland, Belfast, Dept. of Psychology, The Queen's University, 1986, p. 53. (It was in this university department that Bernadette Devlin received her higher education.)
26 Devlin, op. cit., p. 158.
27 Biggs-Davison and Chowdharay-Best, op. cit., p. 377.
28 Devlin, op. cit., p. 206.
29 PRONI D.3543/2/1. Minutes of a meeting convened to consider the formation of the Northern Ireland Family Planning Association, 24 February 1964. (It was

unanimously agreed to form the association. Its first aim was 'to extend the work of family planning in the province by providing material assistance in the formation of new clinics'.)
30 As quoted in T. J. O'Hanlan, *The Irish: Portrait of a People*, London, André Deutsch, 1976, p. 155.
31 *Abortion*, a report to the General Assembly of the Presbyterian Church in Ireland, by its National and International Problems Committee. Published as a discussion document by the Presbyterian Church in Ireland, June 1981, p. 5.
32 ibid., p. 12.
33 'Life (Ireland)', Pregnancy Care Service, Dublin, information leaflet.
34 At the time of writing, it would not be helpful for the party's spokeswoman to be identified.
35 New Ireland Forum submission: C. Clark and E. Evason, 'Women and social policy North and South', Dublin, September 1983, p. 34.
36 O'Hanlan, op. cit., p. 216.
37 Kremer and Curry, op. cit., p. 55.

7 ATTITUDES AND THEIR OUTCOME: SOUTH AND NORTH

1 P. Blanshard, *The Irish and Catholic Power: An American Interpretation*, London, Derek Verschole, 1954, p. 90.
2 Most books that are still banned can be found in *Register of Prohibited Publications*, Dublin, The Stationery Office, 'Published by the Censorship Board in accordance with directions to the Minister for Justice pursuant to sub-section (5) of section 16 of the Censorship of Publications Act, 1946'. Otherwise, up-to-date addenda may be obtained from the Office of Censorship of Publications.
3 Information provided by the Secretary, Office of Censorship of Publications, 11 October 1990.
4 T. O'Hanlon, *The Irish: Portrait of a People*, London, André Deutsch, 1976, p. 158.
5 ibid., p. 157.
6 RS: Noël Browne to author, 12 November 1991.
7 Noël Browne, 'Church and state in modern Ireland', typescript of a lecture delivered at The Queen's University, Belfast, 28 February 1991, p. 15.
8 J. Heenan, *The People's Priest*, London, Sheed & Ward, 1951, pp. 148 and 154.
9 D. Bleakley, *Saidie Patterson, Irish Peacemaker*, Belfast, Blackstaff Press, 1980, p. 25.
10 ibid., p. 40.
11 W. S. Churchill, *Their Finest Hour*, vol. 2 of *The Second World War*, London, Cassell, 1949, p. 287.
12 ibid.
13 Bleakley, op. cit., pp. 42–3.
14 ibid., p. 43.
15 J. M. D. Kremer and C. A. Curry, *Attitudes Towards Women in Northern Ireland*, Belfast, Dept of Psychology, The Queen's University, 1986, p. 19.
16 ibid., p. 51.
17 ibid., p. 33.
18 ibid., p. 49.
19 ibid.
20 ibid., p. 50.
21 M. Ward, 'Marginality and militancy: Cumann na mBan 1914–1936', in A. Morgan

and B. Purdie (eds), *Ireland: Divided Nation – Divided Class*, London, Ink Links, 1980, p. 108.
22 ibid.
23 *Republican News*, 9 February 1974.
24 K. Kelley, *The Longest War: Northern Ireland and the IRA*, London, Zed Books, 1982, p. 320.
25 *Women in the New Ireland*, Belfast, Sinn Féin, 1980.
26 Bleakley, op. cit., p. 72.
27 D. Calvert, *A Decade of the DUP*, Belfast, Crown Publications, n.d., p. 5.
28 ibid., p. 6.
29 Anonymity necessary to protect innocent third party.
30 R. Paisley, *Ian Paisley, My Father*, Basingstoke, Marshall Pickering, 1988, p. 139.
31 ibid.
32 RS: Rhonda Paisley to author, 4 March 1992.
33 David Bleakley, in conversation with author, 22 May 1988. The Rt. Hon. David Bleakley's other offices include being a founder member of the Anglican Consultative Council, General Secretary of the Irish Council of Churches 1980–92, President of the Church Missionary Society and member of the Central Executive of the European Conference of Churches.
34 RS: R. Paisley, tape-recorded interview with author, 21 May 1988.
35 As expressed directly to the author and in Paisley, op. cit., e.g., pp. 31–41, 137–40.
36 Paisley, op. cit., p. 40.
37 For the remainder of this chapter the names of the principal individuals interviewed have had to be withheld. In order to obtain their co-operation it was necessary to assure members of illegal organizations that their identities would not be revealed. They were more afraid of the reaction of their own organizations should they give away too much, than of any other possible outcome of an indiscretion.
38 Kevin McNamara, MP, *Irish News*, 10 January 1985; quoted in *Twelfth Report of the Standing Advisory Commission on Human Rights: Annual Report for 1985–86*, HC 1986–7 (151), p. 112.
39 Ursula Barry, '1916 – What did it mean for Irish Women?', in *Iris, The Republican Magazine*, Easter 1991, no. 15.
40 ibid.
41 ibid.

8 EMANCIPATION AND UNITY

1 Quoted in *Treaty on European Union*, Government of Ireland White Paper (Pl. 8793), Dublin, April 1992, l. 26, p. 13.
2 ibid., l. 31, p. 15.
3 Letter to *Freeman's Journal*, 22 January 1906.
4 RS: Most Revd Michael Smith to author, 28 March 1992.
5 *The Catholic Church in Ireland*, Dublin, Catholic Press and Information Office, 1984, p. 15.
6 L. E. Farquharson, *Ireland's Ideal*, Dublin, Gaelic League (pamphlet no. 31), 1905, p. 4.
7 PRO DO. 35/8033 Question of the Irish Republic rejoining the Commonwealth, G. D. Anderson to W. F. G. Le Bailly, 1 September 1960: '4. The first sign of a move away from this rigidly "non-possumus" attitude towards a Commonwealth link of sorts was made in March 1958 when, in conversation with Lord Home in London, Mr de Valera and Mr Aiken proposed that "Northern Ireland should surrender its direct allegiance to the Queen in return for a United Republic of Ireland within a

Commonwealth recognising the Queen as its Head. The United Kingdom should take the initiative towards such a solution of the problem.'" Students of de Valera will take it for granted that, if everything had gone as he and the Minister for External Affairs had proposed, not long after the United Republic of Ireland had come into existence it would have resigned from the Commonwealth.

8 Shortly after this chapter went to press (and a copy had been sent to President Mary Robinson) a meeting of the two heads of state was arranged. The President visited the Queen on 27 May 1993. Although overshadowed in United Kingdom news coverage by a dramatic cabinet reshuffle, its symbolic value was widely recognized in both countries. It was seen as the precursor of more substantive meetings. British and Irish heads of state are, of course, 'above politics'. But at the time of the devolution referenda for Scotland and Wales the Queen gave forceful expression of her views, which were the same as those of the then Labour government. Her outspokenness was not regarded as unconstitutional.

Were she to broach similar issues with the Irish president, the Queen would be following the example of her grandfather, George V, when he looked forward to the day when 'the Irish people, North and South, under one Parliament or two, as those Parliaments may decide, shall work in common love for Ireland upon the sure foundation of mutual justice and respect'.

BIBLIOGRAPHY

Abbreviations are the same as those used in the Notes.

UNPRINTED SOURCES

Public repositories

Llangollen Town Council: Plas Newydd Papers.

NLI Ir 3996 b15: *Bean na hEireann*: vol. 1, nos 6–25 (1909); vol. 2, nos 23 and 24 (January and February 1911).

NLI MS 4811: Wicklow Papers.

NLI 10464: Alice Stopford Green papers.

NLI 13088: Casement's brief to Counsel.

PRO CO 739/14/15/16: Irish Free State, original correspondence; Atrocities against Protestants in the South; Council of Ireland, administrative powers (in CO 739/15).

PRO DO 35/8033: Question of the Irish Republic rejoining the Commonwealth.

PRO T. 64/362A to 370c: papers from the office of Sir Charles Trevelyan, Assistant Secretary to the Treasury from 1840 to 1859. They are concerned with the administration of Ireland, especially with famine relief.

PRONI D. 1098/2/1/2: North Tyrone Women's Unionist Association, Minute Book for 1907.

PRONI D. 1098/2/3: Women and the wording of the Solemn League and Covenant.

PRONI D. 2479/1/8: Charlotte Despard, diary for 1924.

PRONI D. 2846/1/9/1–47: Letters to Theresa, wife of sixth Marquess of Londonderry, from various women unionists, 1912–19.

PRONI D. 2846/8/23: The need for members of the Women's Unionist Council to avoid being diverted from their principal aim by suffragist activity. The Dowager Marchioness of Dufferin and Ava.

PRONI D. 3074/1/1–2: Francis Sheehy Skeffington letters.

PRONI D. 3099/3/6: Suffrage (1909–13).

PRONI D. 3099/3/12/1–145: 'The Ark'.

PRONI D. 3099/3/38: Women and work in Northern Ireland.

PRONI D. 3099/3/15/52A, 52B and 52C: Michael Collins to Edith, wife of seventh Marquess of Londonderry, cover note, original and fair copy.

PRONI D. 3099/3/20/1–423 (closed): correspondence concerning the border, Ramsay MacDonald (1924–37).

PRONI D. 3370/1–6: Single women and dependants.

PRONI D. 3543/2/1–2: Family planning.

PRONI D. 3543/4/1–3: Family planning.
PRONI T. 2125/32/1–32: 'Unionism and women's suffrage'.
PRONI TP (Tape) 35: Transcript of interview with Miss Margaret Robinson, of Cleggan, Co. Galway, one time suffragette in Belfast, recorded in 1975.

New Ireland Forum submission: C. Clark and E. Evason, 'Women and social policy North and South', typescript, Dublin, September 1983; author's copy provided by the Equal Opportunities Commission for Northern Ireland, Belfast.

Private papers and various unpublished sources

Aylmer Papers, Nunwell House, Brading, Isle of Wight: Louis Spears, typescript.
Browne, Noël, 'Church and state in modern Ireland', typescript of a lecture delivered at The Queen's University, Belfast, 28 February 1991.
Colclough Papers, Cuffsborough, Co. Laois: family history.
Gaelic Society of London (Comunn Na Gaidhlig An Lunnainn): Minutes; Register of members.
Hamwood Papers, Co. Meath: Eleanor Butler's Journal.
Lambeth Palace: Carew MSS (1535, 1544, 1550).
Kavanagh Papers, Borris, Co. Carlow: a largely uncatalogued assortment of documents illustrating the fortunes of the heirs of the Kings of Leinster.
RS: Material in possession of the author. Miscellaneous correspondence: Dr Noël Browne, Richard Colclough, Aideen Gore-Booth, Jaquetta (Guthrie-)James, the Londonderrys, Rhonda Paisley, the Most Revd Michael Smith, Bishop of Meath; and a few temporarily embargoed items; George Russell ('AE') letters. Typescript: Florence O'Donoghue, 'Kerry in the Easter Rising, 1916'. Transcripts of tape-recorded interviews: with Lady Mairi Bury, 10 September 1990; with the Revd Ian Paisley, 26 May 1988; with Rhonda Paisley, 21 May 1988.
Taoiseach, Department of the, Dublin: Frank Thornton memoir (classified).
Wilson, William: 'The Roman Catholic Church and the Eighth Amendment', thesis submitted to The Queen's University, Belfast, 1984.

BRITISH AND IRISH GOVERNMENT PUBLICATIONS

Correspondence from July 1846 to January 1847 Relating to the Measures Adopted for the Relief of the Distress in Ireland: Commissariat Series, HC, 1847 (761) LI.
The First Report for His Majesty's Commissioners for Inquiring into the Condition of the Poorer Classes in Ireland, 1835 (369) XXXII.
Hansard: House of Lords, 30 March 1846 (Famine) House of Commons, 3 May, 17 July 1956 (Casement); 2 July 1984 (New Ireland Forum).
New Ireland Forum, Report, Dublin, Stationery Office, 2 May 1984.
Northern Ireland Constitutional Proposals, 1972–3, (Cmnd. 5259) XXVI, p. 1081.
Register of Prohibited Publications, Censorship Board in accordance with directions of the Minister for Justice, 1986.
Report of Geo. Nicholls, Esq., to His Majesty's Principal Secretary of State for the Home Department on Poor Laws, Ireland, 1837 (690) LI.
Report of the Royal Commission on the Rebellion in Ireland, Minutes and Appendix, 1916 (Cd. 8311) XI.
Treaty on European Union, Government of Ireland White Paper (Pl. 8793) laid before each House of the Oireachtas, Dublin, April 1992.

NEWSPAPERS AND PERIODICALS

Only journals cited in the text, or containing articles or letters having a direct bearing on the argument are listed. Journals and periodicals are shown by volume numbers, newspapers by their dates.

An Claidheamh Solius, 18 July 1903: Pearse and emigrants.

Bean na hEireann, April 1909: twin commitment to separatism and feminism; November 1909: Hanna Sheehy Skeffington, 'Sinn Féin and Irish Women'; September 1909: Inghinidhe na hEireann advocates violence.

Belfast News-Letter, 1 May 1854: accidents to linen-workers; 21 January 1914: women and unionist activity; 2 and 7 October 1959: Sheelagh Murnaghan.

Edinburgh Review, vol. 15: domestic service in Ireland in the nineteenth century.

Eire: The Irish Nation, 19 May 1923: Cumann na Saoirse.

Eriu, XI: St Patrick and the oral traditions of pagan Ireland.

Feminist Review, no. 10, February 1982: M. Ward, account of Irish suffrage movement.

Freeman's Journal, 22 January 1906: Michael Davitt, letter, advocacy of secularism in education.

Guardian, The, 21 June 1991: Dublin as 'European City of Culture': triptych in oils, 'Emerging from the Shamrock'.

Genealogical Tracts, I: Leinster's Queen Maeve.

General Evening Post, The, 20–2 July 1790: The Ladies of Llangollen.

Iris, The Republican Magazine, Easter 1991, no. 15: Ursula Barry on Irish nationalism and 'anti-woman ideology'.

Irish Citizen, The, 15 June 1912: unionism and suffragism; 27 September and 18 October 1913: suffragism and violence; 25 July and 7 November 1914, 22 May 1915: women's rights and separatism.

Irish Figaro, 7 April 1900: Maud Gonne disgraces the Pilchers.

Irish Freedom, November 1913: IRB attitude to women's involvement in separatism; September 1914: Mary Colum on Cumann na mBan; November 1927: Cumann na mBan and policy of destabilization.

Irish Independent, 20 March 1922: de Valera and the civil war.

Irish News, 10 January 1985: strip-searching of women prisoners.

Irish Press, 24 April 1933: de Valera and the 1922 Constitution.

Irish Volunteer, The, 18 April and 17 October 1914, 1 January 1916: Cumann na mBan policy.

Irish Worker's Voice, 21 March 1931: Cumann na mBan and Soviet communism.

Journal of the Butler Society, vol. 1, no. 3: The Ladies of Llangollen.

Leinster Express, 30 December 1905: landlord and tenant.

Morning Post, The, 7 November 1925: Boundary Commission recommendations.

New York Times Book Review, 18 November 1984: Philip Roth, 'A conversation with Edna O'Brien'.

Republican News, January–February 1971: Provisional IRA's attitude to women; 9 February 1974: contraception.

Revue Celtique, XXXIX: criticism of the traditions of ancient Irish sagas.

United Irishman, January 1975: Irish Republican Socialist Party and Bernadette McAlisky.

Zeitschrift für Celtische Philologie, XVII: Leinster's Queen Maeve.

PUBLISHED AND PRIVATELY PRINTED WORKS: GENERAL LIST

For Chapter 3, 'Irish cultural revival', only a few literary publications used as principal examples in the text are listed.

Abortion, Presbyterian Church in Ireland, June 1981.
Abortion Now, Dublin, Life Education and Research Network, 1983.
Aylmer, Sir Fenton, *The Aylmers of Ireland*, London, Mitchell, Hughes & Clarke, 1931.
Bailey, S. D. (ed.), *Human Rights and Responsibilities in Britain and Ireland: a Christian Perspective*, London, Macmillan, 1988.
Beckett, J., *The Anglo-Irish Tradition*, London, Faber & Faber, 1976.
Bell, G. H. (ed.), *The Hamwood Papers of the Ladies of Llangollen and Caroline Hamilton*, London, Macmillan, 1930.
Bence-Jones, M., *Twilight of the Ascendancy*, London, Constable, 1987.
Biggs-Davison, J. and Chowdharay-Best, G., *The Cross of Saint Patrick: the Catholic Unionist Tradition in Ireland*, Bourne End, Kensal Press, 1984.
Birkenhead, Second Earl of, *F. E. The Life of the First Earl of Birkenhead*, London, Eyre & Spottiswoode, 1959.
Blanshard, P., *The Irish and Catholic Power: An American Interpretation*, London, Derek Verschole, 1954.
Bleakley, D., *Saidie Patterson, Irish Peacemaker*, Belfast, Blackstaff Press, 1980.
Boyd, E., *Ireland's Literary Renaissance*, Dublin, Figgis [1916], 3rd edn, 1968.
Browne, N., *Against the Tide*, Dublin, Gill & Macmillan, 1986.
Buchanan, A. W. P., *The Buchanan Book*, Montreal, privately printed, 1911.
Bugge, A. (ed. and tr.), *Caithrein Cellachain Caisil: the Victorious Career of Cellachan of Cashel*, Christiania (Oslo), Norsk Historisk Kjeldeskriftinstitutt, 1905.
Butler, H. J., and Butler, H. E. (eds), *The Black Book of Edgeworthstown and Other Edgeworth Memories 1585–1817*, London, Faber & Gwyer, 1927.
Calvert, D., *A Decade of the DUP*, Belfast, Crown Publications, n.d.
Catholic Church in Ireland, The, Dublin, Catholic Press and Information Office, 1984.
Chambers, A., *Granuaile: the Life and Times of Grace O'Malley*, Dublin, Wolfhound Press, 1979.
Churchill, W. S., *Their Finest Hour*, vol. 2 of *The Second World War* (6 vols), London, Cassell, 1949.
Clark, A. (ed.), *Gleanings from an Old Portfolio*, privately printed for David Douglas, Edinburgh, 1895–8, vol. 3 (of 3 vols).
Clear, C., *Nuns in Nineteenth-Century Ireland*, Dublin, Gill & Macmillan, 1987.
Collis, M., *Somerville and Ross: a Biography*, London, Faber & Faber, 1968.
Colum, M. M., *Life and the Dream*, London, Macmillan, 1947.
Conlon, L., *Cumann na mBan and the Women of Ireland 1913–25*, Kilkenny, Kilkenny People, 1969.
Coogan, T. P., *The IRA*, London, Fontana, revised and expanded edn, 1980.
—— *Michael Collins, a Biography*, London, Hutchinson, 1990.
Coxhead, E., *Daughters of Erin: Five Women of the Irish Renascence*, London, Secker & Warburg, 1965.
Daly, M. S., *The Church and the Second Sex*, London, Chapman, 1968.
de Courcey, A., *Circe: the Life of Edith, Marchioness of Londonderry*, London, Sinclair Stevenson, 1992.
Devlin, B., *The Price of My Soul*, London, André Deutsch, 1969.
Donnelly, J. S. (jun.), *The Land and the People of Nineteenth Century Cork: the Rural Economy and the Land Question*, London, Routledge & Kegan Paul, 1975.

Donovan, K., *Irish Women Writers (Marginalized by Whom?)*, Dublin, Raven Arts Press (Letters from the New Ireland series), 1988.

Doyle, C. M., *Women in Ancient and Modern Ireland*, Dublin, Kilkenny Press, 1917.

Dunbar, J., *Mrs G. B. S.: a Biographical Portrait of Charlotte Shaw*, London, Harrap, 1963.

Dunsany, Lord, *Patches of Sunlight*, London and Toronto, Heinemann, 1938.

Edgeworth, M., *Castle Rackrent, an Hibernian Tale: taken from the Facts and from the Manners of the Irish Squires, before the year 1782*, London, Joseph Johnson, 1800.

——*Castle Rackrent* and *The Absentee*, London, Dent (Everyman's Library), 1910, repr. 1952.

Edwards, R. D., *Patrick Pearse: the Triumph of Failure*, Swords, Poolbeg Press, 1990.

Ervine, St J., *Craigavon: Ulsterman*, London, Allen & Unwin, 1949.

Farquharson, L. E., *Ireland's Ideal*, Dublin, The Gaelic League (pamphlet no. 31), 1905.

Ferguson, S., *Lays of the Red Branch* (New Irish Library), London, T. Fisher Unwin, and Dublin, Sealy, Bryers & Walker, 1897.

Fingall, Elizabeth, Countess of, *Seventy Years Young*, Dublin, Lilliput Press in association with Carty/Lynch, 1991.

Foster, R., *Modern Ireland 1600–1972*, Allen Lane, Penguin Press, 1988.

—— (ed.), *The Oxford Illustrated History of Ireland*, Oxford University Press, 1991.

Gore-Booth, E., *Poems of Eva Gore-Booth*, London, New York and Toronto, Longman's, Green, 1929.

Green, A. S., *The Making of Ireland and its Undoing*, London, Macmillan, 1908.

Green, J. R., *A Short History of the English People*, London and New York, Macmillan, revd edn, 1888.

Gwynn, S., *The History of Ireland*, London, Macmillan, and Dublin, Talbot Press, 1923.

Hawthorne, J. (ed.), *Two Centuries of Irish History*, London, British Broadcasting Corporation, 1976.

Heenan, J., *The People's Priest*, London, Sheed & Ward, 1951.

Hyde, H. Montgomery, *The Londonderrys: a Family Portrait*, London, Hamish Hamilton, 1979.

Jeffares, A. N., *W. B. Yeats: a New Biography*, London, Hutchinson, 1988.

Joyce, J., *Pomes Penyeach*, London, Faber & Faber, 1968.

Kavanagh, P., *Collected Pruse*, London, MacGibbon & Kee, 1967.

Kelley, K., *The Longest War: Northern Ireland and the IRA*, London, Zed Books, 1982.

Kettle, T., *The Open Secret of Ireland*, London, Ham-Smith, 1912.

Kinsella, T. (tr.), *The Tain*, translation of *Tain Bo Cuailnge*, Dublin and Oxford, Oxford University Press in association with Dolmen Press, 1970.

Knowler, W. (ed.), *The Earl of Strafforde's Letters and Dispatches*, Dublin, R. Reilly for Robert Owen, 1739–40, vol. 2 (of 2 vols).

Kremer, J. M. D. and Curry, C. A., *Attitudes Towards Women in Northern Ireland*, Belfast, Dept. of Psychology, The Queen's University, 1986.

La Tocnaye, Bougrenet de (tr. J. Stevenson), *A Frenchman's Walk through Ireland, 1796–7*, Belfast, McCaw, Stevenson & Orr, and Dublin, Hodges, Figgis, 1917.

Levenson, S., *Maud Gonne*, London, Cassell, 1976.

Lewis, G., *Somerville and Ross: the World of the Irish RM*, London, Viking, 1985.

Londonderry, [Edith] The Marchioness of, *Retrospect*, London, Frederick Muller, 1938.

Longford, The Earl of, and O'Neill, T. P., *Eamon de Valera*, London, Hutchinson, 1970.

MacBride, M. Gonne, *A Servant of the Queen*, London, Gollancz, 1938.

McCormack, W., *Ascendancy and Tradition in Anglo-Irish Literary History from 1789 to 1939*, Oxford, Clarendon Press, 1985.

MacCurtain, M. and O'Dowd, M. (eds), *Women in Early Modern Ireland*, Edinburgh, Edinburgh University Press, 1991.

McNeill, *Ulster's Stand for Union*, London, John Murray, 1922.

Maddox, B., *Nora, a Biography of Nora Joyce*, London, Hamish Hamilton, 1988.

Marreco, A., *The Rebel Countess: the Life and Times of Constance Markievicz*, Philadelphia, PA., Chilton Books, 1967.

Mavor, E., *The Ladies of Llangollen: a Study in Romantic Friendship*, London, Michael Joseph, 1971.

—— (ed.), *Life with the Ladies of Llangollen*, London, Viking, 1984; also pubd as *A Year with the Ladies of Llangollen*, Harmondsworth, Penguin, 1986.

Morgan, A. and Purdie, B. (eds), *Ireland: Divided Nation – Divided Class*, London, Ink Links, 1980.

Morgan, Lady (Sydney Owenson), *The Wild Irish Girl*, London, Pandora Press, Routledge & Kegan Paul, 1986.

Nicholls, K., *Gaelic and Gaelicised Ireland in the Middle Ages*, Dublin, Gill & Macmillan, 1972.

Nicolson, H., *Lord Carnock, a Study in the Old Diplomacy*, London, Constable, 1930.

O'Brien, C. Cruise, *States of Ireland*, London, Hutchinson, 1972.

O'Faolain, S., *The Irish: a Character Study*, New York, Devin-Adair, 1949.

O'Grady, S. J., *History of Ireland: the Heroic Period*, London, Sampson Low, Searle, Marston & Rivington, and Dublin, E. Ponsonby, 1878, vol. 1 (of 2 vols).

O'Hanlan, *The Irish: Portrait of a People*, London, André Deutsch, 1976.

O'Hegarty, P. S., *The Victory of Sinn Féin*, Dublin, Talbot Press, 1924.

O'Neill, *Ulster at the Crossroads*, London, Faber & Faber, 1969.

O'Rahilly, T. F., *Early Irish History and Mythology*, Dublin, Dublin Institute for Advanced Studies, 1946.

O'Sullivan, D., *The Irish Free State and its Senate*, London, Faber & Faber, 1940.

Paisley, R., *Ian Paisley, My Father*, Basingstoke, Marshall Pickering, 1988.

Pearce, D. R. (ed.), *The Senate Speeches of W. B. Yeats*, London, Faber & Faber, 1961.

Rees, A. and Rees, B., *Celtic Heritage: Ancient Tradition in Ireland and Wales*, London, Thames & Hudson, 1961, repr. 1978.

Rhys, J., *Celtic Folklore, Welsh and Manx*, Oxford, Clarendon Press, 1901.

Ryan, D., *The Rising: the Complete Story of Easter Week*, Dublin, Golden Eagle Books, 1949.

Ryan-Smolin, W., Mayes, E. and Rogers, J. (eds), *Irish Women Artists: From the Eighteenth Century to the Present day*, Dublin, National Gallery of Ireland and Douglas Hyde Gallery, 1987.

Salaman, R. N., *The History and Social Influence of the Potato*, Cambridge University Press, 1949.

Sinn Féin Rebellion Handbook, Dublin, *The Irish Times*, 1917.

Somerville, E. and Ross, M., *Beggars on Horseback*, Edinburgh and London, Blackwood, 1895.

—— *Irish Memories*, London, Longman's, Green, 1917.

Stephan, E., *Geheimauftrag Irland*, Hamburg, Gerhard Stalling Verlag, 1961.

Stokes, G. T., *Ireland and the Celtic Church*, London, Hodder & Stoughton, 3rd edn, 1892.

Titley, E. B., *Church, State and the Control of Schooling in Ireland, 1900–1944*, Dublin, Gill & Macmillan, 1983.

Ward, M., *Unmanageable Revolutionaries: Women and Irish Nationalism*, London, Pluto Press, 1983.

Wilde, Lady, *Ancient Legends, Mystic Charms, and Superstitions of Ireland*, London, Ward & Downey, 1888.

Woodham-Smith, C., *The Great Hunger: Ireland 1845–1849*, London, Hamish Hamilton, 1962.
Women in the New Ireland, Belfast, Sinn Féin, 1980.
Yeats W. B., *The Countess Cathleen*, London, T. Fisher Unwin, 1892.
—— *Collected Poems*, London, Macmillan, 2nd edn, 1950.
Young A., *Tour in Ireland*, Dublin, T. Cadell & J. Dodsley, 1780.
Young, M. F. (ed.), *The Letters of a Noble Woman (Mrs La Touche of Harristown)*, London, George Allen & Sons, 1908.

The following works of reference were also useful:

Burke's Irish Family Records, London, Burke's Peerage, 1976.
Burke's Landed Gentry of Ireland, various editions.
Catholic Encyclopedia, The, London, The Catholic Encyclopedia, 1912.
Farmer, D. H., *The Oxford Dictionary of Saints*, Oxford, Clarendon Press, 1978.
Grundy, Isobel, and others, *Feminist Companion to Literature in English*, London, Batsford, 1990.
Humana, C., *World Human Rights Guide*, London, Economist Publications, revd edn, 1986, and Oxford University Press, revd edn, 1992.
Pine, L. (ed.), *Burke's Genealogical and Heraldic History of the Peerage, Baronetage and Knightage*, London, Burke's Peerage (102nd edn), 1959.
Who Was Who 1916–1928, London, A. & C. Black, 1929, and various other volumes, both of *Who Was Who* and *Who's Who*.

INDEX

Monteagle, 2nd Baron 44
Morgan, Lady 51
Morgan, Sir Charles 51
Morning Post, The 123
Mount Stewart 45, 124
Mother and Child Scheme 110–14, 154
Muir, Maud 76
Munster, kings of 9, 12
Munster Women's Franchise League
78–9
Murnaghan, Sheelagh 135–6, 178
Muskaus, Prince Puckler 26, 28
Mythological Cycle 3

Naisi (Noisui) 6
National Board of Education 40
National H-Block Committee 134
National Literary Society of Ireland 58
national schools 4, 174
National Volunteers 86
Neave, Airey 134
Nemed 2
Nes 4
Nessa 7
New Ireland Forum 141, 176
Niall of the Nine Hostages 8, 10
Nicolson, Sir Arthur (lst Baron
Carnock) 45
Nicolson, Harold (later Sir) 45
Noah 1
Normans 12, 15, 17, 22, 174
Northern Ireland Assembly 63
Northern Ireland Equal Opportunities
Board 135
Northern Ireland Family Planning
Association 136
Northern Ireland Women's Rights
Movement (NIWRM) 159
Northern Irish Civil Rights Association
(NICRA) 128–9, 130, 133
Northern Resistance Movement 133
Nuada 2
nuns *see* convent life

O'Brien, Edna 70, 149
O'Brien, Conor Cruise 132–3, 134
O'Brien, Kitty 65
O'Brien, Murrough (1st Earl of
Inchiquin) 18
O'Briens and the O'Flahertys, The 51
O'Callaghan, Kate 97
O'Casey, Sean 100
O'Connor, Father Denis 150

O'Conor, Rory, King of Connaught 13
O'Downyll, Lord, the Lord Deputy 12
O'Downyll, Rose 12
O'Farrell, Elizabeth 90, 91
O'Farrelly, Agnes 81
Official IRA *see* Irish Republican Army
O'Flaherty, Donal 16
O'Grady, Standish 3
O'Hegarty, P. S. 73, 79, 80
O'Malley, Grania (Grace) 15–16, 21, 80,
174
O'Neill, Captain Terence 131–2
O'Neyll, and Nelan Connelagh
O'Neyll 12
Open Line Counselling 117
oral tradition 1–2, 3, 5–7, 45, 63, 65
Oriel, King of 9
Ormonde family 12, 24
Ormonde, 1st Duke of 18
Orpen, Sir William 66–7
O'Shea, Katherine 86, 105
O'Shea, Kittie 66
Ota, Queen 11
Owenson, Sydney *see* Morgan, Lady

Paisley, Eileen 162, 163, 164, 165
Paisley, The Reverend Ian 109, 162, 163,
164
Paisley, Rhonda 163–5
palaeolithic period 1
Pankhurst, Emmeline 75, 76, 95
Pankhurst, Sylvia 75, 95
Parent's Assistant, The 50
Parnell, Anna 41, 46, 61, 79, 80
Parnell, Charles Stewart 45, 86, 105
Partholon 2
Patterson, Monica 159–60
Patterson, Saidie 152–5, 160–1, 178
Paul VI, Pope 140
Payne-Townshend, Charlotte (Mrs G.
B. Shaw) 55, 68
Peace People (formerly Peace Women)
159, 160–1
Pearse, Margaret 99
Pearse, Mary Brigid 89
Pearse, Patrick 53, 55, 59, 61, 80, 88, 89,
175
Penal Code 19–20
People's Democracy Party 129–32, 133,
135
People's Priest, The 151–2, 173
Pilcher, Kathleen 55
Pilcher, Major General Thomas David 55